TRIBAL WOMEN OF ARUNACHAL PRADESH

THE AUTHOR

V.M. Rao (*b.* 1954) holds a doctorate in Dairy Economics and is currently working as Professor and HOD, Department of Research & Publications at Vaikunth Mehta National Institute of Cooperative Management, Pune. He has earlier worked with National Institute of Rural Development, Hyderabad (1984-88), and Indian Institute of Management, Ahmedabad (1988-92). On a British Council's fellowship, Prof. Rao visited Belgium, France, Luxembourg, The Netherlands, and United Kingdom. He has authored/co-authored five books: (a) *Dairy Farming: Socio-Economic Analysis of Milk Production (1991)*, (b) *Castor Economy: A Profile and Analysis of India and International Market (1991)*, (c) *International Castor Oil Market: An Econometric Analysis (1994)*, (d) *Developing Agro Enterprises among Farm Women: A Case of Amul (2000)*, and (e) *Empowering Farm Women through Dairy Cooperatives: A Study in Andhra Pradesh and Karnataka*. Besides these books, he has published over 60 research papers. His areas of interest are: (a) animal husbandry economics, (b) agri-business management, and (c) gender related issues. He has completed 16 research studies sponsored by Government of India, ICSSR, and other state governments in the above areas during 1980-02. At present Prof. Rao is engaged in: (a) Evaluation of Women: Dairy Project in Rajasthan, and (b) Integrating Tribal Women into Cooperatives: An Experience of Girijan Cooperative Corporation Limited (Andhra Pradesh).

TRIBAL WOMEN OF ARUNACHAL PRADESH

SOCIO-ECONOMIC STATUS

V. M. Rao

MITTAL PUBLICATIONS
NEW DELHI-110059 [INDIA]

First Edition 2003

ISBN 81-7099-909-X

Editorial Office:
H-13, Bali Nagar,
New Delhi - 110015
Phones: 25163610, 25431361

Showroom:
4594/9, Daryaganj,
New Delhi - 110002
Phone: 23250398

Published and printed by Naurang Rai for Mittal Publications,
A-110, Mohan Garden, New Delhi-110059, India.
Tel.: 25351493, 25351976 *Telefax:* 91-11-25351521
E-Mail : mittalp@ndf.vsnl.net.in *Gram* : Mittalbux
website : www.mittalpublications.com

ACKNOWLEDGEMENTS

The project is funded by the Tribal Development Division of Ministry of Social Justice and Empowerment, Government of India, New Delhi. We are extremely thankful to the ministry for the financial support. The project was sanctioned in the first half of 1998, and as I was involved in three more projects during this period (1998-02), project is delayed. I am extremely sorry for the inconvenience.

I would like to thank Dr. B.B. Barik, Director of the institute for extending administrative support in conducting the study.

During the process of data collection I received immense help from Mrs. D.M. Mallo, Director, Department of Social Welfare, Women and Child Development, Government of Arunachal Pradesh, Naharlagun. It would have been impossible for me to complete the field visits in 40 Anganwadi centres spread over five districts without her support. Once Mrs. Mallo went out of way for accommodating me in Pawanhans (Naharlagun to Roing) by way of requesting one of the passengers to cancel his programme on the scheduled day. I was moved by her timely support and concern.

I am equally thankful to all the Deputy Directors (ICDS), and CDPOs who extended necessary support during field visits. I had the opportunity to have discussions with 10 CDPOs, 42 supervisors/statistical assistants/gramsevikas, 40 anganwadi workers and helpers. I am thankful to each one of them who received with warmth and enlightened on the status of women in the society, problems of women, women's awareness about health, nutrition and other ongoing developmental programmes. These discussions helped me in concretizing ideas, and to have meaningful interviews with women respondents.

My acknowledgements would be incomplete if I don't thank 200 women who spared their valuable time to respond to my lengthy, and trivial questions. They cheerfully shared their experiences, and ungrudgingly provided answers to all my inquiries. The report is a consolidated outcome of their cooperation and support. I was treated as a member of their families and looked after very well. I am also thankful to the male members who neither interfered with interviews nor my stay at their homes.

During 1998-00, I undertook a study on 'Integrated Cooperative Development Project for Arunachal Pradesh' and 75 days were spent in field visits. I visited all 13 districts and 75 villages in that study which gave me a feel of the state, its generous, hospitable, and colourful people. I collected large volume of secondary data from Departments of agriculture, horticulture, animal husbandry and veterinary, fisheries, education, health, rural development, social welfare, women and child development, NABARD, etc. I am thankful to all officers who provided access to the data. Officials of the Directorate of Economics and Statistics too provided data used in the study and I thank them all. I met Dr. D. K. Bora, Director, Directorate of Research during my field visit to Lohit district. Dr. Bora has shown interest in the study and provided reports/articles/old volumes of Reasurn for my office use. I am extremely thankful to Dr. Bora for his support.

I am also thankful to Mr. Vijay Swamy, Secretary, Gyanodaya, a service mission for Arunachal Pradesh. Mr. Swamy briefed me about the existing self-help groups in the state and provided material on their working.

Conducting field visits in 5 districts drawn from different regions of Arunachal Pradesh is challenging and risky. It is so because there are few lateral roads connecting districts and towns. As a result, one has to journey up north from plains of Assam, come down south, and climb up once again in order to enter other district. Public transport including Pawanhans service is irregular on these routes and undependable. Heavy rainfall, landslides, inclement weather, and snowfall are not uncommon. I brought 100 kgs of manuscripts, typed, and printed material, 100 photographs, and impressions to last a life time.

I am thankful to Sh. Atul Sinha, IAS, Secretary, Department of Development of North Eastern Region, Government of India for going through report and providing valuable suggestions.

I am also thankful to my wife Mrs. V. Venkata Ramana, daughters Omkara Lakshmi, and Srividya Rao who provided the necessary moral support for conducting field visits in this hilly, inhospitable, and exceptionally difficult terrain.

Initial chapters of the report were typed by Miss. V. Yagneswari, Miss. Pushpaleela P. Nadar, and Mr. Vasant U. Alone joined in the month of June and completed upto Chapter 8. Chapters 9 and 10 were completed by Ms. Pushpaleela P. Nadar. I thank them all for this support. Finally, all observations and remarks are my own, and for any shortcomings, I am alone responsible.

V.M. RAO

CONTENTS

LIST OF TABLES

LIST OF CHART, MAPS AND APPENDICES

CHART

LIST OF MAPS

LIST OF APPENDICES

1

INTRODUCTION

Preamble

Scheduled tribes constitute the backward segment of the Indian society. The tribal population in India is generally designated as adiwasis/adibasis implying original inhabitants. They constitute 8.08% of the total Indian population (Office of the Registrar of General and Census Commissioner, 1994). They are a virile people who went astray sometimes. Once late Pandit Jawaharlal Nehru said, "in the tribal people, I have found many qualities which I miss in the people of plains, cities, and other parts of India". Pandit Nehru suggested five broad principles for the welfare of tribals : (a) plans in consonance with tribals own genius, (b) safeguarding tribals lands and forests, (c) imparting training to shoulder responsibilities, (d) close coordination between developmental officers and tribals, and (e) evaluation of tribal welfare activities with reference to qualities and character of the human beings involved. Compared to other categories, incidence of poverty is high (53%) in tribal population and literacy is the lowest (16.35%). Realising these inequalities, the constitution has provided certain privileges to tribals under Article 275. It was felt that the concern for tribal development should be oriented towards bridging the gap between tribals and non-tribals so that they become equal partners in development programmes.

The concept of Tribal Sub-plan was introduced during Fifth Five Year Plan (1976) to facilitate monitoring of development programmes for Scheduled Tribes. This was followed by the Integrated Tribal Development Projects

(ITDP) to control, direct, and manage the development activities of various tribals (Verghese, 1983). At the end of Seventh Five Year Plan, the Tribal sub-plan strategy was implemented through 191 ITDPs, 269 pockets of tribal concentration, and 74 primitive tribal group projects (Planning Commission, 1993). These programmes were continued during Eighth and Ninth Five Year Plans. Further, State Tribal Development Cooperative Federations were established to undertake collection and marketing of minor forest produce in such a way as to ensure reasonable returns to tribals. These state level cooperatives are federated to form Tribal Cooperative Marketing Development Federation Limited (TRIFED) at the national level.

Status of Tribal Women

In the tribal socio-economic set up, it is the women[1] who occupy dominant role rather than the men, consequently their social status is much higher when compared to their counterparts in other parts of the country. However, contribution of tribal women to the family starts from childhood and continues unabated till their death. While the ratio of male and female workers to the total population of the country is 5:1, it is 3:1 for tribal population. Among the non-tribal women, 12% are workers and it is 21% among tribal women (Mukhopadhyay, 1992). Among Mishmis, Nishis, Adis, Monpas, Apatanis, etc. of Arunachal Pradesh, women play a major role in agriculture, collection of fuel wood, collection of roots, vegetables, and tubers which supplement family diet and look after livestock. Thus, a woman's initiative is foremost in tribal family affairs.

The primacy of the female principle is reflected in the general belief among various tribes that Mother is the origin of everything. The myths and beliefs of Khasis and Garos of Meghalaya, Noctoes, Singphos, Mishmis, Tangsas, Adis, Sherdukpens, Monpas, Nishis, and many other tribes of Arunachal are based on female divinities. The feminine principle is so overbearing that sun is considered a female and the moon a male; fire is female and ashes male.

Women have freedom to choose their spouse as among Adis of Arunachal Pradesh. The family of the bride is compensated by bridegroom's family as the former suffers a loss of their daughter due to her marriage. This is dowry-in-reverse practice and a testimony of the importance of women. Further, women of this region are independent to a great extent. Their talent finds fulfillment in running the household chores, tending infants tied to their backs while working in the Jhum fields/forests or shopping or even fetching water from a far off source. Women play a major role in Jhum cultivation, providing nearly 70-75% of labour. They spend considerable time in forests for their livelihood and are called guardians of bio-diversity. Their contribution is much more than the menfolk in running various errands and attending to multifarious responsibilities like sowing seeds, watering fields, fencing, transplanting, weeding, harvesting, and preservation of grains/meat/forest produce.

These women are excellent weavers and repositories of cultural and folk traditions. The Bihu dances of Assam, the Bamboo dance of Mizoram, Ponung dance of Arunachal Pradesh, and Hozaigiri dance of Reangs of Tripura have been retained and practised in popularity without contamination from pop and modern variations. The women of the region are hard working and scorn idleness (Bawa, 2001). A popular ballad of Arunachal Pradesh describing the first woman you know-your mother-is given below:

Hi-yun yun-sin la
Ane gu-min-si
Gu-min hi-re-go
Ir-men-la-ju-ka

Built around the motif of cotton picking, this ballad sings of a woman's life; her joys, her sorrows, the inevitability in her life and the hope (Araham, 2000).

Although there are no signs of matriarchy in Arunachal, women hold a high and honourable position. They work on equal terms with men in jhums and make their influence felt in tribal councils (only few tribes have this practice). Women can become shamans and their intimate relations with the unseen world gives them great authority. Adi women, with daos in their hands and wearing sacred ornaments, often lead the ceremonial dances. There was an Aka Rani, wealthy and powerful, and the wives of great Wancho and Nocte nobles are very fine ladies, possed of a natural grace and dignity; they have many privileges and social duties (Elwin, 1959).

Realising the importance of women and their problems, Government of Arunachal Pradesh passed a bill for constitution of state commission for women (2002). The bill aims at providing for the constitution of a women's commission in the state to improve the status of women and to enquire into unfair practices affecting women and matters connected therewith or incidental thereto. It is hoped that such an act would go a long way to protect the fundamental rights of women enshrined in the constitution. The commission has been vested with powers of civil court and its proceedings would be deemed to be judicial. It would submit annual reports to government covering rights and other issues of women. Recommendations of the commission would be placed in the assembly to cause necessary action within 60 days. The government is also required to consult the commission on matters affecting the women of the state. It would work as a watch dog to protect and promote the privileges of women (Kumar, 2002).

Despite their massive contribution, there is no comprehensive study which looked into the socio-economic conditions of these women. A mention about studies conducted by Dutta (1975), Mishra (1991), and Pandey, *et al.* (1997) are in order here. These studies were aimed at socio-economic status of women of Arunachal. Mishra's study was exclusively about the Mishing women of Upper Subansiri and East Kameng. Pandey, *et al.* (1997) provides a description of almost all tribes of Arunachal. Above studies are not empirical and hardly any quantitative data are available. It would be difficult to make meaningful comparisons in the absence of quantitative data. Such an analytical study not only helps in understanding living conditions of tribal women but also provide reasons for success and/or failure of the various developmental programmes being implemented by Government of India/Government of Arunachal Pradesh. Such a study also would provide answers for intervention mechanisms required to uplift tribal women.

Objectives

The overall objective of the study is to capture the socio-economic conditions of tribal women in Arunachal Pradesh. Specific objectives of the study are:

1. to review various governmental programmes for development of tribal women in the state,
2. to study martial, and economic status of selected women,
3. to analyse time allocation, and participation in decision-making process of tribal women,
4. to understand the awareness of respondents about cooperatives, health, ICDS, and government loaning,
5. to observe working of self-help groups in the state and to suggest a financial package for strengthening SHGs, and
6. to document case studies on typical tribal women.

Methodology

The study is conducted in Arunachal Pradesh. It is one of the seven sisters of north-eastern states. The region (NEFA) was formed as a full-fledged state on February 20, 1987. It is skirted by Bhutan in west, Tibet and China in north and north-east, Myanmar to east and Assam in south. It is the largest state, area-wise, in north-eastern region. Monpas, Akas, Apatanis, Adis, Miris, Wangchoos, Mishims, Nocktes, etc. of mangolian descent live here (Dutta, and Dutta 1990). Total population of the state is 10.11 lakhs, and 64% of them are tribals. In all, there are 3257 villages of which 3176 villages have less than 1000 population. Literacy rate is 41.6%. It is the most sparsely populated area of the country with 10 persons/sq.km. However, only 4% of the geographical area is under cultivation and as much as 63% is occupied by forests. Farming (slash and burn), hunting and forestry are their means of livelihood.

Both primary and secondary data were collected to address the stated objectives. Based on concentration of various tribes, 5 districts were selected (Lohit[2], Dibang Valley, Upper Siang, Lower Subansiri, and West Kameng), and 8 Anganwadi centres drawn from two Integrated Child

Development Services (ICDS) area from each district were identified for a detailed study. Location of Arunachal Pradesh in India, various districts of Arunachal, selected districts, and corresponding villages for the study are provided in Maps 1.1 to 1.7. A moderate sample of 5 tribal women were interviewed from each selected Anganwadi centre. Thus, the sample includes 200 women respondents spread over 40 Anganwadi centres, 10 ICDS project areas, and 5 districts. Presence of Anganwadi centre, number of households in the village, spread of distance from district headquarter, and concentration of a major tribe are the

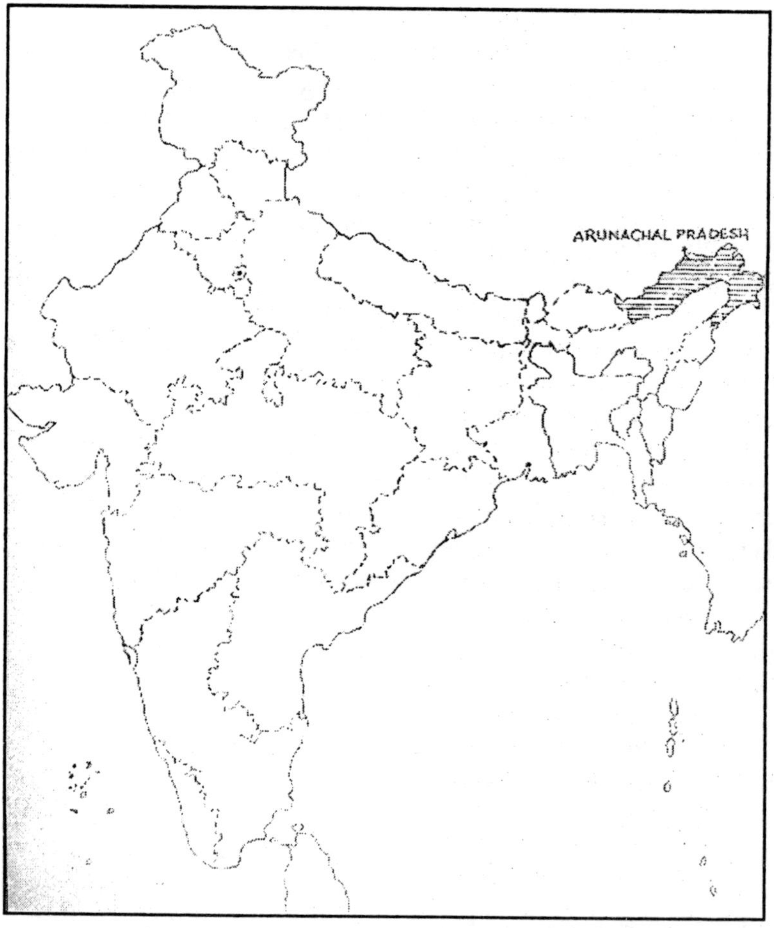

Map 1.1: Location of Arunachal Pradesh in India

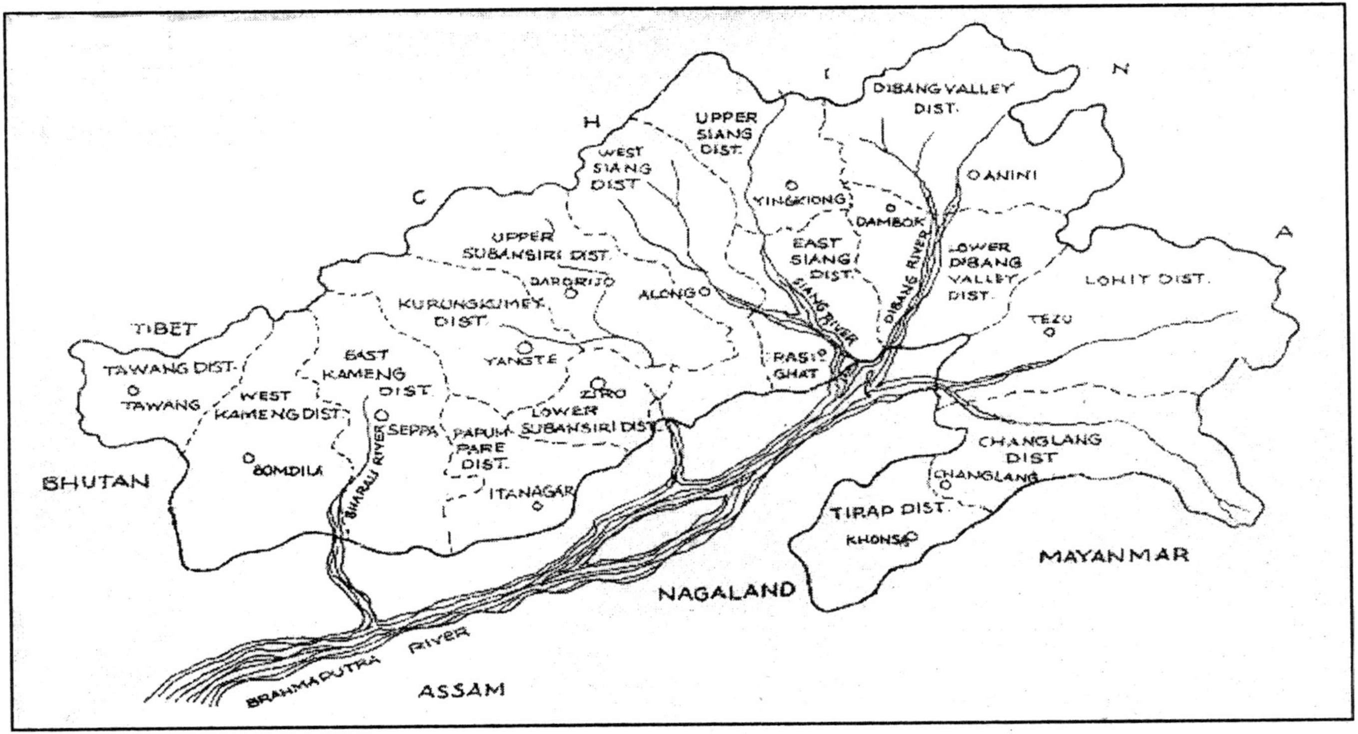

Map 1.2: Location of various districts of Arunachal Pradesh

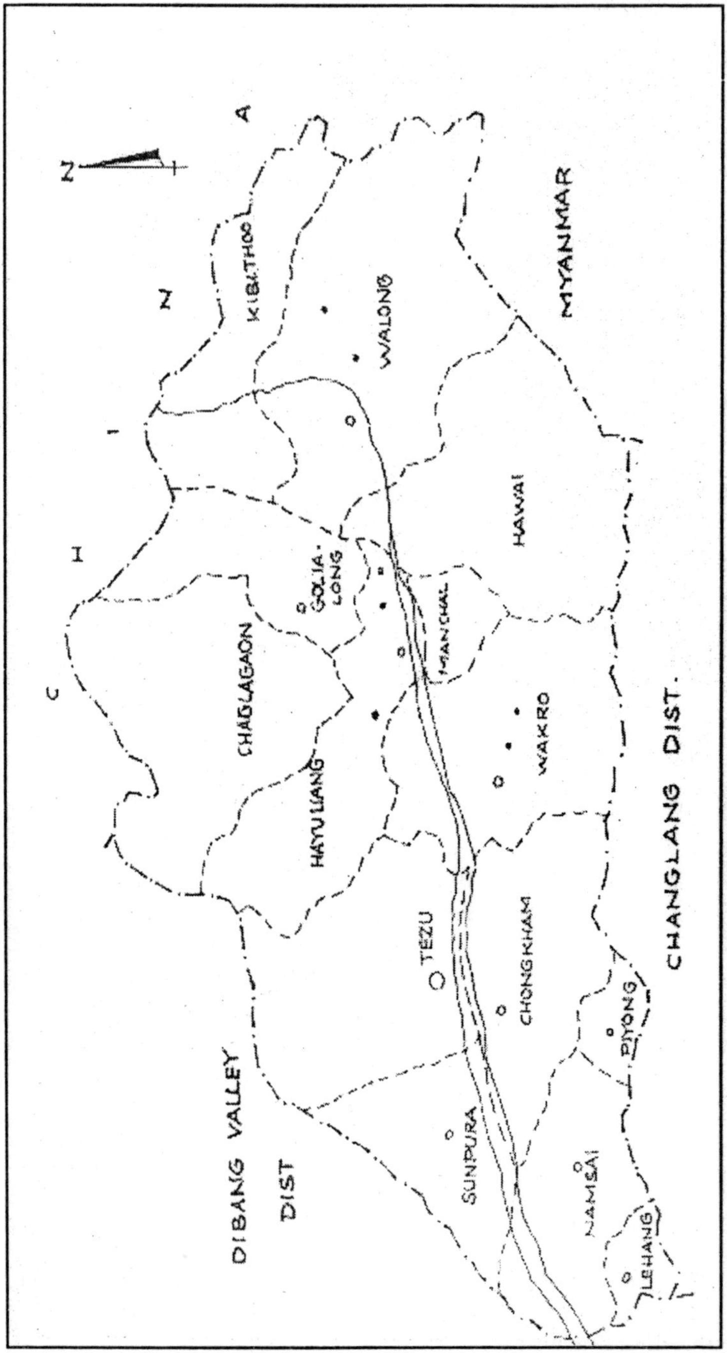

Map 1.3: Location of selected villages in Lohit district

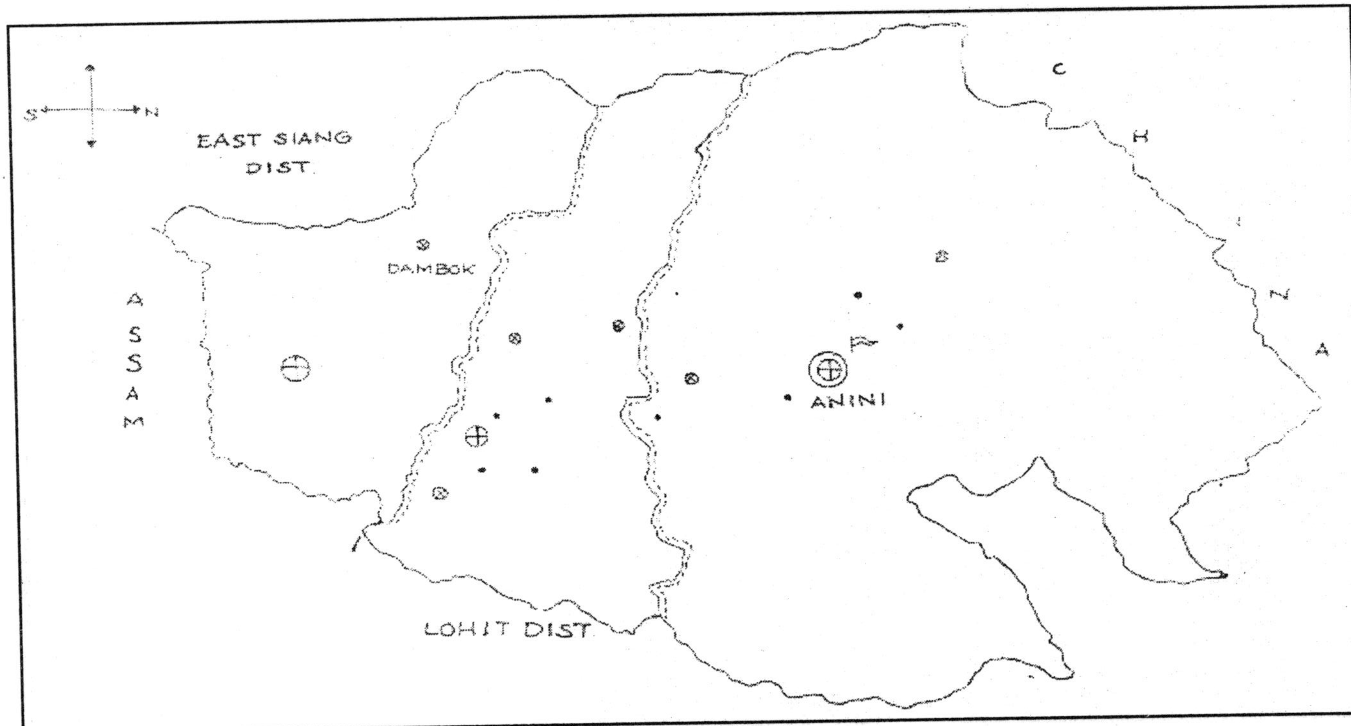

Map 1.4: Location of selected villages in Dibang Valley district

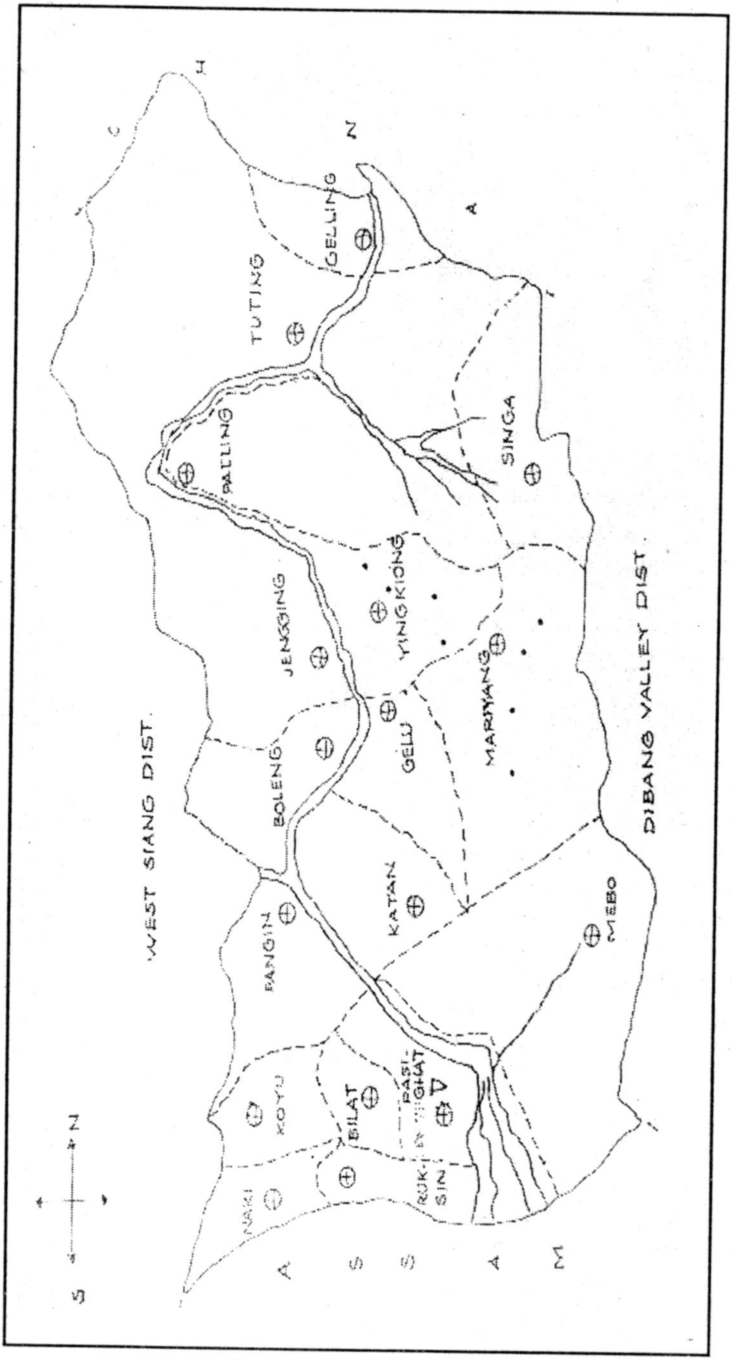

Map 1.5: Location of selected villages in Upper Siang district

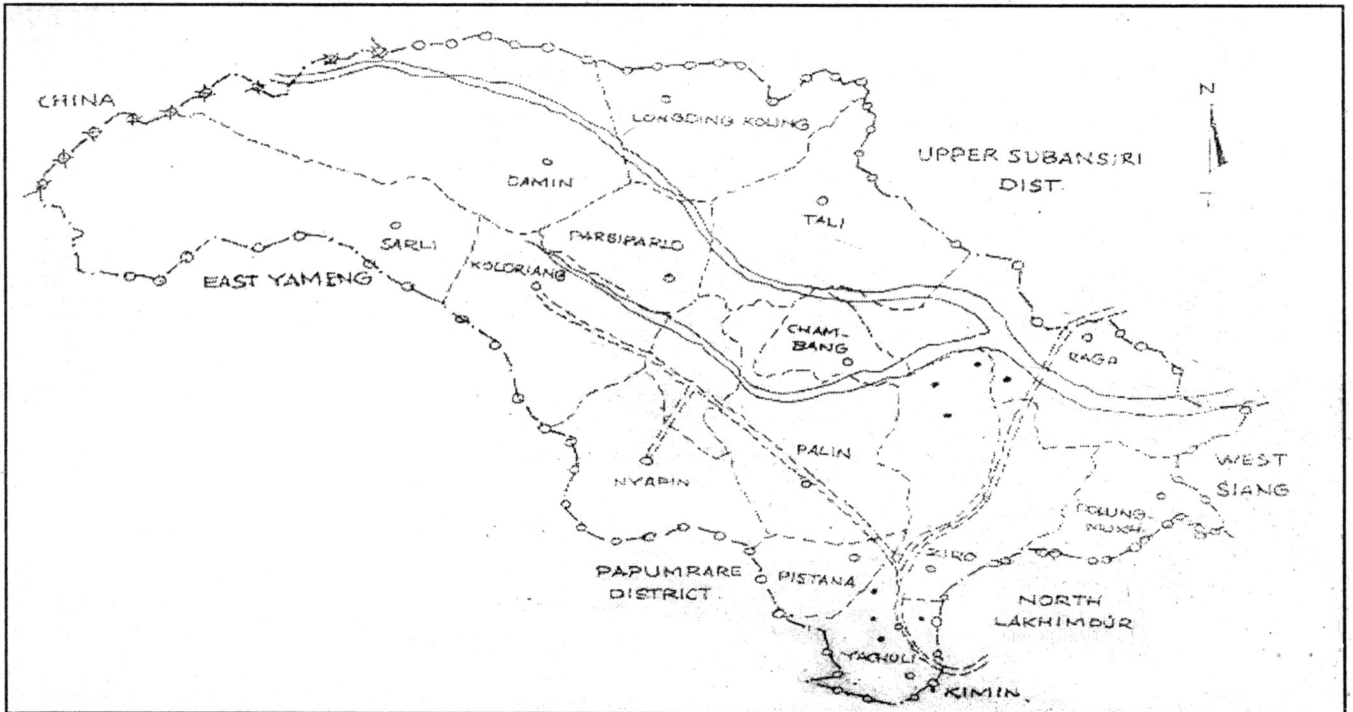

Map 1.6: Location of selected villages in Lower Subansiri district

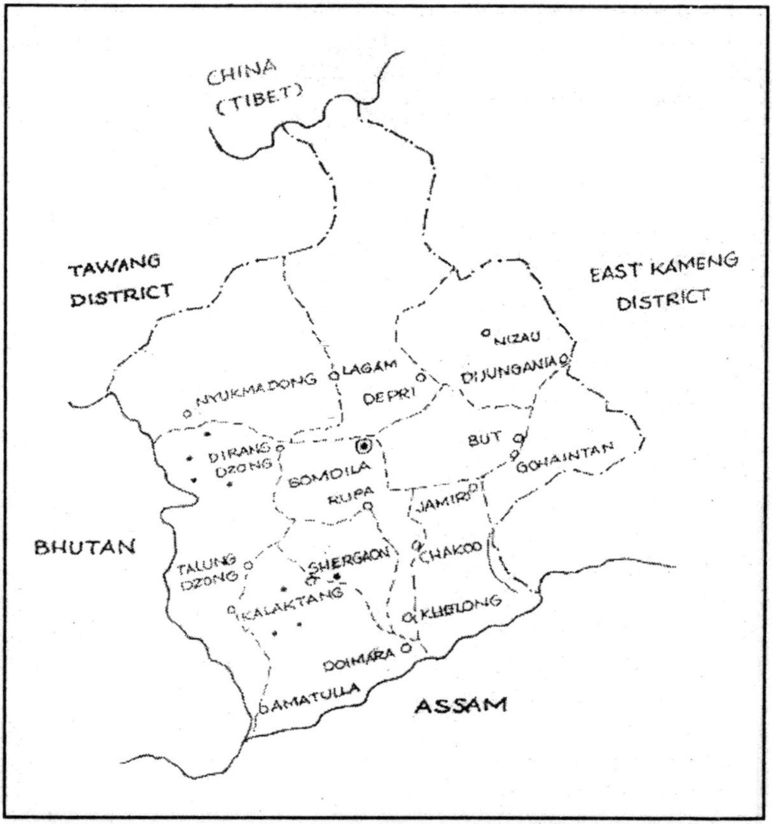

Map 1.7: Location of selected villages in West Kameng district

criteria used for inclusion of villages in the study. Pre-tested questionnaires were used to collect data on age, tribe, educational status, marriage profile, family income, time allocation, awareness about health, cooperatives, ICDS, and developmental programmes, role in household, agriculture, horticulture, animal husbandry, collection of forest produce, decision making process, etc. Primary data are supported by secondary data collected from state departments like social welfare, women and child development, family planning, education, agriculture, horticulture, animal husbandry, health, rural development, etc. Extensive discussions are also held with senior officers incharge of various developmental programmes to elicit their opinions/suggestions to improve status of women in the society. Data are collected during

October 2001-May 2002 and in all 80 days are spent in the field.

Organisation of the Report

The report is presented in ten chapters. Chapter 1 is devoted to introduction to tribal world, status of tribal women, need for the study, objectives, and methodology. A profile of Arunachal Pradesh is presented in Chapter 2. Various developmental programmes aimed at women of Arunachal are discussed in Chapter 3. Chapter 4 provides profiles of selected districts and assistance provided to women under IRDP and DWCRA. Chapter 5 deals with martial, and economic status of women. Workloads, and participation in decision-making process among tribal women is covered in Chapter 6. Chapter 7 is devoted to study awareness of respondents about cooperatives, health, ICDS, and government loaning. Working of women self-help groups is studied in Chapter 8, and individual case studies of selected women are presented in Chapter 9. Summary and recommendations comprised Chapter 10.

NOTES

1. According to Biblical description of creation of women, the word female was made from its root word 'male'. According to another group of scholars origin of word female is from the latin word 'femina' for woman. From that beginning came femella, which passed into French as femelle and then into English female.
2. Initially, Tirap district was formed part of the study. However, due to insurgency and the resultant disturbances, it was replaced by Lohit district.

2

AN OVERVIEW OF ARUNACHAL PRADESH

Introduction

Many Indians and outsiders are not aware of history of Arunachal. Information on Arunachal is scanty and scattered. Further, there are few books which dealt with the subject comprehensively. An attempt is made in this chapter to compile and put together facts in an orderly form for the benefit of the readers. Extensive touring in the state by the author also helped in arranging the material.

Arunachal Pradesh[1] (mountains of rising sun) with a total area of 83743 sq.kms is situated in the north-east extremity of India. Topographically the plains and foothills cover about 10-15% of Arunachal's total area. Broad valleys and plateaus cover about 35% of the area, while steep slopes account for about 35%. Snow clad peaks and pastoral lands occupy 18-20% of the land. Area-wise, it is the largest state in the north-east region of India. It has a long international border with Bhutan to west (160 km), China in north and north-east (1030 km), and Myanmar to east (440 km). The neighbouring states of Assam and Nagaland are in south. The state has a vital significance because of its distinctive, ethnic, linguistic, and religious features. It is lying between 26°4'-29°3' north latitude and 89°-97.5° east longitude representing a beautiful scenery with irregular mountainous topography. Besides streams, rivers, mountains, and peaks,[2] its endless variations in scenic beauty are the first to greet sunrise in the country. It was here that Parasurama washed away his sins, Vyasa meditated, Bhishmaka founded his kingdom,

Lord Krishna married his consort Rukmini, and king Balinarayana drew men for his armies from among the hardy people. The 6th Dalai Lama was born, and the 13th found refuge on this soil.

History and Evolution

Arunachal has practically no written records relating to tribal[3] history, except some. Late Verrier Elwin put it in his inimitable style that 'the history of what is known as oral literature and a number of historical ruins lying in foothills along the region.[4] The North-East Frontier Agency (Arunachal Pradesh) ascends for hundreds of years into the mist of tradition and mythology'. References to early Ahom[5] Buranjies as well as other records tell about the relations between Arunachal and Assam and influence exercised by Ahom Kings over these areas.

The British came to Assam during Anglo-Burmese war of 1824-26 and occupied it as a conquered territory. After the final expulsion of the Burmese troops the British had to take over the charges of administration of Assam as stipulated in the treaty of Yandaboo (1926). This event forced British Assam government to deal with hill tribes of Arunachal Pradesh as the tribemen had age old prescriptive claims over the plains of Assam bordering hills and were accustomed to collect taxes annually from Assamese inhabitants. Between 1826-61, it was kept as a non-regulation area and the post of chief commissionership for Assam was constituted in 1874 (till that time it was a part of Bengal). Scheduled districts regulation was also passed during the same year.[6] Lieutenant R. Wilcox extensively surveyed the land of Arunachal during 1826-28. During the last quarter of 19th century British expedited a number of primitive expeditions against Arunachalis. Jack Francis Needham of the Bengal police was appointed as Assistant Political Officer under the Deputy Commissioner of Lakhimpur with headquarters as Sadiya in 1882. He was advised to acquaint himself and deal with frontier tribes. Later British established an outpost at Pasighat in 1912. During British period the territory was economically backward and politically fragmented. Intentionally Britishers kept these people aloof from the rest of the country with a view to 'keep them politically unconscious'.

These tribals used to collect 'posa'[7] in the neighbouring plains of Assam during Ahoms period which continued, reluctantly, during early British regime too. Britishers organised number of expeditions to bring hill people under their control. Till 1875 Arunachal as a geographical unit was indefinite. Inner Line Regulation[8] was laid down (1873) in: (a) Balipara Frontier Tract, (b) Sadiya Frontier Tract and Lakhimpur, and (c) Sibsagar sub-divisions (map 2.1). With the boundary with Assam fixed, tribes beyond inner line were left to themselves, engaged so far in extracting and/or blackmail from Assam villages near foothills. Political officers were appointed who could collect from village headmen, wherever possible, a token toll tax or house tax. This introduction of administration, though loose, started the process of knitting tribes into a geographical unit, for every extending till other boundary with Tibet and China was demarcated with the McMahon Line in 1914 (map 2.2). The chief commissioner of Assam proposed to Government of India for division of frontier tracts, which after Simla conference was supposed to extend upto international border (McMahon Line), into three sub-sectors as recommended by Major General H. Bower.

Arunachal acquired an identity of its own for the first time in 1914, when some tribal areas were separated from the then Darrang and Lakhimpur districts of Assam to form North East Frontier Tract (NEFT). The NEFT was further sub-divided, from east to west, into the Balipara Frontier Tract, the Sadiya Frontier Tract, and the Tirap Frontier Tract during various stages of evolution between 1914-43 (Appendix 2.1)[9]. All the frontier tracts of Assam were declared as backward tracts in 1921 where only such laws would operate as the Governor in Council might direct. At the time of independence, present territory of Arunachal was in part B of sixth schedule of the constitution as tribal areas of Assam. Part B includes north-east frontier tract including: (a) Balipara Frontier Tract, the Tirap Frontier Tract, the Abor Hills district, and the Mishmi Hills district, and (b) the Naga tribal area. Together, they were renamed as North-East Frontier Agency (NEFA) in 1951.

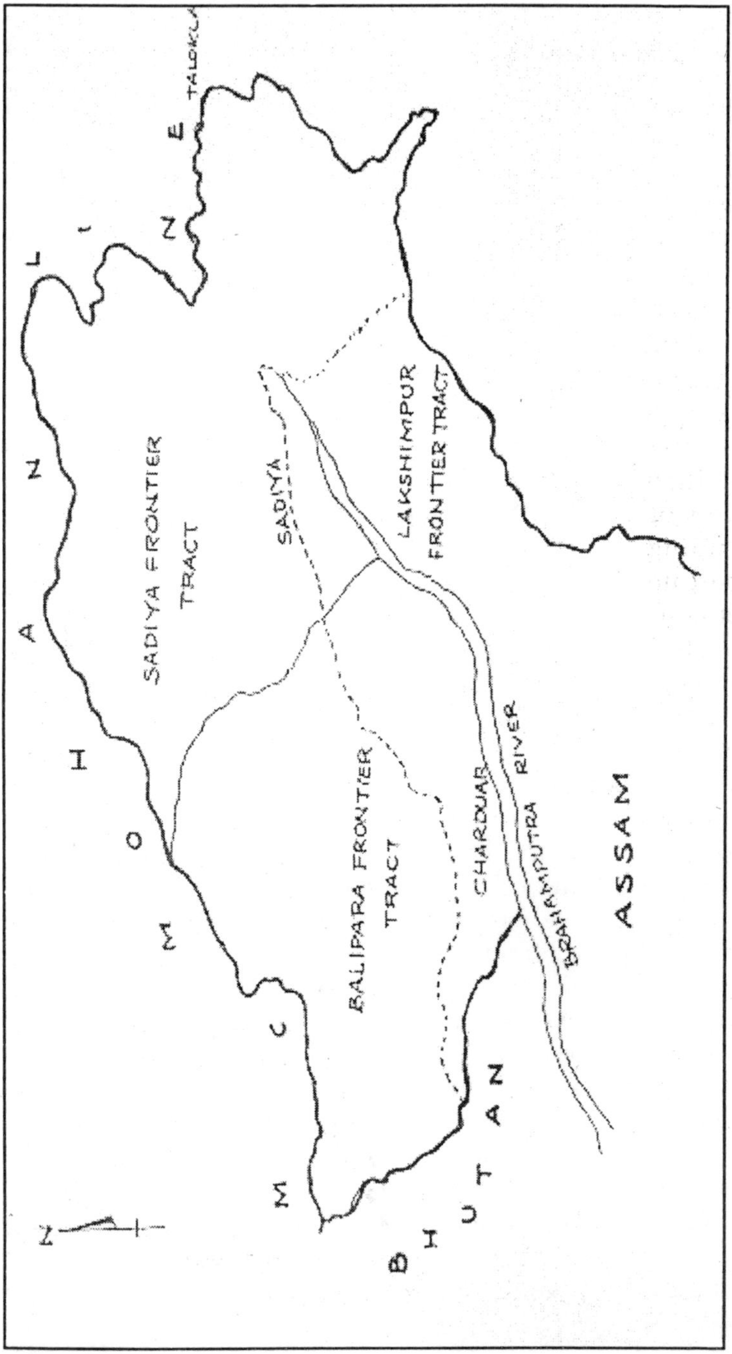

Map 2.1: North-East Frontier Tract, 1919

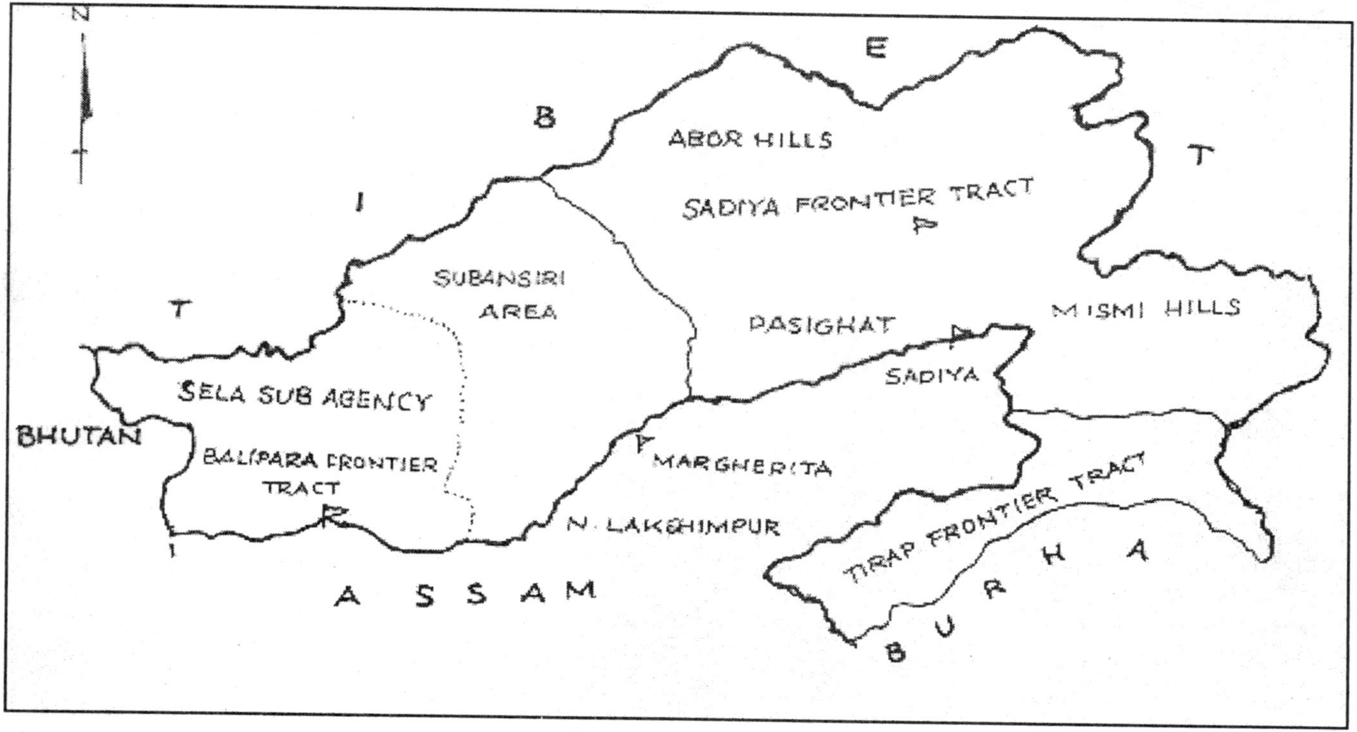

Map 2.2: North-East Frontier Tract, 1914

The NEFA was reconstituted [North-east Frontier Areas (Administration) Regulation of 1954] into Kameng Frontier Division, Subansiri Frontier Division (Balipara Frontier Tract), Siang Frontier Division (Abor Hills District), Lohit Frontier Division (Mishmi Hills District), Tirap Frontier Division (Tirap Frontier Tract), and Tuesang Frontier Division (Naga Tribal area). The later was separated from NEFA in 1957 and merged with newly constituted Nagar Hills (Tuensang area now forms the state of Nagaland). While NEFA was scheduled[10] as part of Assam during 1950-65, its administration was carried out by Governor of Assam as Agnet of President of India under general supervision and control of the Ministry of External Affairs. The Governor of Assam was assisted by an Advisor to look after the affairs of Arunachal whose office was at Shillong, former capital of Assam, now the capital of Meghalaya. Later, based on the recommendations of Daying Ering Commission (1965), the responsibility was passed on to Ministry of Home Affairs in 1965. Subsequently, five sub-divisions of the territory (Kameng, Subansiri, Siang, Lohit, and Tirap) became five districts. Four districts were added in 1980 and two in 1984. These districts have been further sub-divided, with the passage of time, and the territory presently (2002) has 15 districts.

Following the recommendations of Daying Ering Commission (1965), North-East Frontier Agency Panchyat Raj Regulation was passed to be implemented in 1967. As per this regulation, Agency council was formed at the apex level followed by Zilla Parishads, Anchal Samitis, and Gram Panchayats at the bottom. The village councils which were already recognised under North-East Frontier Administration of Justice Regulation, 1945, were accorded the status of Gram Panchayats. Adult franchise was introduced in 1972 and panchyat bodies including Gram Panchayats were made elective. The region was upgraded as Union Territory of Arunachal Pradesh on January 21, 1972 by the North-east Frontier Areas (Reorganisation) Act of 1971 and placed under the charge of a Chief Commissioner with his headquarters at Shillong which was later shifted to Itanagar in 1974. Subsequently, Agency council was replaced by Pradesh council which inturn was converted into a provisional legislative assembly in 1975. The Chief Commissioner was replaced by Lt. Governor as the administrator assisted by a Chief Minister and a cabinet of four ministers to run the union territory. The first election to a 30 member legislative assembly was held in 1978. Finally, it became a full fledged state on February 20, 1987. On attainment of statehood the Lieutenant Governor was redesignated as Governor and the number of seats in legislative assembly had been increased to 60 accordingly.

McMahon Line

China attacked India in the cold winter of 1962 and captured large part of Arunachal Pradesh. China returned to the pre-war position, after ceasefire. The Chinese invasion of 1962 was a turning point in the history of Arunachal Pradesh. Since then top priority was given to hitherto hidden land. In the contest of Indo-China border dispute Arunachal is most important for various points of view. China has not only refused formal recognition of McMahon Line[11] but claimed all of Arunachal Pradesh up to Himalayan foothills and declared as a 'disputed area'.

Flora and Fauna

Forest cover extends over 51540 sq. km., accounting for about 62% of the total area. Of the total forest area, 15% is reserved and the rest being state forests. Vast climatic variations in the region have resulted in existence of all most all types of timber wealth ranging from tropical teak in foothill jungles to coniferous and alpine of high mountains. Cane, bamboo, and soft wood are grown in the state. Timber varieties like champ, sissa, bhola, khoir, bansum, sal, amari, simul, hollack, hollang, khokan, gamari, sonaru, bogipoma, velum, kadam, chirpine, bluepine, nahar, ajhar, etc. are grown in these forests. The state is famous for rare species of orchids, which are found in all types of forests, altitudinal ranges, and rainfall conditions. More than 500 species of orchids are found in the state. The flora of this remote hill state has medicinal values which are utilised by indigenous people for providing cures without any after-or-side effects like modern medicines. Medicinal herbs such as adhatodavasica, amomum, aromation, coptis teeta, dhatura, clavatum, citronella, rauvolfia, etc. are available in this region. Medicinal plants like boch (cures headache and giddiness), kalmegh (cure for worm dysentery), chhatim saptaparna (cure for dermatitis including leprosy), daruharidra (cure for haemorrhage), nayanatara sadabahar (cure for diabetes, cancer, menorrhagia), amlaki adiphal (cures diarrhea and dysentery), and yathu (cures asthma, bronchitis, and tuberculosis) are also available in this land.

The many unspoiled tree clad slopes contain tigers, leopards, elephants, block panther, deer, bears, monkey, langur, and apes. The mithun (bos frontails) exists both in wild and semi-domesticated form. Mithun is highly valued as a source of wealth and meat. Mithun is a browser and prefers tender shoots and younger leaves of forests to grass of open country. It wanders freely in the jungle finding its own food and brought home only when it is to be slaughtered, exchanged in barter or gifted in marriage. Arunachal is also happy home of hornbill, the extraordinary bird with an inordinately large beak. The white winged wood duck, a rare and endangered species has been sheltered in Namdapha National Park (Changlang district). Takins (ox-goat species) are found in Upper Siang. Both sexes bear identical horns which are almost like those of buffalo.

People and Culture

Racial affiliation of Arunachalis has been described as mangoloid, Indo-mangoloid, Kiratas, protomangoloid, and so on. The people of Arunachal Pradesh are called Indo-Mongoloids by anthropologists while kirata is the generic name given by Indologists. Though we find stray references to these people in Sabhaparva of Mahabharata, periplus of Erythream Sea (a work of first century A.D.), Geography of Ptolemy[12], Kalikapurana, Vishnu Purana, Katha Sarita Sagara, Ramayana, The Tempest, etc. but those do not give sufficient clues to study social formation of these tribes. They are divided into several sub-tribal groups because hills and rivers cut off communities from their neighbors. Perhaps no other region of India has as varied a tapestry of people as Arunachal. There are 25 major tribes and over 100 sub-tribes speaking over 50 dialects. Thus, it is a conglomeration of number of tribes, cultures, socio-economic conditions, and topography. Most of these tribes are individualistic to their core. A list of tribes of Arunachal is provided in Appendix 2.2. According to 1961 census, total number of tribes in Arunachal were only 80, it increased to 110 in 1971 and 111 in 1981. Principle tribes of the state are Monpa, Miji, Aka, Sherdukpen, Nishing, Apatani, Nishi, Tagin, Hill-Miri, Adi, Digaru Mishmi, Idu Mishmi, Miju Mishmi, Khamti, Nocte, Tangsa, and Wancho.

Monpas received Buddhism from Padma Sambhava and are gentle cultured. The Tyongi (Sherdukpens) traces their chief's relationships with powers in the valley to a thousand years back. The proud Bangni-Nishi and the Tagin typifying the ancient Indian ideal of the honourable warrior; the Adis and Mishmis are eager to build academics and careers; the Apatanis with their marvels of wet rice cultivation, the Khamti in their magnificent ceremonial robes; and the peaceful progressive Nocte, Wancho and Tangsa are some of the qualities of this hill people.

Most of these communities are ethnically similar, having derived from an original common stock. But due to geographical isolation certain distinctive characteristics of each tribe in language, dress, and custom can be noticed. They may broadly be divided into three cultural groups on the basis of their socio-religious affinities. Monpas and Sherdukpens (Tawang and West Kameng) follow lamaistic tradition of Mahayana Buddhism. Noted for their religious flavour, villages of these communities have richly decorated Buddhist temples, locally called Gompas. Though largely agriculturists practising terrace cultivation, many of these people are pastoral and breed herds of yak and mountain sheep. Culturally similar to them are Membas and Khambas (East Siang) who live in high mountains along northern borders. Khamtis and Singphos (Tirap and Changlang) inhibiting eastern part of the state are Buddhists of Hinayana sect. They are said to have migrated from Thailand and Burma long ago and still using ancient scripts derived from their original homeland.

The second group of people are Adis, Akas, Apatanis, Nishing, Mishmis, Tangsa, etc. who worship sun and moon god, namely, Donyi-Polo and Apatani, the original ancestor for most of these tribes. Their religious rituals largely coincide with phases of agricultural cycles. They invoke nature dieties and make animal sacrifices. They traditionally practice jhumming or shifting cultivation. The third group comprises Nocte and Wanchos of Tirap and adjoining Nagaland. These are hardy people known for their strictly structured village society in which the hereditary village chief still plays a vital role. The Noctes also practise elementary form of Vaishnavism.

Usually, members of a tribe marry within it (endogamous), and members of a clan always marry outside it (exogamous). Society is patriarchal and primogeniture. Polygamy is common and there are traces of polyandry in some tribes. Marriages are arranged by parents with certain kin or on a basis of exchange, though love marriages are not infrequent. There is a good deal of premartial freedom among younger people, but there is a high standard of fidelity within marriage bond, though divorce is permitted. Local institutions maintain law and order, decides disputes, and take up welfare activities. This institution is known as Kabang in Adis, Bulyang of Apatanis, Male of Akas, Ngothum of Noctes, Wangsu-Wangsa of Wanchoos, Abbala of Idu Mishmis, Yallung-Gandu of Nishis, Tsargan of Monpas, Jung of Sherdukpens, Mokechup of Khamtis, Khaptongwa of Tangsas, Pharai of Miju Mishmis, Ira-Tangdai of Singpho, Bango of Hill-Miri, etc. The chieftain system is also prevalent among Wanchoos, and Noctes.

Arts and Crafts

Artistic craftsmanship in Arunachal has been passed on from one generation to other. The Buddhist tribes make beautiful masks. They also periodically stage pantomimes and masked dances. They make exquisite carpets, painted wooden vessels and silver articles. People from central part of the state are experts in cane and bamboo. They weave articles that are in common use in their daily lives. The shawls and jackets, shoulder bags, and coats all stand for perfection that the people have attained in this art. The people of the south-eastern part of the territory are famous for their wooden carvings. They weave beautiful bags and loincloths too. Goat's hair, ivory, beads of agate and other stones as well as of brass and glass are the specialties of the people of this part of the region.

The womenfolk throughout the territory have an excellent sense of colour. The basic colours that dominate weaver are black, yellow, dark blue, green, and scarlet–all put together in the most fascinating combinations. The weaving designs are essentially geometric varying from a formal arrangement to lines and bands. Most of the domestic requirements are made of cane and bamboo. Hats, baskets, cane vessels, cane belts (woven and plain), bamboo mugswith carvings, a wide variety of ornaments, and jewelry items are crafted by workmen. A specialty of Monpas, the Buddhist community, is carpet weaving, with exotic designs of dragons, geometric and floral patterns. Besides, Monpa wood carver scoops out beautiful cups, dishes, fruit bowls, and magnificent ceremonial masks for dances.

Crafting ornaments is another art widely practiced by Arunachalis. Besides multicoloured beads, feathers of birds and wings of the green beetles are also used as embellishments. The Monpas also make papers for writing religious prayers etc. from pulp of trees called susko or the paper trees. The Akas make bamboo bangles and ear- rings, which are occasionally decorated with various designs. The Khamtis carve out beautiful religious images, figures of dancers, toys and other objects. Beautiful rugs are woven in Adi area. Apatanis, Hill Miris, and Adis make attractive articles in cane and bamboo. The Wanchoos are famous for their wood, and bamboo carved figurines.

Major Fairs and Festivals

Losar is the New Years' Celebration of the Monpas. During the five days of festivities, prayers are offered, religious flags are hoisted atop their homes, Buddhist scriptures are read in every home and butter lamps are lit in houses and the campuses. Reh is essentially associated with the Idu Mishmis, the six-day celebrations special attraction is the Priest dance.

During Tamladu, the Digaru Mishmis offers prayers to the God of the Earth and the God of the Water. The supreme God Jebmalu is also worshipped. Khan is significant because of a ceremony where the priest ties a piece of wool around everybody's neck. During Sangken, people sprinkle water on each other as a sign of merriment. Smearing of rice powder on each other's face marks the beginning of the five day celebrations of Mopin (Table 2.1). From highly stylized religious dance-dramas of Buddhists to the martial steps and colourful performances of the Noctes and Wanchos, dances are the source of real joy. Teams of young girls in perfect rhythmic unison perform the Ponung dance of the Adis. Similar group dances in colourful costumes are performed in Upper and Lower Subansiris.

Table 2.1 : Major Fairs and Festivals of Arunachalis

Occasion	*Tribe involved*	*Month*	*Place(s)*
Losar	Monpas	February/March	Dirang, Tawang, Bomdila
Khan	Mijis	February/March	Bomdila, Bichom
Nechido	Akas	November	Bomdila, Bhalukpang
Nyokum	Nishis	February 26	Itanagar, Ziro, Koloriang, Raga, Palin, Nyapin, Seppa
Mopin	Gallong	April 5, 6	Itanagar, Daporijo, Along, Pasighat, Roing
Sulung	Adi	September 1, 2	Itanagar, Along, Pasighat, Yingkiong
Dree	Apatani	July 5	Itanagar, Ziro
Reh	Idu Mishmis	February-March	Roing, Anini, Tezu
Si- Donyi	Tagin	January 6	Daporijo
Boori- Boot	Hill-Miri	February 6	Daporijo
Aaran	Adi	March 7	Pasighat
Tamladu	Digaru Mishmi	February 15	Tezu
Sangken	Khamtis, Singphos	April 15	Tezu
Makar Sankranti	(all)	January 14	Parasuram Kund
Ojiyale	Wanchoos	March- April	Khonsa, Changlang
Waniyee	Sulung		Koloriang, Toli
Mioko	Apatani	March 1-5	Ziro, Itanagar

Source: Compiled by the author.

Great Earthquake of 1950[13]

It is all happened at 19.39 p.m. of August 15, 1950. The entire upper and central Assam along with the northern hills of the then undivided Assam, which now constitutes the state of Arunachal Pradesh shook by the tremor of a devastating earthquake. According to seismological report the tremor was 8.6[1] in Richter Scale. The epicentre of this earthquake could be located at 20.7 kms north-west of Tajobum (Arunachal Pradesh) a place in the then Mishmi hills in the Indo-China Border. The shock is said to have lasted about 4 to 8 minutes. As usual August being the month of summer, there used to be rain all along and on the fateful day the sky was overcast, right from the morning hours there were intermittent showers. In no time the big buildings were brought down, roads caved in and river course at many a place got diverted from their original course. As if that was not enough, immediately on the aftermath of the earthquake, a devastating flood swept away whatever had remained. The misery of the people knew no bounds. The devastation caused by this earthquake as well as by the flash flood was so great that perhaps no one will ever be able to tell how many people actually lost their lives and the quantum of property lost in the hills.

The most affected areas were the then Abor[14] and Mishmi[15] hills districts of NEFA, a nomenclature applied to the present state of Arunachal Pradesh till 1972. It was reported in a press trust of India dispatch published in Assam Tribune that "terrific land slides, never recorded in world's history had taken place in this district of North-East Frontier of India and all attempts to establish contact with this region inhabited by over a lakh of tribals have failed". Further, it was also reported that an Idu Mishmi village (Adai) was completely wiped out with its estimated number of one hundred fifty villagers (*Amrit Bazar Patrika*, October 9, 1950). Sadiya, the then headquarters of the Mishmi Hills district, itself could be contacted after 45 days of isolation. It was also reported further that the 'topography of the region has undergone tremendous changes and the Abor Hills may have to be mapped a-new' (*Assam Tribune*, October 8, 1950). In Pasighat, new and old official buildings and private buildings as well were extensively damaged (*The Nutan Aromiya*, August 18, 1950). Pasighat is reported to have experienced forty two tremors of the quake. In all, 1526 deaths were recorded in both Arunachal Pradesh and Assam.

Indo-China War of 1962[16]

A mention about 1962 war is essential here as it has changed the pace of development in Arunachal. Background for demarcation of McMahon Line was discussed in an earlier section of this chapter. Late Jawaharlal Nehru believed that India and China freed from foreign domination and had to work hand in hand towards enlightened Asianism. Both countries signed an agreement in 1952 on trade and intercourse between Tibet region of China and India. Under the agreement, India relinquished extra-territorial rights she inherited by the Anglo-Tibetan Trade Regulations (1914). Above all, India recognised Tibet as an integral part of China. However, this friendship could not last for long. Chinese started (1956-57) constructing a motorable road from Sinkiang to Gartok through a considerable portion of Aksai Chin of Indian territory. India conveyed her displeasure while India was told that, 'not the Chinese but the Indian troops had unlawfully intruded into Chinese territory'. They asserted that Aksai Chin had always under Chinese jurisdiction. Border disputes at Bora Hoti, Khurnak Fort, and Lohit valley damped our friendship. The Chinese atlas (The China pictorial 1958) had shown, among others, NEFA as part of China. When the matter was brought to the notice of Chou-en-lai it was reported that these maps were merely reproduction of Kuomintang maps. India was further told that though China objected to McMahon Line, they had accepted the line on the border between China and Burma, and intended to accept it in case of India too.

During this period (March 1959), Dalai Lama took shelter in India. This was the turning point in Indo-China relations and India incurred the displeasure of Chinese government. Soon after arrival of Dalai Lama, a number of clashes took place between the two troops. Chou-en-lai on September 8, 1959 categorically denied that Sino-Indian boundary was ever delimited and said that 'the so called McMahon Line was a product of the British policy of aggression and never been recognised by any Chinese central government and is therefore illegal'. Nehru referred Simla agreement and said that the frontier claimed by India had been determined by history, geography, custom, and tradition. Indian public opinion was roused when on October 20, 1959 nine Indian soldiers on patrol were killed near Kongka Pass (Chang Chenmo valley of Ladakh sector) and 10 taken as prisoners. During this period Chinese laid formal claim 50000 sq. miles of Indian territory in Ladakh and NEFA. Further foreseeing Indo Chinese War, China made friendship with Burma (January 1960), Nepal (March 1960), and Pakistan.

Under these circumstances, Nehru supported by Krishna Menon and B.M. Kaul (Chief of General Staff) decided a forward policy and asked Indian army to advance outposts to check further infiltration of Chinese.

In this direction, Indian soldiers setup a post at Dhola in May-June 1962 which Chinese said that it was in their side. Chinese crossed Thagla ridge and invested Dhola Post (Tawang sector) at 8.00 a.m. on September 8, 1962. A massive Chinese attack began on October 20, 1962 which compelled Indian detachment at Dhola post to beat a hasty retreat. The Thagla confrontation ended in massive Chinese attack on October 20, 1962. This period can be divided into four phases. The first phase, from September 8 to 20 was the advance to contact, ending in exchanging of fire between regular battalians of India and China. The second phase lasted from September 20 to October 3 during which time a scratch force was hurriedly marshaled at Lumpu (Tawang sector), and government and army high command insisting on eviction of the Chinese intruders regardless of the consequences. The third phase from October 3 to 10 marked the replacement of Lt. General Umrao Singh (33 corps commander) and the appointment of Lt. General B.M. Kaul with the task of speeding up operations, and move of 7 Brigade to Namka Chu, culminating in major skirmish of October 10 at Tseng Jong. The fourth and final phase from October 10 to 20 witnessed 7 Brigade helplessly tithered to the Namka Chu valley until it was destroyed on the morning of October 20.

Khinzemane, Longju, Tawang, Jang, and Bomdila fell in rapid succession. Chinese forced Indian troops to withdraw from Galawan, Chief Chap Valley and Pangong lake areas (western sector). Indian troops evacuated Kibitoo and Walong in Lohit valley and Chinese penetrated upto Hayuliang. On the central front, Chinese occupied Tuting, Gelling, Singga, Tato, Manigong, and Mechuka. In the utter despair and anguish, Nehru appealed for military aid on November 19, 1962 to friendly powers. On the midnight of November 20, 1962, India was told by the Chinese premier that on the following day the Chinese frontier guards will cease to fire along the entire Indo-China frontier, and from December 21, 1962 they will withdrew to positions 20 kms behind the lines of actual control which existed on November 7, 1959. He wanted Indian forces to be removed 20 kms from the line of actual control, otherwise, he said, the Chinese reserved the right to strike.

Indian casualities was put at 2420. A number of soldiers shown exemplary bravery in this war. A mention about Subedar Joginder Singh[17] and Riffleman Jaswant Singh is in order here. Subedar Joginder Singh was the commander of a platoon of 1 Sikh, holding a defensive position at a ridge near Tangpen La in NEFA. At 5.30 a.m. on October 23rd, 1962, the Chinese opened a very heavy attack on the Bumla axis with the intention of breaking through to Tawang. The leading battalion of the enemy attacked the ridge in three waves, each above 200 strong. Subedar Joginder Singh and his men mowed down the first wave and the enemy was temporarily halted by the heavy losses it suffered. Within a few minutes a second wave came over and was dealt with similarly. But the platoon had by then lost half of its men.

Subedar Joginder Singh was wounded in the thigh but refused to be evacuated. Under his inspiring leadership the platoon stubbornly held its ground and would not withdrew. Meanwhile, the position was attacked for the third time. Joginder Singh himself manned a light machine gun and shot down a number of soldiers. The Chinese, however, continued to advance despite heavy losses. When the situation became untenable, Joginder Singh with his few men emerged from their position with fixed bayonets and charged the advancing Chinese, bayoneting a number of them before he and his comrades were overpowered. Throughout his action,

Mr. Singh displayed devotion to duty, inspiring leadership, and bravery of the highest order and finally made the supreme sacrifice.

Following the withdrawal of troops from Tawang, 4 Garh Rifles was ordered to deploy in the Jaswantgarh area to facilitate preparation of main defenses in Sela. The BW was disposed with 'A' Coy in Jaswantgarh. 'D' Coy to its right across the road, 'B' Coy to its east and BN HQ with 'C' Coy in the area of Bridge III, about 1500 metres to the east of Jaswantgarh.

A Chinese attempt to infiltrate into the defenses in the guise of local Monpas was thwarted by an alert JCO of this Coy at about 5 a.m. on November 17, 1962. The enemy simultaneously attacked the coy from its left and front in three waves. This was effectively beaten back and the enemy withdrew. This was followed by two more attacks supported by artillery, mortars, and medium machine guns at 7.45 a.m. and 9.10 a.m. respectively. Our troops held their ground and these attacks too met the same fate. The Chinese who were better equipped and had not suffered reverses so far, were more determined when they launched their fourth attack. They moved up a medium machine gun about 40 metres close to the left platoon of this coy and brought down heavy volume of fire on our positions preventing our light machine guns from engaging them.

Lance-naik Trilok Singh, Riffleman Jaswant Singh and Riffleman Gopal Singh volunteered to silence the menancing medium machine guns. By physically neutralising it Jaswant and Gopal armed only with hand grenades, in total disregard for their personal safety crawled under heavy enemy fire to close in with medium machine gun. Trilok provided covering fire with his stun gun. From about 15 metres they hurled hand grenades to silence the medium machine gun and then physically assaulted the position to find two Chinese killed and a third wounded. But still holding on to the weapon, Jaswant, using both his hands snatched the medium machine gun and crawled back. Just as he was about to reach his trench, he was hit by a fatal bullet on his head. Trilok, in the meantime, was spotted by the Chinese and killed by a long burst from an automatic weapon. Gopal badly wounded, managed to drag the captured medium machine gun back to his trench. This entire action took only 15 minutes but the courage of this men charged the course of the battle. Our weapons came alive once again and conclusively beat back the 4th Chinese attack at 11.40 a.m.

Indo-China war had far reaching effects on NEFA. Indian government realized the strategic importance of the region and seriously began to think for the welfare of the people.

Developmental Efforts

Development (materialistic development) came late to Arunachal Pradesh. Primarily due to historical reasons, the region inherited a primitive economic structure at the time of independence. Small self governing communities had perpetuated at a low level of equilibrium, encased, as it were, in a time capsule. With hardly any division of labour and specialisation, the economy presented a picture of self-sufficient households and villages with minimal barter links outside their traditional boundaries. Superimposed on this economic structure was a wide variety of tribal customs and beliefs, with each tribal group fiercely proud of its heritage and naturally wary about alien influences and cultures.

The decision to breach this isolation was indeed monumental. The challenges of initiating development in this area were tremendous and complex. It was a delicate task in social engineering, whereby the conflict of cultures had to be minimised and a transition from primitive environment into a modern technological world effected with minimum friction. Initially, policy towards these excluded and other partially excluded areas was formulated on the basis of excluded areas sub-committee headed by Shri G.N. Bordoloi (1946). The committee felt that 'hill people have not yet been assimilated with people of the plains of Assam and the future of these hills does not seem to lie in absorption rather the evolution should come as far as possible from tribals itself'. The committee recommended 'for protection of tribal rights on land and forest and also tribal customs and traditions'. It sought economic and administrative integration of frontier tribes allowing scope for cultural plurality to co-exist with them. The committee neither justified the continuation of inner line nor did it oppose but emphasised importance of controlling the immigration of non-tribals in hills. The committee advocated a change not suddenly brought to them from outside but a gradual change from within. Late Verrier Elwin was entrusted to look after these tribal affairs in NEFA in 1953 by Late Jawaharlal Nehru as a mark of recognition of his dedicated work among the tribes of central India. Drawing inferences from the Bordoloi Committee, Elwin concritised development policy towards frontier tribals. Foundations for this transition were spelt out in five fundamental principles enunciated by late Prime Minister Jawaharlal Nehru in his forward to Late Verrier Elwin's 'A Philosophy for NEFA' (1957) as:

(1) people should develop along with the lines of their own genius and we should avoid imposing anything on them. We should try to encourage in every way their own traditional art and culture,

(2) tribal rights in land and forests should be respected,

(3) we should try to train and build up a team of their own people to do the work of administration and development. Some technical personnel from outside will, no doubt, be needed especially in the beginning. But we should avoid introducing too many outsiders into the territory,

(4) we should not over administer these areas or overwhelm them with a multiplicity of schemes. We should rather work through, and not in rivalry to, their own social and cultural institutions, and

(5) we should judge results, not by statistics or the amount of money spent, but the quality of human character that is evolved.

These humane principles are the bed-rock on which Arunachal Pradesh raises today. Though planning era commenced in 1951, investment in Arunachal remained insignificant till the end of fourth five year plan. The problem was further compounded by high cost of transporting materials, and sustaining an administrative infrastructure in difficult and inhospitable terrain. There was a shift in the policies pursued during late Prime Minister Mrs. Indira

Gandhi and Arunachal Pradesh took a big leap during Fifth Five Year Plan, and has never looked back since.

Development During 1951-00

An attempt is made in the following paragraphs to highlight achievements of the state in various sub-sectors. Area-wise, Arunachal Pradesh is the largest among seven sisters of north-east India. It has 2.6% of area and 0.1% population of the country (Table 2.2) which led to lower density of population (10 persons/sq. km.) while Assam has as many as 286. Further, literacy rate (41.59%), and sex ratio (859) are the lowest in Arunachal Pradesh compared to her neighbours and the country as whole too. Against all these drawbacks,

Table 2.2 : Profile of North-Eastern States of India

State	*Area (000 ha)*	*Population (000)*	*Density of popul-ation*	*Literacy (%)*	*Sex ratio (%)*	*Work parti-cipation rate (%)*
Arunachal Pradesh	84.00	864	10	41.59	859	46.24
Assam	78.00	22414	286	52.89	923	36.09
Manipur	22.00	1837	82	59.89	958	72.18
Meghalaya	22.00	1775	79	49.10	955	42.67
Mizoram	21.00	690	33	82.27	921	48.91
Nagaland	16.00	1029	73	61.65	886	37.53
Tripura	10.00	2757	263	60.44	945	31.14
All India	3287.00	846303	273	52.21	927	37.46

Source: North Eastern Council (various years).

the work participation is 46% which is much higher than national average. Of the total workers, cultivators occupied as much as 60%, 'others' (34.32%), and agricultural labourers (5.13%) in 1991. More or less similar pattern was noticed in the neighbouring states (Table 2.3).

Net Domestic Product

Net State Domestic Product (NSDP) is regarded as a measure of economic development of the concerned state. Higher the level of NSDP more is the growth and vice versa. NSDP of Arunachal Pradesh in 1980-81 was Rs. 97.70 crores of which 47.5% was in primary sector, 22% in secondary sector and 30.5% was accounted for by tertiary sector (Table 2.4). At

Table 2.3 : Occupational Distribution of Workers (%) in North-eastern India

State	*Cultivators*		*Agricultural labourers*		*HIMPS**		*Others*	
	1981	*1991*	*1981*	*1991*	*1981*	*1991*	*1981*	*1991*
Arunachal Pradesh	71.26	60.36	2.49	5.13	0.32	0.19	25.93	34.32
Assam	NA	50.50	NA	12.08	NA	0.88	NA	36.14
Manipur	63.60	61.77	4.99	6.69	9.68	5.80	21.70	25.84
Meghalaya	62.56	55.31	9.99	12.51	0.84	0.40	26.62	31.78
Mizoram	70.63	61.35	2.49	3.28	0.85	1.02	26.03	34.35
Nagaland	72.18	72.65	6.81	1.41	0.40	0.38	26.51	25.56
Tripura	43.29	38.09	24.00	23.38	1.44	1.42	31.27	37.11

Source: Same as Table 2.2.
* Household industry, manufacturing, processing, and services.

Table 2.4 : Net State Domestic Product at Factor Cost by Economic Activity, 1981-00 (Current Prices)

Year	*Sector*			*Total*	*Per capita (Rs.)*
	Primary	*Secondary*	*Tertiary*		
		(Rs. lakhs)			
1980-81	4619 (47.3)	2170 (22.2)	2981 (30.5)	9770 (110)	1571
1981-82	6809 (51.9)	2460 (18.8)	3849 (29.3)	13118 (100)	2040
1982-83	7530 (49.5)	3067 (20.2)	4610 (30.3)	15207 (100)	2294
1983-84	9677 (56.0)	2295 (13.3)	5305 (30.7)	17277 (100)	2526
1984-85	10957 (54.0)	3263 (16.1)	6060 (29.9)	20280 (100)	2877
1985-86	13955 (56.4)	4015 (16.2)	6772 (27.4)	24742 (100)	3403
1986-87	15532 (55.5)	3993 (14.3)	8475 (30.2)	28000 (100)	3733
1987-88	15228 (50.9)	4715 (15.8)	9980 (33.3)	29923 (100)	3866
1988-89	18440 (52.4)	5102 (14.5)	11672 (33.1)	35214 (100)	4407
1989-90	17330 (47.0)	6707 (18.2)	12809 (34.8)	36846 (100)	4461
1990-91	21381 (46.4)	8383 (18.2)	16281 (35.4)	46045 (100)	5398
1991-92	26124 (45.6)	10049 (17.6)	21063 (36.8)	57236 (100)	6526
1992-93	31644 (46.8)	10646 (15.8)	25264 (37.4)	67554 (100)	7514
1993-94	35695 (43.8)	17175 (21.1)	28663 (35.1)	81533 (100)	8853
1994-95	37168 (41.8)	19831 (22.3)	31901 (35.9)	88900 (100)	9417
1995-96	38723 (43.6)	33920 (38.2)	36659 (41.2)	109302 (100)	11303
1996-97	41955 (35.1)	35773 (30.0)	41631 (34.9)	119359 (100)	12032
1997-98	47652 (34.9)	38699 (28.3)	50171 (36.8)	136522 (100)	13424
1998-99	49439 (38.4)	25626 (19.9)	53584 (41.7)	128649 (100)	15038
1999-00	55326 (36.1)	28331 (18.5)	69618 (45.4)	153275 (100)	15887

Sources: (a) State income unit (1998).
(b) State income unit (1999).
(c) Directorate of Economics and Statistics (2002).

current prices, NSDP increased to Rs. 1365.22 crores showing an annual average growth rate of 72%. Of the total NSDP in 1997-98, primary state accounted for 34.9%, 28.3% by secondary sector, and 36.8% by tertiary sector. Further, across the study period, NSDP shows a falling trends of growth in primary sector, fluctuating trend in secondary sector, and an increasing trend in tertiary sector. The NSDP per capita income at current prices increased from Rs. 1571 in 1980-81 to Rs. 4461 in 1989-90 and further to Rs. 13424 in 1997-98. Percentage increase over the years is 754 with an annual average growth rate of 41.9%.

Data on growth in population of the state are presented in Table 2.5. Population has increased from 3.37 lakhs in 1961 to 8.65 lakhs in 1991, more than 100% increase during 30 years period. But the percentage of ST population to total population has decreased from 88.67 to 63.66 during the same period. Appointing a number of non-tribals from plains was the major factor for this.

Table 2.5 : Growth in Population, 1961-01

Year	*Male*	*Female*	*Total*	*ST population*	*ST population as % of total population*
1961	177680	158878	336558	298439	88.67
1971	251231	216280	468511	369408	78.85
1981	339322	292517	631839	441167	69.82
1991	465004	379554	864558	550351	63.66
2001	573951	517951	1091117	NA	NA

Sources: (a) Directorate of Economics and Statistics (various issues).
(b) Banthia (2001).

Distribution of Various Tribes

The first ever census in Arunachal Pradesh were conducted in 1961 and the entire state was treated as rural. Total population of the state increased from a mere 3.37 lakhs in 1961 to 10.91 lakhs in 2001. There has been a steady decline in the percentage of ST population in the total population of the state (Table 2.5). As mentioned in the Chapter, a number of tribes inhabit this land of five rivers (Subansiri, Siang,

Lohit, Dihang, and Tirap). In absolute numbers, Adi, Nishing, Monpa, Wancho, Mishmi, Tagin, Tangsa, Nocte, Apatani, and Hill-Miri are major tribes (Table 2.6). The state has 13 districts whose names along with headquarters and population in

Table 2.6 : Tribe-wise Distribution of Population, 1961-91

Sl.No.	Name of the tribe	1961	1971	1981	1991
1.	Adi	77187	93959	120839	158059
2.	Aka	2239	2345	2947	3531
3.	Apatani	10793	12888	16580	22526
4.	Deori	NA	2683	3608	5200
5.	Hill-Miri	2442	8174	6936	11017
6.	Khamba	1110	848	342	1333
7.	Khamti	2644	4115	7010	8339
8.	Khowa (Bugun)	659	703	625	1046
9.	Memba	2431	2486	2679	1169
10.	Miji	2079	3549	4074	5779
11.	Mikir	543	1298	598	NA
12.	Mishing	2817	3359	5201	5899
13.	Mishmi	19722	22561	24596	31329
14.	Monpa	20799	28209	32902	38862
15.	Nishing	51023	82178	87075	116258
16.	Nocte	19287	23416	26257	33720
17.	Sherdukpen	1144	1639	2096	2547
18.	Sulung	1781	4288	4233	5443
19.	Singpho	957	1567	2353	2978
20.	Tagin	24055	22107	27124	28860
21.	Tangsa	6741	13447	18921	26016
22.	Wancho	23382	28650	32441	38528
23.	Yobin or lisu	78	926	5	1530
24.	Zekhering	NA	23	14	NA

Source: Chowdhury (1996).

1981, 1991 and 2001 are presented in Table 2.7. Lower Subansiri and Upper Siang were created after 1991 and figures for these two districts are not separately available.

Concentration of various tribes, physical location, and potential in each district are provided in Table 2.8. East and West Siangs, and Changlang district have many tribes living in their territory. Almost all the districts are located in

Table 2.7 : District-wise Population, 1981-01

District	*Headquarter*	*Total population*			*Literacy*
		1981	*1991*	*2001*	
Tawang	Tawang	21735	28287	33146	41.14
West Kameng	Bomdila	41567	56421	74595	61.67
East Kameng	Seppa	42736	50395	57065	40.89
Lower Subansiri	Ziro	NA	83167	97614	45.01
Papum Pare	Itanagar	112650	72811	121750	70.89
Upper Subansiri	Daporijo	39410	50086	54995	50.89
West Siang	Along	68320	89936	103575	60.31
East Siang	Pasighat	76295	71864	87430	60.22
Upper Siang	Yingkiong	NA	27779	33146	49.80
Dibang Valley	Anini	30978	43068	57543	59.45
Lohit	Tezu	69498	109706	143478	56.05
Changlang	Changlang	62211	95530	124994	51.98
Tirap	Khonsa	66439	85508	103575	42.01
Arunachal Pradesh	Itanagar	631839	864558	1091117	54.74

Sources: (a) Duarah (1998).
(b) Directorate of Census Operations (2001).

mountainous regions with varying heights and poor infrastructure. Farther the distance from Inner Line, more difficult region it is. There is scope for hydroelectricity, integrated fish farming, few cash crops, and horticultural crops in the region.

Sex-ratio, literacy rates, and density of population over 1961-01 are presented in Table 2.9. Sex ratio (number of women per 1000 male population) declined from 894 in 1961 to 901 in 2001. Gradual improvement can be noticed in literacy rate and also density of population. District-wise details on villages, circles, community development blocks, literacy, sex ratio, density of population, etc. are presented in Table 2.10. Literacy is the highest in Papum Pare while density of population is more in East Kameng (962 women/ 1000 males).

Land Use Pattern

Net area sown is around ha. 1.65 lakhs, and West, and East Siangs have larger portion of this (Table 2.11). About ha. 65000 land is fallow which can be put to productive use and 21%

Table 2.8 : Concentration of Various Tribes and Potential Across Districts

District	*Major tribes*	*Location*	*Potential*
Tawang	Monpas	2/3rd of the district comprises high mountaineous region (22500 feet)	Tourism, potato, and apples
West Kameng	Monpas, Mijis, Akas, Sherdukpens, and Khawas	Mountaineous with maximum altitude up to 15000 feet	Tourism, handicrafts, and off-season vegetables
East Kameng	Bongnis, Akas, Nishis, Mijis, and Puroites	Inadequate road and communication facilities	Hydroelectricity
Papum Pare	Nishing, and Mikir or Karbi	Mountaineous terrain with varied topography	Handicrafts
Lower Subansiri	Apatani, Bangaro, Hill Miri, Sulung, Tagin, and Nishing	Mountaineous ranging from 200 to 1600 metres	Integrated fish culture, hydroelectricity and ginger
Upper Subansiri	Tagin, Gallongs, and Hill Miri	Mountaineous and road connections are yet to be developed	Hydroelectricity
West Siang	Adis, Membas, Gallongs, Minyong, Bori, Bokar, Pailibo, and Ramo	Mountaineous terrain and inadequate road communication facilities	Potato, ginger, garlic, sugarcane, citrus, citronella, tea, and rubber
East Siang	Adi, Minyongs, Padampassi, Karko, Panjins, Simongs, Mishings, Gallongs, Millangs, and Idu Mishimis	Hilly with altitudes varying from 200 to 5250 feet	Foodgrains, oilseeds, citrus, and tea
Upper Siang	Adia, Membas, and Khambas	Poor communication and infrastructure facilities	Large Cardamom, hydroelectricity, handicrafts
Dibang Valley	Idus, Adis, and Mishings	Many areas are inaccessible	Tourism, ginger, and mustard
Lohit	Mishimis, Khamtis, and Singphos	Mostly hilly with inadequate transport facilities	Tea, and hydel power stations
Changlang	Tangsa, Tutsa, Nocte, Singpho, Millang, Yobin, and Panthai	Half the area is plains	Coal, oil, tea, oilseeds, and ginger
Tirap	Wanchos, and Noctes	Hilly with altitudes varying from 150 to 4615 feet	Coffee, and tea

Source: Compiled from NABARD (1998).

Table 2.9 : Changes in Sex Ratio and Literacy, 1961-01

Year	*Sex ratio*		*Literacy (%)*		*Density/ sq. km.*
	General	*ST*	*General*	*ST*	
1961	894	1013	7.13	2.51	NA
1971	861	1007	11.27	5.20	6
1981	862	1005	20.75	14.04	8
1991	859	998	41.59	34.45	10
2001	901	NA	54.74	NA	13

Source: Same as Table 2.5.

Table 2.10 : District-wise Distribution of Few Developmental Indicators

District	*Area (sq.km.)*	*Population (1991)*	*CD Blocks*	*Circles*	*Villages*	*Sex ratio (1991)*	*Literacy (general) (1991)*	*Density population (1991)*
Tawang	2172	28287	3	6	162	844	29.50	13
West Kameng	7422	56421	3	9	170	822	46.31	8
East Kameng	4134	50395	4	9	275	962	26.20	12
Papum Pare	2875	72811	2	7	252	831	55.11	25
Lower Subansiri	10135	83167	9	15	595	957	30.07	8
Upper Subansiri	7032	50086	5	11	418	867	38.31	7
West Siang	8325	89936	7	17	408	873	45.64	11
East Siang	45.70	71864	4	10	132	877	44.30	10
Upper Siang	56.23	27779	4	10	72	862	44.30	NA
Dibang Valley	13029	43068	3	9	238	788	46.88	3
Lohit	11402	109706	5	13	487	797	49.21	10
Changlang	4662	95530	4	11	285	863	43.20	20
Tirap	2362	85508	3	8	155	862	32.06	36
Total	83743	864558	56	135	3649	859	41.59	10

Source: Compiled by the author.

Table 2.11 : District-wise Classification of Land-use, 1997-98

District	*Geographical area (lakh ha)*	*Net area sown (ha)*	*Fallow land (ha)*	*Land not available for cultivation (ha)*	*Net irrigated area by canals (ha)*
Tawang	21.72	3255	524	815	452
West Kameng	74.22	6445	2786	892	117
East Kameng	41.34	9394	9549	1181	2390
Papum Pare	28.75	11239	4367	2495	1471
Lower Subansiri	101.35	18030	7666	7541	3142
Upper Suansiri	70.32	6531	13517	2646	349
West Siang	83.25	26779	6438	2360	6661
East Siang	45.70	25465	7082	20396	9795
Upper Siang	56.23	NA	NA	NA	NA
Dibang Valley	130.29	13534	828	39	2820
Lohit	114.02	16544	2157	2777	3154
Changlang	46.62	14501	2869	1558	3788
Tirap	23.62	13002	6847	1316	616
Total	837.43	64719	64630	44016	34755

Source: Same as Table 2.5.

of the net sown area is irrigated. As mentioned earlier, it is a high rainfall area with erratic nature (Table 2.12). Five major rivers (Kameng, Subansiri, Siang, Lohit, and Tirap) with a large number of tributaries have drained the waters of this

Table 2.12 : District-wise Annual Rainfall, 1992-99

District	*1992*	*1993*	*1994*	*1995*	*1996*	*1997*	*1998*	*1999*
Tawang	2423	2670	2697	2697	2688	2581	2760	2862
Bomdila	1411	1709	1409	1908	1694	1880	711	1539
Seppa	1605	2212	1407	1954	648	1777	2596	1445
Ziro	1108	1081	1245	1223	775	1075	NA	1008
Itanagar	4033	6484	6084	2845	2338	3459	5171	3738
Daporijo	3091	2038	1666	1513	825	897	756	1558
Along	2998	2291	1939	2193	2413	3270	2608	1987
Pasighat	4961	2885	823	4654	4671	3036	5571	5591
Yingkiong	NA	NA	NA	NA	NA	2775	2818	2910
Anini	2150	2505	2513	NA	NA	1239	5278	3851
Tezu	2850	3194	2469	3225	NA	3811	4259	3034
Changlang	2931	2837	2415	4188	2914	3159	2083	3783
Khonsa	1155	5174	3884	2996	2059	3249	6209	3724

Source: Same as Table 2.5.

vast area to empty in the Brahmaputra. These rivers, besides being an important source of protein rich fish, have of late begun to provide hydel powers to illuminate the hitherto formidable land.

Agriculture

Agriculture is the primary occupation of Arunachalis. From time immemorial, they have been following slash and burn cultivation (jhumming) with no out of pocket expenses. It is locally known as Rong-Ngo where patches of forests are annually cut, burnt, and seeds are sown in the resulting ash cover. Land having thick vegetation is selected to provide enough ash as top cover. Ash content in the soil reduces acidity and balances its fertility. This kind of agriculture is completely dependent on human energy. Cut down forests are mostly burnt out during night to destroy insects and pests by attracting them to the light of fire.

Agricultural demonstration farms established by British India, during later part of 19th century at trading posts, educated tribesmen. However, seeds of development were sown by British forces, during early 1900s, employed in building roads and cultivating rice (terraces or wet rice cultivation on plain lands). The examples of forces were followed by tribals, which benefited them. Later, agricultural demonstrators were employed to educate people in improved methods of cultivation, and improved varieties of seeds were supplied in some areas to impress upon tribal folk. This spirit of British India could not be continued due to two world wars. Appointment of J.P. Mills as advisor to the Governor of Assam for tribal affairs in 1943 marked beginning of a new era of development in Arunachal Pradesh. He can be termed as founder of modern Arunachal because it is in his policy there lies the foundation of various developmental departments (medical, education, agriculture, engineering, administration, etc.).

Department of Agriculture was created in 1946 with the appointment of an Agricultural Officer[18] followed by Director of Agriculture in 1956. To demonstrate latest techniques for agriculture, several demonstration farms were started. A Gram Sevak Training Centre was set up at Pasighat to cater basic training needs of farmers and field functionaries. Further, five farmers training centres (Salari in East Kameng, Pasighat in East Siang, Ziro in Lower Subansiri, Namsang in Tirap, and Khern in Lohit) were set up to provide short term programmes to farmers. Area, and production of major crops during 1978-00 are provided in Tables 2.13 and 2.14. An area of ha. 1.39 lakhs was under various crops in 1977-78 and 72% of it was allocated to cereals. Area under commercial crops

Table 2.13 : Changes in Area (Hectares) Under Major Crops, 1978-00

Crop	*1978*	*1994*	*1995*	*1996*	*1997*	*1998*	*2000*
Rice	78229	122000	109408	118678	115817	120000	122740
Maize	28790	35500	34684	32860	31201	34504	35637
Millets	15678	22420	22471	20783	18563	18467	19800
Wheat	2050	4700	4517	4630	4333	3785	3896
Pulses	910	5820	6227	6111	6644	6452	NA
Oilseeds	7417	24500	26885	24754	26201	26118	27748
Potato	807	5100	4484	4623	4508	4494	4960
Ginger	211	2500	2571	2730	3330	4187	4399
Turmeric	58	390	385	347	460	300	404
Chilli	431	1093	1121	1138	1149	1280	1499
Sugarcane	468	450	640	702	807	681	809
Vegetables	1342	13890	15547	11191	13763	12365	16219

Source: Same as Table 2.5.

Table 2.14 : Changes in Production (Tonnes) of Major Crops, 1978-00

Crop	*1978*	*1994*	*1995*	*1996*	*1997*	*1998*	*2000*
Rice	113253	104400	105800	124464	129387	129505	134807
Maize	26142	46700	46680	45381	45844	58025	48346
Millets	12086	21500	22500	20566	17774	18032	17123
Wheat	2596	8500	7635	7286	6052	5725	5069
Pulses*	709	5350	5819	5724	6667	6598	NA
Oilseeds**	5018	27200	24600	25219	24234	24290	27228
Potato	4055	37800	36340	34689	32911	33269	32434
Ginger	652	16500	16880	19445	24336	32078	34890
Turmeric	175	1250	1126	1165	1150	1034	1473
Chilli	667	1375	1280	1404	1466	1551	1696
Sugarcane	1368	12500	15700	15818	17867	15806	16219
Vegetables	4239	38500	37130	38729	44270	35100	37060

* Pulses include rajma, lentil, and other pulses.

** Oilseeds include mustard, groundnut, sesamum, soybean, and sunflower.

Source: Same as Table 2.4.

was too less at ha. 10734. Dramatic changes can be noticed after two decades, 1997-98. Of the total cultivated area in 1997-98, 78.8% is under foodgrains followed by oilseeds (11.2%), vegetables (5.3%), and ginger (1.8%). Thus, food grains again dominated cropping pattern in the state. Productivity of all crops, except paddy, has increased during 1979-98 and the increase is more than 100%. Yield improvements in commercial crops is much higher than cereals. Thus, rice, maize, potato, oilseeds, and sugarcane are the major crops grown in the state.

Horticulture

Diversity in lands, typical topography, and peculiar agro-climatic conditions provide scope for growing both temperate and sub-tropical fruits. Horticultural activities in the state are aimed at utilization of waste lands, reducing shifting cultivation, improving socio-economic conditions of tribals, and prevent soil erosion. Due to inadequate technical manpower and other infrastructure, horticulture has a long way to go. Area, and production of principle horticultural crops for 1994-00 is provided in Tables 2.15 and 2.16. Apple, citrus, pineapple, banana, and walnut are the major crops cultivated in the state. Citrus occupied as much as 24% under

Table 2.15 : Changes in Area (Hectares) Under Horticultural Crops, 1994-00

Crop	*1994*	*1995*	*1996*	*1997*	*1998*	*2000*
Apple	5523 (23.3)	5709 (20.5)	5970 (20.2)	6186 (20.4)	6370 (20.3)	6601 (15.9)
Citrus	5725 (24.1)	6850 (24.6)	6970 (23.6)	7258 (23.9)	7643 (24.3)	8593 (20.6)
Pineapple	3869 (16.3)	6700 (24.1)	7125 (24.2)	7143 (23.5)	7230 (23.0)	7314 (17.6)
Banana	2210 (9.3)	2825 (10.1)	3082 (10.5)	3198 (10.5)	3350 (10.7)	3489 (8.4)
Walnut	1450 (6.1)	1790 (6.4)	2013 (6.8)	2038 (6.7)	2076 (6.6)	2199 (5.3)
Others	4948 (20.9)	3969 (14.3)	4322 (14.7)	4534 (14.9)	4740 (15.1)	13405 (32.2)
Total	23725 (100.0)	27843 (100.0)	29482 (100.0)	30357 (100.0)	31409 (100.0)	41601 (100.0)

Source: Same as Table 2.5.

Table 2.16 : Changes in Production (Tonnes) of Horticultural Crops, 1994-00

Crop	*1994*	*1995*	*1996*	*1997*	*1998*	*2000*
Apple	9730 (19.3)	9250 (15.7)	12993 (19.3)	14500 (17.1)	15255 (17.1)	8265 (7.7)
Citrus	9357 (18.6)	10250 (17.4)	13635 (20.4)	18500 (21.8)	19795 (22.2)	11315 (0.6)
Pineapple	13869 (27.5)	17000 (28.9)	22105 (32.9)	28000 (33.0)	29400 (33.0)	31980 (29.9)
Banana	8540 (16.9)	11081 (18.9)	7525 (11.2)	10500 (12.3)	11025 (12.4)	12270 (11.5)
Walnut	210 (0.4)	713 (1.2)	700 (1.0)	940 (1.1)	958 (1.0)	50 (0.1)
Others	8703 17.3)	10500 (17.9)	10211 (15.2)	12500 (14.7)	12715 (14.3)	43213 (40.2)
Total	50409 (100.0)	58794 (100.0)	67169 (100.0)	84940 (100.0)	89148 (100.0)	107093 (100.0)

Source: Same as Table 2.5.

area and contributed 22% to production. Similarly, pineapple occupied 23% of the total area and contributed 33% to production. Other crops included black pepper, cardamom, pears, papaya, plum, etc. A regional apple nursery at Dirang (West Kameng), and a horticultural processing unit at Nagmoi (West Siang) have been set up in the state.

Due to remoteness of the fruit growing areas from main markets of Assam and also due to inadequate communication facilities, emphasis has been laid on low volume high value horticultural crops (large cardamom, ginger, turmeric, chilli, black pepper, etc.). Of late cultivation of edible mushrooms is spreading in the remote rural areas. Mushroom development centre at Itanagar has been strengthened with 500 kgs fresh mushrooms, 10000 spawn cultivation, and training to 150 growers annually. To boost up production of fruits in the state, more than 15000 peoples horticultural garden units were developed.

Forestry

The habitations of Arunachalis are surrounded by forests. They live in forests, they dance in forests, they decorate their figures with forests, they worship forests, they practice jhumming in forests, some mothers have deliveries in the interior forests, they hunt in forests, and dead bodies are buried in forests. There is no life without forests. Thus, Arunachalis cannot be separated from forests as fish from water.

As mentioned earlier, forest cover of Arunachal Pradesh is about 62% of its geographical area and is a natural eco-system having multi-species and multi-aged trees. Apart from various timber species, a large variety of cane, bamboo, medicinal plants, etc. are available. They serve as a supply base to ply-wood and veneer industries. District-wise area under reserved forest and total forests are given in Table 2.17. Of the total forest area of 24012 sq.km., 40% is reserved forest. Maximum forest area is located in Lohit, Dibang Valley, Changlang, and East Kameng. District-wise forest ranges are also presented in Table 2.17. These forests increase infiltration of water, regulate stream flows, check soil erosion, reduce floods, help in recharge of groundwater acquirers, moderate the climate, and maintain soil-water values in many ways. However, due to indiscriminate jhumming, felling of trees, and other unsustainable exploitation, forest land is increasingly threatened. Forest department should focus on: (a) introduction of tea, rubber, bamboo, and cane plantation

Table 2.17 : Distribution of Forest Area (sq. km.), 2000

District	*Reserved forest*	*Total forest area*	*Forest ranges*
Tawang	0.00	5.98	3
West Kameng	708.35	1520.57	8
East Kameng	1083.86	1963.78	14
Papum Pare	810.50	1255.24	27
Lower Subansiri	347.07	1141.99	6
Upper Subansiri	504.00	506.00	3
West Siang	248.18	734.18	7
East Siang	467.39	817.64	7
Upper Siang	0.00	483.00	6
Dibang Valley	515.96	5101.45	1
Lohit	4233.53	7356.52	18
Changlang	653.48	2877.08	13
Tirap	0.00	247.48	5
Total	9572.32	24010.91	118

Source: Same as Table 2.5.

to generate surplus, (b) scientific management of forest to yield necessary firewood and other minor forest produce, (c) identifying commercially exploitable herbs and medicinal plants and managing their supply through commercial cultivation, (d) managing forest resources and spreading awareness among locals about forest management and regeneration, and (e) preserving primary forests in selected areas, aiding forest based tourism and reducing timber extraction.

The situation has considerably improved with introduction of Anchal forests (1975-76) under departmental management on 50% profit sharing basis, and creation of wild life wing (1977-78) for protection of fauna in the state. Further, Arunachal Pradesh Forest Corporation was established (1978-79) for institutional finance in forest management and elimination of contractors to check illegal fellings. Van Vignan Kendra was established in 1991-92 to carry out research work in forestry. Progress achieved through all these measures was less than desired and the Honourable Supreme Court pronounced a ban in 1996 on tree felling in Arunachal Pradesh. Such a ban has put a severe strain on the economy of Arunachal. Tribals, hitherto, getting easy money on timber trade have found it very difficult to cope up. Further, there are hardly any avenue for industrial development. In the absence of gainful employment, slowly they are shifting towards horticultural crops, and coffee/tea plantation.

Livestock

Livestock plays a vital role in Arunachal economy[19]. Tribals have been rearing livestock (mithun, cattle, buffalo, pig, sheep, goat, yak, poultry, dzo-dzomo (a cross between yak and hill cattle)), etc. from time immemorial. Baring few, all most all are non-vegetarians and beef is the easily available and cheap source at present. Apart from socio-economic considerations, socio-religious life of tribals centres around livestock. Mithun serves them, by and large, as a store of wealth, medium of barter trade, and reservoir of meat, as insurance against rainy days and crop failures. It serves as a medium for fulfillment of social, moral, ceremonial, and religious obligations. Vast forest resources provide ample opportunities for grazing. Trends in livestock during 1979-98 are provided in Table 2.18. There is appreciable increase in cattle, 'other livestock', goats and poultry. Changing food habits, developmental activities, dwindling forests, etc. could be reasons for changes. Department of Animal Husbandry and Veterinary has been emphasising on (a) livestock

Table 2.18 : Trends in Livestock Population (lakhs), 1979-98.

Category	*1978-79*	*1988-89*	*1992-93*	*1997-98*
Cattle	1.68	3.11	3.47	4.49
Buffaloes	0.11	0.12	0.10	0.11
Mithun	0.85	0.99	1.06	1.24
Yak	0.06	0.07	0.10	0.09
Sheep	0.20	0.29	0.33	0.28
Goat	0.76	1.08	1.28	1.83
Horses/ponies	0.05	0.05	0.06	0.07
Pigs	2.13	2.43	2.39	2.75
Other livestock*	0.05	0.08	1.56	3.23
Poultry	9.71	11.21	10.98	11.57

* others include dzo-dzomo, elephant, mules, donkey, dogs, and ducks (data on dogs and ducks were not available for 1978-79 and 1988-89).

Source: Records of Directorate of Animal Husbandry and Veterinary.

development and production, (b) animal health coverage, (c) dairy development, and (d) training and education. As of livestock development and production, a number of subsidy based schemes (cattle, sheep and goat, pigs, etc.) are being implemented for economic development of tribals. For effective health coverage veterinary institutions at different levels are being established (Table 2.19). There are 153 veterinary aid centres at village level with a trained functionary. Minor ailments treated and artificial inseminations provided at these institutions. There are 13 mobile veterinary units at district level.

As of dairy development, Integrated Dairy Development Project (IDDP) was initiated in 1993-94 with Rs. 4.58 crores for five years. The project is being implemented at East Siang, and Papum Pare districts. Following are the objectives of IDDP:

Table 2.19 : Particulars of Veterinary Institutions, 2000

Institution	*Number*
Veterinary hospital	01
Veterinary dispensary	93
Veterinary aid centre	155
Mobile veterinary unit	13
Central vaccine depot	01
Disease investigation lab	03
District diagnostic lab	12
Reindeerpest check post	01
Reindeerpest vigilence unit	01

Source: Same as Table 2.5.

1. to organise 50 dairy cooperative societies (DCSs) in Papum Pare and East Siang districts and to create marketing infrastructure to producers to enable them getting remunerative prices for their produce,
2. to support DCSs with essential technical inputs which will help augmenting milk production in the project area,
3. to provide veterinary health cover to animals covered in the project area,
4. to improve productivity of animals through artificial insemination, and natural breeding,
5. to provide training to personnel involved in animal husbandry and to farmers,
6. to establish 5000 litres/day dairy plant at Itanagar, and two chilling centres of 2000 litres/day at Pasighat and Balijan, and
7. to ensure regular supply of processed milk to consumers of Itanagar and Pasighat at reasonable price.

The area selected contains large number of dairy animals and the farmers are relatively progressive. The project is based on 'Anand pattern' dairy cooperatives with two tier system. Cattle feed at reasonable rate is being supplied to producer members in the project area. Efforts are being made to complete the project with the help of NDDB. Under education and training, efforts are being made for training of in-service personnel both within and outside the state. A school of veterinary science and animal husbandry has been functioning at Pasighat for conducting courses to veterinary field assistants. Besides, training programmes to progressive farmers are also being conducted to acquaint them with improved animal husbandry and poultry. Production of milk, eggs, and wool are given in Table 2.20.

Table 2.20 : Growth in Production of Husbandry Products, 1989-98

Year	*Milk (000 tonnes)*	*Eggs (million)*	*Wool (000 kgs)*
1988-89	38.5	29.0	56.0
1989-90	40.0	30.0	57.0
1990-91	40.5	30.5	57.2
1991-92	41.0	31.0	57.4
1992-93	41.5	31.5	57.6
1993-94	42.0	32.0	57.8
1994-95	42.5	32.5	58.0
1995-96	43.0	33.0	58.2
1996-97	43.7	33.7	58.5
1997-98	44.3	41.3	58.9

Source: Same as Table 2.5.

In order to improve productivity of local cattle, cross breeding programme has been taken up. There are 120 cattle upgrading centres, a key village block (with 30 sub-centres) and 10 cattle breeding farms. Improvement in poultry is being achieved through scientific breeding with the help of central poultry farm and central hatchery located at Nirjuli. Central hatchery is catering to requirements of eggs and broilers with capacity to hatch 150000 chicks at a time. Chicks procured from central hatchery are reared for further multiplication.

Regional sheep breeding farm was set up at Sangti (West Kameng) in 1975 to improve quality of wool and mutton. Piggery programme emphasizes on upgrading of local stock through crossbreeding with exotic animals (White Hampshire). A central pig breeding farm at Karsingsa, and regional exotic pig breeding farm at Loiliang have been functioning to produce pure breed of stock for distribution, demonstration, and impart training. The department has been implementing a number of centrally sponsored programmes: (1) rinder pest surveillance and containment vaccination programme, (2) foot and mouth disease programme, (3) systematic control of livestock diseases of national importance, (4) animal disease surveillance, (5) strengthening arrangements for statistics, (6) seed and fodder development, and (7) extension of frozen semen technology.

Fisheries

Fish is an important food of Arunachalis. Fishing is not only a hobby or sport but also a subsidiary occupation here. It is also connected with religious activities involving taboos. According to them, success or failure of ceremonial fishing depends on good or bad harvest. Methods followed by locals to catch fish included poisoning or harpooning. Fish culture was not known to them. Scientific pisciculture is, however, a recent development in the state. A fishery development programme was initiated in 1958-59 on a modest scale. With the passage of time and expansion of programme, pisciculture has taken a firm root in the state. Initially, the department was part of the directorate of agriculture. There are five fisheries cooperatives registered in the state whose health is not satisfactory.

Involvement of the state in fisheries activities started in 1958-59 under the department of agriculture. It remained the responsibility of the department of agriculture till 1980, when a separate department of fisheries was carved out of the department of agriculture. Programme for development pisciculture included following schemes: (a) intensive fish farming, (b) expansion and improvement of existing fish seed farms, (c) paddy-cum-fish culture, (d) reclamation of swamps and natural lakes, (e) trout culture, (f) supply of fishing gear and tackles on 50% subsidy, (g) marketing, and (h) education and training. Two regional fish farmers development agencies (FFDA) are working in the state. Major objective of FFDA is to increase fish production and generate self employment in rural areas. FFDA-I consists of East Kameng, Lower Subansiri, Papum Pare, Dibang Valley, Lohit and Changlang, while FFDA-II includes Upper Subansiri, West Siang, East Siang, Upper Siang, and Tirap. FFDA is a centrally sponsored scheme with 50:50 expenditure basis. In all 1500 farmers were trained under FFDA in 1997-98 (for more details on fisheries, see Table 2.21).

Table 2.21 : Progress in Fish Production, 1991-01

Year	*Area (ha)*	*Fry (millions)*	*Fingerlings (millions)*	*Fish (tonnes)*
1990-91	1206	18.00	5.50	1246
1991-92	1150	19.09	6.00	1499
1992-93	1065	19.90	6.00	1605
1993-94	907	19.70	6.31	1702
1994-95	1075	19.09	6.35	1801
1995-96	1182	21.00	7.00	1852
1996-97	1480	21.80	7.30	2002
1997-98	1612	24.00	7.50	2130
1998-99	1755	26.25	7.60	2320
1999-00	1849	28.30	7.90	2510
2000-01	2050	30.29	8.20	2875

Source: Same as Table 2.5.

Industries

To promote tribal arts and crafts, Department of Cottage Industries was established in 1953-54 with superintendent as its head. Departmental efforts were mainly confined to promotion of traditional handicrafts, handlooms, khadi and village, etc. up to fourth five year plan period. The post was re-designated as Chief Industries Officer and in 1977 the post of Director of Industries created. The pace of development quickened from fifth five year plan with establishment of District Industries Centres in 1978-79. The Department has taken up: (a) sericulture and silk weaving, (b) skill development, (c) established a rock solt unit at Changlang, (d) established aromatic grass plant, and (e) conducted feasibility study on agro and forest based industries.

There were 10 crafts centres in 1953 and their number increased to 21 by 1972. A significant development had taken place during 1972-87. As many as 14 medium industries, 1625 small scale industries, and 64 craft/weaving centres along with 25 sericulture centres were established during this period. There were 19 medium industries, 336 small/village industries, 88 craft/weaving centres, and 26 sericulture centres at the end of 1997.

To promote industries along with development of marketing of facilities, Arunachal Pradesh Industrial

Development and Financial Corporation Limited was established in 1978. Further, Arunachal Pradesh Khadi and Village Industries Board was set up in 1990 to promote rural industries in the state. Department of Industries was bifurcated into (a) Handlooms and Handicrafts, and (b) Geology and Mining.

Health

Medical department was started in 1911 and a hospital was established at Pasighat in 1912. There were 12 health units in 1947. Department is headed by chief medical officer, with headquarters at Pasighat. It was shifted to Shillong in 1956 and later to Naharlagun. Performance of health facilities are provided in Table 2.22. There is substantial improvement in the facilities over the last 30 years.

Table 2.22 : Performance of Health Facilities, 1972-01

Item	*1972*	*1987*	*1997*	*2001*
Hospital	13	15	14	12
Health Unit	NA	12	5	-
Dispensaries	NA	31	11	3
Community Health Centre	NA	7	13	25
Primary Health Centre	NA	28	50	65
Sub-Centre	NA	73	325	350
Doctors	144	210	258	385
Nursing staff	226	251	471	556

Source: Same as Table 2.5.

Education

Education department was started in 1947 and Mrs. Indira Miri was the first Education Officer. There were 4 primary schools in the entire NEFA in 1947. Due to concerted efforts the facilities have increased leaps and bounds. There were 503 primary schools, 11 higher secondary schools and a college by 1972. Arunachal University was added in 1984. By 1997, the state has a university, an Engineering Institute, six colleges, and 1256 primary schools (Table 2.23). District wise number of students enrolled (both boys and girls) is provided

Table 2.23 : Development of Educational Institutions, 1956-01

Institution	*1956*	*1972*	*1982*	*1987*	*1997*	*2001*
University	0	0	0	0	1	1
Engineering college	0	0	0	0	1	1
College	0	1	2	3	6	7
Higher secondary school	0	7	15	28	67	68
High school/ Secondary	2	11	32	46	90	116
Middle school	16	45	120	181	301	333
Primary school	152	503	916	1004	1256	1303
Nursery school	0	3	49	249	137	57
School for handicapped	0	0	0	0	0	1

Source: Same as Table 2.5.

in (Table 2.24). On the whole the dropouts in girls is more than boys. In all around 2.85 lakhs students are enrolled in 2001 (Table 2.24).

Table 2.24 : Enrollment of Boys and Girls in Various Stages of Schooling, 2001

District	*Pre-Primary*		*Primary*		*Middle (VI-VIII)*		*Secondary (IX-X)*		*Higher Secondary (XI-XII)*		*Total*
	Boys	*Girls*	*Boys*	*Girls*	*Boys*	*Girls*	*Boys*	*Girls*	*Boys*	*Girls*	
Tawang	782	688	2047	1837	495	455	252	212	68	44	6880
West Kameng	509	421	4925	4255	1130	1049	544	396	263	153	13645
East Kameng	1709	1261	4789	3731	1586	922	720	318	308	150	15494
Papumpare	6520	5210	11827	9449	4056	3344	2212	1486	1145	695	45944
Lower Subansiri	975	780	13548	11417	3080	2584	1898	1423	891	697	37293
Upper Subansiri	869	768	4944	4426	1400	1086	673	381	329	102	14978
West Siang	596	560	12010	11174	4603	4762	1574	1070	676	337	37362
East Siang	2024	1569	7490	6780	3053	2851	1294	1037	709	458	27265
Upper Siang	541	536	2456	2438	843	681	398	232	201	53	8379
Lohit	1880	1398	7253	5822	2626	1901	1079	687	550	304	23500
Changlang	1276	970	7415	5293	2533	2063	1165	860	430	259	22264
Dibang Valley	747	613	3809	3060	1501	1195	687	458	344	198	12612
Tirap	2344	1565	6327	4019	2006	1415	685	412	306	179	19258
Total	20772	16339	88840	73701	28912	24308	13181	8972	6220	3629	284874

Source: Same as Table 2.5.

Banking and Credit

Banking service is relatively new to Arunachal. There were five branches of State Bank of India (Bomdila, Ziro, Pasighat, Tezu, and Khonsa) at beginning of 1972 with total deposits of Rs. 34.57 crores. There are (1998) 99 branches of various nationalised banks, and Arunachal Pradesh Cooperative Apex Bank with a total deposits of Rs. 476.58 crores. District-wise coverage of banks, average population/branch, demand, collection, and recovery are provided in Table 2.25. Maximum branches are located at Papum Pare (state headquarter is located in this district) followed by East and West Siangs. Average population served/branch is the highest in East Kameng followed by Tirap, Changlang, Upper Subansiri and Lohit. Recovery is the highest (83%) in Tawang and the lowest in Lower Subansiri.

Table 2.25 : Performance of Credit Delivery System Across Districts, 1997-98

District	*Number of banks*	*Number of branches*	*Average no. of villages/ branch*	*Average popu-lation/ branch*	*Average deposits/ branch (Rs.)*	*Demand (Rs. lakhs)*	*Collec-tion (Rs.*	*Re-covery (%)*
Tawang	2	5	32	5657	315.99	50.19	41.64	83
West Kameng	2	8	21	7052	341.63	57.44	17.88	31
East Kameng	2	3	91	16798	338.86	60.25	12.00	20
Papumpare	3	17	15	4283	989.17	300.91	100.35	33
Lower Subansiri	3	8	72	10396	234.60	111.35	5.25	05
Upper Subansiri	3	4	100	12990	385.54	95.88	27.18	28
West Siang	3	11	37	8176	323.05	101.95	54.51	54
East Siang	2	11	14	6533	286.06	79.20	34.14	43
Upper Siang	NA	NA	NA	NA	NA	NA	NA	NA
Dibang valley	2	4	60	10767	571.00	111.43	30.42	27
Lohit	2	9	109	12190	510.90	400.76	104.60	26
Changlang	2	7	64	13647	372.93	34.13	8.30	24
Tirap	2	6	32	14251	787.36	47.88	10.20	21

Source: Records of the Office of Director (Rural Development).

Tourism

Arunachal Pradesh is the land of dawn-lit-mountains. The state has some of the finest tourist attractions such as the orchid museum, and the Ganga Seki lake. The state has five major rivers which are ideal for sailing, boating and rafting and its terrain is suitable for trekking, hiking and holidaying in a serene atmosphere. There are eight wild life sanctuaries and two national parks in the state. Important places of tourist interest include Parasuram Kund, Bhishmaknagar, Namdapha, Bomdila, Sela Pass, Tawang, Pangkong Teng Tso (popularly known as Madhuri Lake), Along, Malinithan, Anini, Yingkiang, etc. Ecotourism[20] has a special relevance for the state because of its unique topography, floral and faunal diversity, deep georges, lofty mountains, snow clad peaks, and idyllic natural settings. With proper development of the infrastructure, the state with its vast natural endowments can convert its scenic locations into important tourist spots, earning a substantial income. State government has embarked on a drive to make the picturesque hill state a major tourist destination for both domestic and international tourists. Government had been trying to develop tourism with various river festivals (Brahmaputra Darshana at Roing, and Pasighat). The Buddha Mahotsava at Tawang was aimed at boosting tourism. Developing appropriate infrastructure, encouraging tour operators, and sensitizing people besides promoting private entrepreneurs would go a long way in this direction.

Cooperatives

Cooperation is an inherent quality of Arunachalis. However, the movement has taken birth, formally, during 1957-58 by establishing Pasighat Cooperative General Stores limited at Pasighat. Initially movement was started to provide essential commodities to employees of the state. Number of societies have increased from 12 in 1957-58 to 115 in 1970-71 and 243 by 1997-98. Of the 243, 107 are in profits, and 79 are loss making. The movement has a membership of about 54000 with an annual turnover of Rs. 146.26 crores. It is the second largest employment provider in the state. It is a pioneer to render immense services like supply of essential consumer goods, road transport for passenger traffic, agricultural credit, processing and marketing of agricultural commodities, fisheries, dairying, handicrafts, etc. From among the cooperatives, LAMPs at Daporijo, Khonsa, Pasighat, Roing, Tawang, Miao, and Namsai needs special appreciation (for more details on cooperative movement, see Rao (2000 a)),

Rao (2000 b), Rao (2001 a), and (Rao 2001 b). Over the period, societies started spreading and now tribals need to travel at the most a day which was more than a week sometimes back, to procure essential commodities. Looking at the progress and need, Government of India sanctioned Rs. 22.50 crores to implement 'Integrated Cooperative Development Project' for overall development of cooperative movement in the state. Looking at government's support, the number of societies increased to about 400 by 2002.

Summary

People are changing and they are no longer what they were 50 years ago. The change was introduced by the administration and people are heading towards larger affiliation with nation to share its development and prosperity. This is basic for wider cohesion which goes to make a nation. The physiological integration is the greatest achievement to the credit of administrative policy followed in this region. In the new environment, new class alignment in offing; ministers and legislatures, officers and employees in government service; newly educated people; contractors; agents; traders; etc. have began to live a different life of their own forming a class of elites of society. Their mode of life in houses made of bricks, morthers, R.C.C. buildings, window curtains, bathrooms and kitchens with most modern amenities, TV sets, VCR, cordless phones, air conditioners, maruti cars, gypsies, dress, diet, etc. are different from the rank and file who are still living age-old life in far flung areas.

A close observation of above discussion reveals that considerable amount of development has taken place during the planned era and lot more needs to carried out. It is to be considered as a joint effort of people, government, politicians, officials, state, and central governments. A holistic approach; by taking locals into confidence, and with their active participation; would go a long way in making this region a paradise.

NOTES

1. The name was suggested by Sh. B. Das Shastri, ex-Director of Research (NEFA) and formally declared by Smt. Indira Gandhi on January 20, 1972 at Ziro, headquarters of erstwhile Subansiri district.

2. Kante in Tawang is the highest peak (7090 metres) and Deomali in Tirap is the lowest peak (135 metres). About 64% of the total geographical area lie above 1200 metres and only 1.7% below 150 metres above the mean sea level. Minimum temperature varies between 0^0C-2^0C winter in south, and below 0^0 in the higher elevation. Summers are moderate and temperature ranges between 35^0-40^0C. There is a fall in temperature with an increase in height (i.e.) 1.7^0C/300 metres in altitude.
3. The term tribe is derived from the latin word 'tribus'. Earlier Romans used this word to designate divisions in a society. Later use suggests that it meant for poor people. The term 'tribal' is nowhere defined in the constitution and infact there is no satisfactory definition. To the ordinary man it suggests simple folk living in hills and forests; to people who are a little better informed, it signifies colourful folk famous for their dance and song; to an administrator it means a group of citizens who are the special responsibility of the President of India; and to an anthropologist it indicates a special field for study of a social phenomenon. The current popular meaning of a tribe in India is a category of people included in the list of scheduled tribes. As these groups are presumed to form the oldest ethnological sector of the population, the term 'Adivasi' (Adi = original, and vasi = inhabitant) has become current among certain people. Words like Vanyajati, Vanavasi, Pahari, Adimjati, Anusuchitjati, etc have been coined to designate these people. The names of tribes like Kurumba, Irula, Paniya in south India, Asur, Faora, Oraon, Gond, Santhal, Bhil in central India, Bodo, Ahom in north east India, occur in our old classical India literature.
4. This section is based on the information obtained from: (a) Bhattacharya (2000), (b) Bose (1997), (c) Chowdhury (1996), (d) Dutta, (ed.) (1997), (e) Elwin (1959), (f) Osik (1996), (g) Osik (1999), (h) Pandey (1997), (i) Pandey (ed.) (1997), (j) Riba (2000), (k) Tayeng (2001), and (l) various issues of Arunachal Review.
5. Ahoms from upper Burma established their kingdom in upper Assam during the early 13th century. They crossed Patkoi range in 1228 and settled at Charaideo near Sibsagar (Assam). They gradually expanded their power and empire, conquered their main rivals, Kacharis, in 1540. In course of time they expanded their rule over the whole of Bramhaputra valley. According to most historians, the name Assam has been derived from the word Ahom or Asom names by which local tribes referred to the conquerors. Ahoms ruled Assam almost uninterruptedly for 600 years. Rulers of Ahom dynasty came in contact with hill tribes at the borders of their kingdom. In the chronicles of Ahoms (Ahom Buranjies) there occur references to these tribes, to their frequent predatory raids in the plains, to punitive expeditions carried out by the Ahoms, and finally to their paying allegiance and tribute to the king and serving in their army.
6. British thought of protecting indigenous people by bringing a regulation in 1833. Scheduled area regulation was passed in 1874 whereby the local government was empowered to declare in respect of the tracts specified in the act what enactments were or were not in force and to notify, the application with modifications or restrictions, if necessary,

of any enactment in force at the time in any part of British India. In due course the idea of a distinct and special arrangement in non-regulated areas was accepted. By the act of 1919, the idea of wholly excluded area and partially excluded area emerged where tribal population was concentrated.

7. Posa strictly denotes the subscription raised by villagers in order to meet customary demands of hill people introduced during the reign of Pratap Singh (1603-41) when the Ahom king wanted to reserve his energies for checking the Mughal incursions into the valley. Some of the Britishers called it as black mail. Hill people collected Posa once in a year in kind which was replaced by money during British period.

8. Inner line regulation of 1873 gave power to prescribe a line for frontier districts beyond which no British subject or foreign resident could pass without a license. Economic and commercial objectives of inner line were: (a) to regulate trade in Indian rubber between hills and British traders, (b) to control extension of tea plantation into hill areas, and (c) to regulate transfer of land in hill districts. The line was marked at intervals by frontier posts held by military police and commanding roads access to the tracts beyond. Any person from the plains, who had received permission to cross inner line had to present his/her pass at these posts. The term 'inner line' was originated from a suggestion of Arthur Hobhouse who observed in his draft for the regulation of 1873 and north-east frontier territories as a separate entity began to develop since then. Currently, the line effectively controls population movement into this region. While tribal communities have freedom of movement all over India and can compete for employment/enterprise, they are guarded against more aggressive and better placed trading and migrant farming communities from rest of India. National Council of Applied Economic Research (1967) advocated for 'a relaxation of inner line regulations backed by measures to protect tribal interest in a fast changing situation. The author too had the privilege of crossing inner line several times. It is not at all required in the changing environment . People at the inner line (checkgates) are mostly illiterate and rarely verifies the validity. They simply look at the form and allows persons to enter Arunachal. I am of the opinion that it should be abolished. Deletion of inner line regulation attracts more visitors which inturn bring income in various forms. The government, rather, should try to strictly prohibit outsiders to do business, trading, and other activities. All out efforts should be made to encourage locals in all these fields.

9. Initial administrative structure was laid out by the Government of Assam assisted by secretariat set up in 1936. After independence, administrative work was shifted from Governor's secretariat to the state government of Assam by an act of 1947 and remained so until 1950 which was renamed as NEFA in 1951 and was again brought directly under the Governor of Assam, who acted as the agent of the President of India.

10. Indian Statutory Commission (Simon Commission, 1930) suggested to create 'excluded' and 'partially excluded' areas to take aboriginal areas towards removal of poverty and towards economic and educational

betterment. This was also designed to prevent application of unsuitable legislation, to permit making special rules and regulations required for any different system of administration needed, and for provision of funds at the discretion of the Governor of these areas. They are well defined areas populated either predominantly or to a considerable extent by aboriginals. They, however, do not by any means cover entire population of tribal origin, and in many cases represent only a comparatively small proportion of aboriginal population, the rest of them being scattered over non-excluded areas. Sections 91 and 92 of Government of India Act, 1935 provided for declaration by any order of council of 'excluded areas', and 'partially excluded areas'. No act of federal legislature or provential legisiature would apply to these areas except on the direction of the Governor, who was empowered to make such exceptions and modifications as he considered necessary. The frontier tracts were declared to be 'excluded areas' in 1936.

11. The present border line between Arunachal and Tibet (China) is known as McMahon Line and was accepted at a Tripatriate conference (Great Britain (British India), China, and Tibet) held at Simla in 1914. At this conference, British government proposed that an imaginary line be drawn from the Himalayan crest towards eastern extremity of Lohit division and this proposal was approved as the boundary between India and Tibet. The word imaginary was used for the reason that in those days it was not physically possible to reach snow covered mountain peaks. The proposal was drafted by Sir Henry McMahon, Foreign Secretary to Political Department of British India and Lonchen Satra represented Tibet. Therefore, boundary line between India and Tibet (China) is known as McMahon Line. Tibetan representative accepted the proposal and signed it while Chinese representative went back to consult his government. Later Mr. Ivan Chen, representing China, backed out of the agreement being dissatisfied with the demarcation between Tibet and China, but happy with India-Tibet border. When there remained no other alternative, Tibet and India signed the convention on July 3, 1914. Simla convention of 1914 was published in Aitchison's work entitled a collection of treaties, engagements, and sanads relating to India and neighbouring countries (1929) and was never challenged by China. However, it raised the issue after 10 years of India's independence and declared entire Arunachal Pradesh as 'disputed area'. A brief on Indo-China war of 1962 is provided elsewhere in the chapter.

12. Claudius Ptolemaeus, popularly known as Ptolemy, was a great geographer of the Roman empire during 100-165 AD. Ptolemy's geography opens with an excellent theory of map collection. The book contains a list of places and their longitudes and latitudes as well as 26 colour maps and a map of the world.

13. This section is based on Bora (2002) and a website on great earthquakes.

14. Abor hills has been reorganised into East Siang, West Siang, and Upper Siang.

15. Mishmi Hills has been reogranised into Dibang Valley and Lohit districts.

16. This section is based on the information obtained from Dalvi (undated), Government of India (1963a) and (1963b), Hangen (1963), Kaul (1967), Kaul (1976), Khera (1968), Mankekar (1968), Ministry of Information and Broadcasting (1963a, 1963b, and 1965), and Osik (1999).
17. This information is based on my visits to war memorials at Tawang, Jaswantghar, and Walong.
18. For more details, see Rao, V.M. (1999), Development of agriculture in Arunachal Pradesh, paper accepted for presented at conference on 'Potential and constraints for agricultural development in different agro-ecological regions', held at University of Agricultural Sciences, Dharwad (Karnataka) during October 6-7.
19. For more details on livestock sector, see Rao, V.M. (2000), Livestock economy of Arunachal Pradesh, paper presented at conference on 'Livestock in different farming systems' held at Tamil Nadu Veterinary and Animal Science University, Chennai during December 7-8.
20. It is defined as 'travel with a concern for the environment and with an appreciation of natural attractions being the prime purpose of the visit'.

3

DEVELOPMENTAL PROGRAMMES FOR WOMEN

Introduction

Government of India and the respective state governments have a number of schemes/ programmes for the weaker sections (SCs, STs, women, handicapped, etc.) of the society. A number of ministries at the centre as also at the state are entrusted with the responsibility of implementing these programmes. An attempt is made in this chapter to have a look at these programmes[1] aimed at women and their progress in Arunachal Pradesh.

Developmental activities for women in the state are being taken care of by Department of Social Welfare, Women, and Child Development. The present department was conceived in the year 1999 which underwent number of changes in the nomenclature. It was known as Department of Social Welfare, and Cultural Affairs during 1992-99, and Department of Rural Development during 1983-92. Prior to that, it was a part of Department of Agriculture during 1977-83, and was under Department of Health till 1977.

ICDS

Integrated Child Development Services (ICDS) Scheme was conceived in 1975 with an integrated delivery package of services to improve the nutritional and health status of vulnerable groups including pre-school children, pregnant women and nursing mothers. It envisaged supplementary nutrition, pre-school education, immunization, health checkup, referral services and health education. Also, ICDS scheme sought effective convergence of inter-sectoral services through community-based Anganwadi workers and helpers, supportive community structures/women's groups through Anganwadi centres, the health system and within the community. Besides, Anganwadi is a meeting ground where women or mothers' groups can come together with other frontline workers to promote awareness and joint action for child development and women's empowerment.

Growth

Initially, it was launched in 33 blocks across the country. During sixth five year plan, the scheme witnessed expansion with sanction of 1037 projects. The Seventh Plan continued the strategy of promoting early childhood survival and development through programmes in different sections, universal immunisation, maternal and child care services, nutrition, pre-school education, protected drinking water, environmental sanitation, and hygiene and family planning.

ICDS continued to be the main integrated national programme for early childhood survival and development. The number of sanctioned ICDS projects was 2,594 by 1992, and out of them, 1,656 were in rural areas, 711 in tribal areas, and 227 in urban slums. By the end of March 2000, about 30 million beneficiaries had been covered under the scheme including about 189 lakh children below 6 years of age. More than 38 lakh pregnant and nursing mothers were getting supplementary nutrition under ICDS.[2] About 113 lakh children of 3-6 years of age are getting pre-school education services under ICDS.

Main focus during the Ninth Five Year Plan was on human development with policies and programmes for child survival and development receiving high priority. The Ninth Plan views children as the nation's future human resources and child development as an investment in the country's future and in improving the nation's high priority to family and community based preventive services to combat infant and early childhood mortality and morbidity. In this context, ICDS is being viewed as a preventive and developmental effort to extend deeper into community than existing health and education systems. Now ICDS is effective in 4388 community development blocks and major urban slums across the country. As against 2.27 crore beneficiaries until March 1997, there were 3.40 crore beneficiaries by March, 2001. The scheme reaches out to about 54 lakh expectant and nursing mothers and 288 lakh children under six years of age belonging to the disadvantaged groups in all parts of the country.

Impact

The impact of ICDS, however, has been quite distinct on the health of the participant families. As a service delivery programme, ICDS has certain unique features which constitute its areas of strength. The programme is village-based and conducted by workers (Anganwadi workers and helpers), who are normally residents of the same village. The workers maintain close contact with individual households of the village, thus taking away the impersonal approach generally found in Government-run programmes. The programme enlists the active help and participation of voluntary organisations, social activists, academic institutions and professionals and there is a built-in scope for convergence of health, nutrition, and childhood education services at Anganwadi level. Two-thirds of the population covered by the ICDS programme comprise of SCs, STs, and OBCs. The impact of the programme is evident from the remarkable improvements made in child survival and development indicators. There is a decrease in prevalence of malnutrition among pre-school children and immunisation coverage in ICDS areas has improved. The infant mortality rate has decreased in these areas, while school enrolment has improved. The school dropout rate has also come down in ICDS areas.

New Initiatives

ICDS today provides vital services to 2.88 crore children and 54 lakh women in 4388 blocks and major urban slums. The Government has approved a proposal to extend ICDS services in 390 projects with domestic support, and 461 projects with support from the World Bank. In a phased manner, it is committed to universalise the scheme as early as possible during the Ninth Plan. In consonance with the life-cycle approach of development, a nation-wide unique intervention aimed at empowerment of adolescent girls was also tried in all community development blocks in the country during Ninth Plan period. It is estimated that 12.8 lakh adolescent girls from the deprived sections of the society will be benefited under the scheme renamed as Kishori Shakti Yojana.

A new initiative in the form of Pradhan Mantri Gramodaya Yojana (PMGY) has been introduced in order to achieve the objective of sustainable human development at the village level. PMGY envisages allocations for additional central assistance to the states and union territories for basic minimum services in order to focus on certain priority areas including nutrition. The allocation under the nutrition component of PMGY is to be made under the supplementary nutrition programme component of ICDS. It has been specifically outlined with the objective of eradicating malnutrition among children under 3 by increased nutritional coverage of supplementary feeding through ICDS.

ICDS in Arunachal Pradesh

Integrated Child Development Scheme (ICDS) was introduced in Arunachal Pradesh with launching one ICDS project at Niausa in Tirap district in 1979-80. The Scheme has thereafter been extended to other CD blocks in the state and at the end of 2001-02, 57 CD blocks were côvered under the Scheme. Out of 58 projects, 1 project could not be launched so far, in absence of specific clarifications/approval from Government of India (Table 3.1).

Anganwadi Centres under ICDS are the village level institutions where: (a) non-formal pre-school education, (b) health check-up, (c) immunization, (d) referral service, (e) special nutrition, and (f) health and nutrition education services are delivered. A total of 2339 Anganwadi Centres have been sanctioned in 58 projects out of which 2327 Anganwadi Centres have already been made operationalised in 57 projects by the end of 2000-01. The Social Welfare, Women and Child Development Department (nodal department) is responsible for pre-school education, and SNP

Table 3.1 : Status of Coverage of ICDSs in Arunachal Pradesh, 2001

District	*CDPOs*	*Anganwadis*	*Villages to be covered*
Tawang	3	95	26
West Kameng	4	111	35
East Kameng	4	205	60
Papumpare	2	115	37
Lower Subansiri	3	120	64
Kurug Krimey	6	189	84
Upper Subansiri	5	195	86
West Siang	7	332	80
Upper Siang	2	50	33
East Siang	4	171	37
Dibang Valley	3	75	35
Lohit	5	228	41
Changlang	4	216	42
Tirap	5	225	45
Total	57	2327	705

* Data on Hayuliang, Lazu, and Zimitaung are not readily available.
Source: Records of the Office of Director, Department of Social Welfare and Women and Child Development, Naharlagun.

in Anganwadi centres including administration. Health department is responsible for health component like health check-up, immunization, and referral service. Food and Nutrition Extension unit, Itanagar under the Department of Women and Child Development, Government of India is also giving co-operation to the nodal department.

At district level, the state has established a total of 6 divisional ICDS Cells to cover all 14 districts. These cells are headed by Dy. Director (ICDS) under Deputy Commissioner. Similarly, CDPOs are the project level officers, assisted by Supervisors, Extension Officers, Gramsevikas, and Anganwadi workers. These Anganwadi workers are the grass root and key functionaries responsible for running of Anganwadi. Anganwadi workers are assisted by Anganwadi Helpers. Anganwadi centres provide health care facilities to children and pregnant women. They supply medicines, nutritious foods (channa, groundnut, peas, biscuits, kichiri, etc.) to pregnant, lactating, and children. Children are also taught, depending upon the age, games, english, hindi, and maths. Provision of such midday meals attracts children's enrollment, particularly girls, in the Anganwadi centres. The scheme is implemented as per schematic pattern and ceiling limit prescribed for it. All projects are tribal projects and entirely funded by Government of India. SNP is one of the components of ICDS, entirely funded by State budget. District-wise SNP beneficiaries in ICDS project area is provided in Table 3.2. In all, 1.33 lakh women, and children are covered under ICDS in 2000-01.

Table 3.2 : District-wise SNP Beneficiaries in ICDS Projects, 2000-01

Name of district	*Projects*	*SNP beneficiaries*		
		Pregnant and nursing mothers	*Children 0 m–3 yrs.*	*Children 3 yrs.-6 yrs.*
Tirap	5	1778	6227	4309
Changlang	4	1227	4211	3819
Lohit	5	1114	4770	4126
Diabang Valley	3	1046	1346	1337
East Siang	4	1100	4533	4032
West Siang	7	2549	7728	5995
Upper Siang	2	373	1876	1493
Upper Subansiri	5	1171	5087	4401
Lower Subansiri	3	5003	16071	8870
Papumpare	2	677	2381	2132
East Kameng	4	1979	7309	4602
West Kameng	4	1213	3539	2341
Tawang	3	166	500	469
Total	51	19396	65578	47926

Source: Same as Table 3.1.

Other components, namely, providing safe drinking water to Anganwadi and infrastructure facilities are the liabilities of Public Health Engineering (PHE) Department of the state government. The Rural Development (RD) Department is providing financial assistance for constructing Anganwadi buildings through JRY and other schemes. Due to lack of finance, the achievement by PHE and RD is not satisfactory. Only 1425 Anganwadies have been provided with safe water, and 115 Anganwadies out of 2145 have their own buildings. The other Anganwadi centres are run in rented houses as per Government of India's approved rent @ Rs. 25p.m.

ICDS in the Study Area

As mentioned in the methodology, all 40 villages selected are drawn from the ICDS project area. In all, 10 CDPOs, 15 supervisors, and 25 gramsevikas were contacted during the field visits. CDPOs in a region are controlled by a Deputy Director and there are 4 such DDs in the state. The organisational chart of Regional Dy. Director is given in chart 3.1.

Chart 3.1 : Organisational Chart of Deputy Director (ICDS)

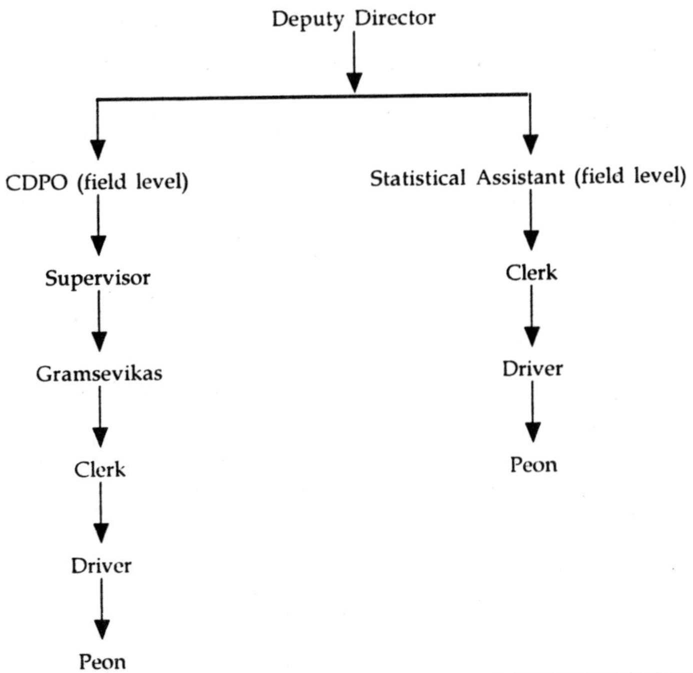

The post of CDPO is the rank of a gazetted officer having drawing and disbursement powers and almost all the CDPOs are provided with a vehicle. Nine out of the ten CDPOs contacted are graduates and one of them is from home science. Depending upon the request from villagers CDPO, organises Anganwadi centres in a village with help of village leaders, gramsevikas/supervisors. A literate lady, preferably from the village, is selected and trained as Anganwadi Worker. Training centres are located in Neharlagun, Pasighat, and Bomdila. It is a 3 months training programme where women workers are trained in adult education, human nutrition, health, sanitation, first aid, child care, etc. On successful completion of training they are posted as a Anganwadi Workers with a monthly salary Rs. 480/month. It is very difficult to get a 10th passed lady in this area for a paltry amount of Rs. 480/month.

The worker is assisted by a helper who also hails from the same village. As per the provisions of the ICDS, villagers are to arrange accommodation while honorarium to worker and helper as also day to day maintenance of the Anganwadi centre is being looked after by the Government of India. There is a token rent of Rs. 25 in case villagers hire a house for this purpose. Play materials, posters, SNP items, medicines, first-aid kit, furniture, etc. are also provided by the Government of India. Anganwadi centres are generally kept open for 2-3 hours during morning. All the employees of the ICDS are happy with the scheme and are willing to work in the rural areas. About 65% of them are trained. Percentage of untrained personnel is more in gramsevikas and supervisors. They all work as a team in organising, supervising, and guiding Anganwadi workers. Anganwadi centres in this part of the country are popularly known as 'chana-badam schools' and are familiar to most of the women.

Discussions with the CDPOs, and supervisors/gramsevikas revealed the following facts and the same are provided in Table 3.3. A close observation of Table 3.3 reveals that there is no provision for accommodation (office and residential quarters) to the employees of ICDS. In the absence of owned residential quarters, CDPOs and accompanying staff are to either hire private accommodation, which is very costly, or else frequently request the Deputy Commissioner for allotment.

All the respondents invariably mentioned it as a major problem being faced in the field. Interestingly, need for human resource development was stressed and vast majority of the respondents expressed desire for regular training

Table 3.3 : Grievances Reported by ICDC Staff

Sr. No.	Grievances	CDPOs (n=10)		Supervisors (n=10)	
		Frequency	% to total	Frequency	% to total
1.	Residential accommodation	10	100.0	40	100.0
2.	Provision for regular training	10	100.0	35	87.5
3.	Increase in house rent allowances	89	90.0	30	75.0
4.	Flexibility in purchasing items locally available for SNP	8	80.0	20	50.0
5.	Supply of sufficient quality of medicines and SNP items	8	80.0	35	87.5
6.	Enhanced winter allowances	6	60.0	30	75.0
7.	Water connection in Anganwadi centres	5	50.0	25	62.5
8.	Enhanced tour allowances	4	40.0	37	92.5
9.	Provision for vehicle	1	10.0	0	00.0

Source: Same as Table 3.1.

programmes. They are trained by NIPCED (New Delhi or Guwahati) but what they wanted is to make the training as a process. Such a step would go a long way in updating their knowledge and to have interaction with personnel working in other parts of the country. Other difficulties mentioned by them include hike in house rent allowances, flexibility in procuring locally available items to be given under SNP, supply of quality medicines and SNP items, etc. It is to be mentioned here that supply of medicines is very irregular, inadequate, and some times, it was reported that expired medicines are distributed. Similarly quality of SNP items too is less than desirable and most of them requested for quality items. A mention about tour allowances is also in order here. CDPO is provided with a vehicle[3] while the supervisors/ gramsevikas are paid a fixed travelling allowances. As the communication and transport facilities are less than desired, they spend more than what is given to them. The CDPOs may allot the vehicle 3-4 days to the field staff so as to enable them to cover as many Anganwadi centres as possible. Some of the Anganwadi centres are located as far as 150 kms away from the head quarter and gramsevikas face numerous problems in reaching such centres. Some of the supervisors/ gramsevikas complained about non-receipt of winter firewood allowances. Thus, employees of ICDS indicated both internal and external problems which are hindering progress of the scheme.

As mentioned above, Anganwadi workers/helpers are gross root level people involved in implementing the scheme. The success and or failure of the scheme depends, to great extent, on these people. They should be committed, sincere, dedicated and should have keenness to know and disseminate the same to villagers. They should act as change agents. It is possible only when they are educated and paid a reasonable honorarium. Present honorarium, Rs. 480/ month, is too inadequate and needs to be enhanced at least to Rs. 1000/month. Arunachal Pradesh is classified as expensive area and hence such hike is all the more essential.

IRDP

Integrated Rural Development Programme, which was a loan linked and subsidy oriented programme, was first initiated in 1978 in selected districts of the country and extended to all over the country by 1980. Basic objective of IRDP was to enable identified families in rural areas to cross the poverty line (Government of India, 1981). By 1990 IRDP was implemented in all the 11 districts of the state. However, credit linkage was started only in 1987-88. As the coverage extended to remote and far off areas, the ratio of credit disbursement started declining. On an average women formed 30% of the total beneficiaries (Table 3.4). Since there were multiplicity of programmes associated with rural poor, Swarnajayanti Gram Swarozgar Yojana (SGSY) was launched on April 1, 1999 by clubbing all the existing rural development programmes. SGSY is a major self employment program under implementation in the entire rural areas of the country. It aims at creating self employment opportunities for rural poor with emphasis on Self Help Groups (SHGs) by providing them assistance through government subsidy and bank credit.

Table 3.4 : Source-wise Distribution of Loans Under IRDP, 1991-01

Year	*Baneficiaries*		*Source-wise credit disbursed (Rs. lakhs)*				*Subsidy (Rs. lakhs)*
	Men	*Women*	*Commercial banks*	*Cooperative banks*	*RRBs*	*Total*	
1990-91	6065	2358	NA	NA	NA	113.05	159.02
1991-92	6815	4073	56.14	30.74	13.27	100.15	164.09
1992-93	9215	4427	66.40	35.59	19.92	121.91	274.95
1993-94	10320	4887	60.35	48.57	19.65	128.57	308.81
1994-95	10822	7942	47.50	26.37	21.55	95.42	386.36
1995-96	8097	6284	55.13	41.04	30.98	127.15	329.41
1996-97	6523	4172	85.36	45.32	48.05	178.73	341.08
1997-98	7319	5480	98.26	75.48	89.91	263.65	409.71
1998-99	5552	6880	99.98	58.16	63.58	221.72	367.85
1999-00*	2065	1169	43.79	27.90	2.79	74.48	240.22
2000-01	796	607	47.04	12.10	53.32	112.36	119.82

Source: Records of Office of the Director, Department of Rural Development, Naharlagun.
* Figures related to SGSY.

The objective is to bring every assisted family above poverty line in three years.

DWCRA

Development of women and children in Rural Areas was started in 1982-83. Women who were not in a position to take advantage of schemes under IRDP were organised into homogeneous groups of 15 to 20 (Planning Commission 1985). It was aimed at improving living conditions of women and thereby of children through provision of opportunities for self-employment and access to basic social services. The strategy adopted under this program was to facilitate access for poor women to employment, skill upgradation, training, credit, and other support services so that these women as a group can take up income generating activities for supplementing their incomes. There were about 2 lakh groups organised under DWCRA throughout the country (Puri, 2000). Such activities included weaving, fish vending, broom and rope making, brick making, candle making, etc. DWCRA was started in 1986-87 in Arunachal Pradesh. East Kameng district was the first to have implemented this program. Subsequently, it was extended to West Siang, Tirap, Tawang, etc. over the period. Groups organised, membership and amount disbursed steadily increased (Table 3.5). Activities covered included weaving, carpet making, knitting, tailoring, poultry, piggery, fish ponds etc. As mentioned earlier, DWCRA was clubbed with SGSY in 1998-99.

Table 3.5 : Progress of DWCRA in Arunachal Pradesh, 1991-99

Year	*No of groups formed*	*Membership*	*Amount distributed (Rs. lakhs)*
1990-91	235	2752	28.54
1991-92	195	2212	22.34
1992-93	200	2751	33.21
1993-94	280	2849	30.00
1994-95	100	1045	18.31
1995-96	173	1865	29.79
1996-97	126	1141	26.10
1997-98	154	1158	42.95
1998-99	70	546	19.26

Source: Same as Table 3.5.

Mahila Swayam Siddha (MSS)

This was previously known as Indira Mahila Yojana (1995), and is being implemented in Tezu block. It is aimed at ensuing empowerment to ST women by encouraging thrift through small savings Government of India recasted the programme and sanctioned 5 new blocks for implementation of Sawayam Siddha Scheme for 2001-2002. These five blocks are Sagalee-Mangio (Papumpare), Buragaon (West Kameng), Dambuk-Roing (Dibang Valley), Pangin (East Siang) and Seppa (East Kameng). Out of six sanctioned, 120 IMKs exists in Tezu-Namsai project.

It is proposed to recast the MSS into an Integrated women's empowerment programme (IWEP) and to expand it from the 238 blocks to 650 blocks by March 2002 in the country. The long term objective of the IWEP is empowerment of women (socially and economically) by ensuring direct access to and control over resources through a sustained process of mobilisation and convergence of all ongoing sectoral programmes. Its immediate objectives are: (a) to establish self-reliance women's SHGs, (b) to create confidence and awareness among members of SHGs regarding women status, health, nutrition, education, sanitation, and hygiene, legal rights, economic upliftment, and other social, economic, and political issues, (c) strengthening and institutionalizing the savings habit in rural women and their control over economic resources, (d) improvement of access to micro credits, (e) improvement of women in local level planning, and (f) convergence of services of department of women and child development and other related departments. It is proposed to cover 650 blocks, to organise 53100 SHGs with 9.29 lakh womens by the end of March 2002.

Balika Samridhi Yojna (BSY)

Under this scheme Rs. 500 as bonus given to each girl child born after 1998 August whose parents belong to below the poverty line. A total of 1660 beneficiaries are benefited from this scheme till March, 2001.

Udisha

This is a training scheme under ICDS funded by World Bank. Udisha is a new scheme of training scheme introduced in 1999-2000 by the Government of India for imparting training to all field functionaries under ICDS. Under Udisha, state government has established 5 training centres in 5 districts recently, and 1 centre at Itanagar functioning since 1985. A total of 850 Anganwadi workers have so far been trained, and 280 were given refresher training. A training calendar was prepared for various centres so as to cover all untrained Anganwadi workers and helpers of all projects by the end of 2002-03.

Kisor Shakti Yojana

This programme launched by Government of India. Twenty blocks are selected in Arunachal Pradesh and work is in progress. The list of blocks and corresponding districts are provided in Table 3.6.

National Social Assistance Programme (NSAP)

The NSAP has got three components namely, (i) National Old Age Pension (NSAP), (ii) National Family Benefit Scheme (NFBS), and (iii) National Maternity Benefit Schemes (NMBS).

Table 3.6 : Selected Blocks for KSY in Arunachal Pradesh

Block	*District*
Tawang	Tawang
Nefra	West Kameng
Seppa	East Kameng
Chayangtajo	East Kameng
Kimin Doimukh	Papumpare
Sagalee	Papumpare
Pangin-Boleng	East Siang
Pasighat	East Siang
Koloriang	Lower Subansiri
Dumporijo	Upper Subansiri
Daporijo	Upper Subansiri
Along	West Siang
Basar	West Siang
Yingking	Upper Siang
Dombuk-Roing	Dibang Valley
Anini	Dibang Valley
Tezu	Lohit
Hayuliang	Lohit
Changlang	Changlang
Khonsa	Tirap

Source: Same as Table 3.1.

(i) **National Old Age Pension Scheme (NOAPS):** Under this scheme as old age persons above 65 years of age and living below the poverty line is provided @ Rs. 75/ month.

(ii) **National Family Benefit Scheme (NFBS):** Under the scheme an amount of Rs. 10,000 is provided as one time grant to kin in case of death of a primary bread winner of the family.

(iii) **National Maternity Benefit Scheme (NMBS):** Under this scheme an amount of Rs. 500 as one time grant is provided to pregnant mother for health-care of the new born baby.

Summary

A review of ongoing developmental programmes for women revealed that both central and state governments have been providing assistance under various heads. Prominent among them are integrated child development services, IRDP/SGSY, DWCRA, MSS, BSY, etc. There are 57 ICDS projects operational in the state with 2327 Anganwadi centres. As many as 1.33 lakh women, and children are covered under this scheme. The CDPOs, supervisors, and gramsevikas complained about non-availability of certain facilities which are hindering successful implementation of the scheme. Both IRDP and DWCRA programmes are now merged and are known as SGSY which is being implementing in the state since 1999-00. There are number of other schemes too for the benefit of women in the state.

NOTES

1. Since ICDS is the most important scheme for women, the progress of ICDP at the centre too is reviewed here.
2. Recently (2002) a National Nutrition Mission has been designed to combat chronic malnutrition through intergenerational approach of focusing on education of girls and young mothers. Under this project, beneficiaries would be given food free of cost as part of the Government of India's bid to control nutritional deficiencies among target groups.
3. The CDPO at Mariyang is not provided with a vehicle. As a result she is put to lot of innocence in touring Anganwadi centers. The centres are located far away from the headquarter and no public transport is available on these roads. Hence, there is an urgent need to provide a vehicle to the concerned CDPO.

4

PROFILES OF SELECTED DISTRICTS

Introduction

This chapter is aimed at providing profiles of selected districts and reviewing progress of IRDP and DWCRA with emphasis on women in these districts. This sector is based on the information obtained from various statistical abstracts, socio-economic review reports, and data obtained from offices of the Project Directors of selected districts. Districts are arranged from east to west, and are presented in the following sections.

Lohit District

The district is named after one of its principle river, Lohit[1] which was earlier known as Lauhitya. The river rises from eastern Tibet and enters India near Dichu in Kibithoo. Locally it is known as 'pagal nala' as it changes its direction frequently and creates havoc with heavy currents during monsoons. The name of this district underwent a series of changes. This area was part of 'central and eastern section' of NEFT in 1914. It was renamed as Sadiya Frontier Tract in 1919. A part of the Sadiya Frontier Tract was named as Mishmi Hills district in 1948 which was once again renamed as Lohit Frontier Division in 1954. It was named as Lohit district in 1965. During 1980, the district was bifurcated as Lohit district and Dibang Valley district.

The district lies in the eastern part of the state between 95°15' and 97°24' east longitudes, and 27°23' to 29°22' north latitudes. Geographical area of the district is 11402 sq. kms.

It is bounded by China along the McMahon line and part of Dibang Valley district in the north, Changlang district to the south, China and Myanmar to the east, and Assam and part of Dibang Valley district to the west. The district consists of chain of hills and maintains with altitudes ranging from 500 metres to 5000 metres.

Lohit, Kamlang, and Noa-Dihing are the rivers that flow through the district. While flowing through foot hill areas, these rivers frequently change their courses resulting in heavy erosion. In the process they pose serious challenge to communication system and as a result the district is cutoff from the mainland for 6-7 months during monsoons. A pumping (floating) bridge was constructed by BRTF to cross Noa-Dining-Kamling which is closed during 5 p.m. to 6 a.m. due to security reasons. Air communication also depends on the mercy of weather. As a result, the tempo of development activities cannot be taken up during this period. The administration is to face numerous problems for transportation of food stuffs and other essential commodities to headquarters as also to far-flung outposts. Tezu, district headquarter, is cut off from the main land for about 4 months a year.

The district has five community development blocks (Tezu, Namsai, Wakro, Hayuliang, and Walong[2] with 487 villages. It has a population of 1.10 lakhs with a sex ratio of 797. Density of population is 9 persons/sq. km. and the percentage of literacy is 49.21. Mishmis (Digaru and Miju), Khamties, and Singphoes inhibit the district. Both Khamties and Singphoes are Buddhists by religion and live in Chougkham, and Namsai area, while Mishmis believe in spirits and concentrated in Hayuliang, Tezu, and Wakro regions.

Agriculture

Agriculture is the main occupation of the locals, 1/4th of the total population are cultivators. Jhumming is followed in the upper hilly region while Khamties and Singphoes of plains practice wet rice cultivation. Cultivators of Namsai-Chowkham (plains) are now growing crops like sugarcane, mustard, soybean, and ginger apart from paddy, maize and potato. Horticulture crops like oranges, pineapples, guava, pear, etc. are also grown in this area.

A large natural lake (glowlake) lies in the Wakro block (around 25 km. from Wakro) at an altitude of 1400 metres. Parasuram Kund and Brahma Kund are located near Wakro in the lower reaches of Lohit river. They are religious places visited by people all over the country on Makar Sankranti day for a holy dip. Common belief is that a dip on that day in the kund washes away one's sins. It is mentioned in the Kalika Purana that it was here the sage Parasurama[3] washed away his sin of having killed his own mother, Renuka. Hawa and Sewak passes are also worth visiting and are located between Tezu and Hayuliang.

Progress of IRDP and DWCRA

Beneficiaries covered, subsidy, and loan amounts released under IRDP during 1994-01 are presented in Table 4.1. As many as 8250 beneficiaries covering 4745 men, and 3505 women were covered under IRDP. An amount of Rs. 210.50 lakhs as loan and Rs. 65.23 lakhs as subsidy were disbursed under this scheme during 1994-01. Thus, on an average, Rs. 3342 were given as loan subsidy during the study period. This amount/beneficiary appears to be inadequate to bring them above the poverty line.

Table 4.1 : Progress of IRDP in Lohit, 1994-01

Year	*No. of schemes implemented*	*No. of beneficiaries*		*Subsidy (Rs. lakhs)*	*Bank loan (Rs. lakhs)*
		Men	*Women*		
1993-94	1029	424	605	22.20	12.88
1994-95	1417	816	601	28.50	9.55
1995-96	1489	800	689	22.94	3.60
1996-97	997	890	107	39.13	3.09
1997-98	1936	1127	809	55.59	1.63
1998-99	1220	556	665	25.74	2.28
1999-00	0	0	0	0	0
2000-01	161	132	29	16.10	32.20

Source: Records of the Project Director (DRDA).

As regards DWCRA, the picture is far from satisfactory. As many as 53 groups with a total membership of 407 were organised, and Rs. 12.06 lakhs were given as revolving fund

(Table 4.2). Thus, on an average, Rs. 2963 were given/ beneficiary as revolving fund.

Table 4.2 : Progress of DWCRA Activities in Lohit, 1994-99

Year	*No. of groups*	*Membership*	*Amount sanctioned (Rs. lakhs)*	*Activities*	
1993-94	Nil	Nil	Nil	-	-
1994-95	Nil	Nil	Nil	-	-
1995-96	27	254	5.86	Handloom	5
				Dairy	3
				Goatery	6
				Duckery	7
				Piggery	2
				Poultry	2
				Weaving	1
1996-97	21	128	4.95	Piggery	5
				Goatery	7
				Weaving	4
				Fish Pond	1
				Dairy	3
				Poultry	1
1997-98	5	25	1.25	Goatery	1
				Piggery	1
				Fish Pond	1
				Knitting	1
				Weaving	1
1998-99	Nil	Nil	Nil	-	-

Source: Records of the Project Director (DRDA).

Dibang Valley district

Dibang Valley derives its name from river Dibang which is originating from glacial lakes below Gorichen and flows through heart of the district. The river finally debauches into plains where it meets Lohit near Sadiya. The district has a wild mountainous area and present a remarkable topographical variety. It is bounded on the north by China, on the south partly by Assam and partly by Lohit district, on the east by China and Lohit district, and on the west by East and West Siang districts. It stretches from snow capped mountains in the north to plains of Brahmaputra valley in the south. The district is situated approximately between 95° 15′ to 97° 30′ east longitudes, and 37° 33′ to 29°30′ north latitudes.

Prior to June 1980, Dibang Valley was a part of Lohit district. It became an independent district with headquarters at Anini in 1980. Area of the district is 13029 sq. kms. with a population of 43068 (1991). Thus, it is the biggest district in area, and second smallest district in population. Dibang Valley was very badly affected by the great earthquake of 1950. Dibang river completely changed its course sweeping the old Sadiya town. Anini is situated at a height of 1698 metres above the mean sea level on a beautiful plateau between Dri and Mathun rivers. There are 238 villages in the district and they are grouped under three community development blocks (Anini-Italin, Hunli-Kronli-Desali, and Roing-Dambuk).

The district has a sub-tropical climate. Summers are pleasant while winters are very cool. Inhabitants of the district comprises of Idu Mishmis, Adis, and Mishing. Adi tribe is mostly concentrated in lower part of the district while Idu Mishmis are inhabitants of upper, middle, and lower parts of the district. Main festivals of the district are Reh, Sulung, Arang, and Pime. Shri Mukut Mithi, Honorable Chief Minister of Arunachal Pradesh hails from Dibang Valley.

The district has a number of tourist places. They include Dri Valley, Magawia, Mehao wild life sanctuary, Bhishmaknagar[4], Rukmini Nati, Ita Phukuri, Roing forest park, Kampona Pond, Mayodeo, etc. Roing is in the lower Dibang Valley while the district's headquarters is in Upper Dibang Valley. The distance between the two is 230 kms. There was no metal road connecting these two important places till 1987. In the absence of load link, sorties were the only mode of transport in those days. Though accommodation is provided to all employees at Anini, due to lack of facilities (education, recreation, inclement weather, etc.) most of them stay at Roing and visit Anini. During his visit to Anini, late Shri Rajiv Gandhi directed authorities to construct a road within about five years. Initially the construction work was assigned to PWD and later handed over to BRTF. The road was finally opened to public in 1998. However, due to adverse climatic conditions, the road is closed half the year either due to heavy landslides or heavy snow fall. Tata sumos, gypsy, and trucks are the mode of transport on this road. On a normal day, it takes about 12 hours to cover the distance. Mayodeo[5], Hunli, Arzoo, and Etalin are the important places on the way.

Agriculture

Unfavourable terrain, remoteness, inaccessibility, scattered population, and long isolation from the mainland are main constraints in economic development of the district. Agriculture is the principle occupation of the people of the district. Out of the total population of 43068, 50% of them are cultivators. Shifting cultivation is followed in Anini-Etalin, and Hunli-Kronli blocks while permanent cultivation is followed in Roing-Dambuk block. The district has a net cultivated area of ha. 13534 with 4944 holdings. Farmers of both lower and upper Dibang Valley grow paddy, maize, and millets. Ginger, rape seed, potato, etc. are also cultivated in the lower region. Horticultural crops like oranges, pineapple, banana, guava, plums, etc. are grown in the district. The district has been bifurcated into Lower Dibang Valley and Upper Dibang Valley through an official notification issued in the month of December 2001.

Progress of IRDP and DWCRA

DRDA has assisted 3962 beneficiaries under IRDP during 1994-01 (Table 4.3). An amount of Rs. 94.53 lakhs as loan and Rs. 48.56 lakhs as subsidy were made available under this scheme. Thus, on an average, Rs. 3612/beneficiary was provided under IRDP during 1994-01. Once again, the amount

Table 4.3 : Progress of IRDP in Dibang Valley, 1994-01

Year	*No. of schemes implemented*	*No. of beneficiaries*		*Subsidy (Rs. lakhs)*	*Bank loan (Rs. lakhs)*
		Men	*Women*		
1993-94	405	243	162	8.05	7.41
1994-95	471	245	226	9.77	3.60
1995-96	397	239	158	8.05	2.71
1996-97	623	523	100	14.72	6.81
1997-98	656	446	210	14.09	2.97
1998-99	1337	845	492	31.52	8.17
1999-00	No scheme implemented under IRDP during this year as new scheme namely SGSY introduced				
2000-01	73*	58	15	8.33	16.89

* includes a group of 15 women members.

Source: Records of the Project Director (DRDA).

appears to be inadequate to bring the people above poverty line.

The performance of DWCRA is not satisfactory (Table 4.4). In all, 64 groups with 877 members were organised. Average membership/group was 13. An amount of Rs. 11.10 lakhs were given as revolving fund giving Rs. 1265/ beneficiary. This is a paltry amount in an expensive area like Arunachal Pradesh. Thus, amount given both under IRDP and DWCRA is not satisfactory.

Table 4.4 : Progress of DWCRA Activities in Dibang Valley, 1994-99

Year	*No. of groups*	*Membership*	*Amount sanctioned (Rs. lakhs)*	*Activities*	
1993-94	21	273	3.19 @ Rs. 15,200/group	Knitting	5
				Tailoring	4
				Ginger cultivation	9
				Domestic fish pond	1
				Loin loom	1
				Duckery	1
1994-95	23	299	3.50 @ Rs. 15,200/group	Loin loom	21
				Tailoring	1
				Knitting	1
1995-96	6	90	0.91@ Rs. 15,200/group	Ginger cultivation	1
				Vegetable garden	1
				Duckery	1
1996-97	8	120	2.00@ Rs. 25,000/group	Loin loom	3
				Domestic fish pond	1
				Ginger cultivation	1
				Duckery	1
				Weaving	1
				Mushroom	1
				cultivation	1
1997-98	2	32	0.50 @ Rs. 25,000/group	Potato cultivation	1
				Sugarcane	1
1998-99	4	63	1.00 @ Rs. 25,000/group	Duckery	2
				Piggery	1
				Weaving	1

Source: Records of the Project Director (DRDA).

Upper Siang District

Name of the district is derived from river Siang[6] which flows through the district. This area was part of the central section of the NEFT in 1914. Central section along with eastern section of the NEFT was renamed as Sadiya Frontier Tract (SFT) in 1919 with headquarters at Sadiya. SFT was bifurcated into two administrative charges (Abor Hills District, and Mishmi Hills District) in 1948 and Upper Siang region was part of the Abor Hills district. Under the regulation of 1954, Abor Hills district was renamed as Siang Frontier Division (SFD). The area (SFD) was again renamed as Siang district in 1965 with headquarter at Along. Siang district was divided into East and West Siangs in 1980 and the present Upper Siang was part of East Siang district with headquarter at Pasighat. Upper Siang district was carved out from the East Siang in 1994 with headquarter at Yingkiong.[7]

The district is situated in the remote north upper most part of the state. A greater part of the district falls within higher mountain zone consisting of tangled peaks and valleys. The district lies roughly between 94°-95° northern latitude and 28°-29° eastern longitude with an area of roughly 6188 sq. kms. It is bounded by Dibang Valley in east, East Siang in west, McMahon line on north (China), and West Siang in west.

It has four community development blocks (Yingkiong, Jengging, Mariyang, and Tuting) with 822 villages. Cadastal survey has not been conducted so far and revenue system in villages is yet to be introduced. As such each area with locally recognised boundaries is considered as a village. Thus, a village in this area or in the entire Arunachal as well may comprise even one house/household only. Each village is an independent unit for local administration. Age old village council called Kebang is still functioning. The village governing authority consists of Head Gaon Burah and few village elders exercising maximum authority in council's deliberations. Failure with regard to administration of Justice, both civil and criminal cases, in village council will be referred to inter village council. This is called Banggo Kebang comprising two or more villages. Cases which are not settled through these councils are referred to Administrative Officers of concerned jurisdiction. Kebang is the life force of Adi society where from emanates all activities starting from day to day social affairs to the highest political matters. The district is inhabited by Adis (Pasi, Padam, Panggi, Kimkar, Shimong, Karko, Millang, etc.), Membas, Khambas, and Idu Mishmis. The district has a population of 27779 with a density of population of 4 persons/sq.km. (out of the total area of 6188 sq.kms., as much as 4005 sq.kms. is inaccessible). Sex ratio is 822 females/1000 males and literacy rate is 35.3%.

Agriculture

Agriculture occupies a central position in the district followed by forestry, hunting, and gathering. Vast majority of agriculture is based on Jhumming. It has been the usual practice in Jhumming that male would perform activities like felling of tries, burning and clearing, and largely making field ready for sowing. Women are valued for both production and reproduction. Due to broad and narrow valleys, cultivated area is confined to 3% of the total geographical area. Paddy, millets, and maize followed by ginger, chillies, sugarcane, potato, etc. are grown in the district. Mariyang, Yingkiong, Jengging, and Tuting are beautiful places with pleasant climatic conditions.

Horticulture

The district has scope for growing varieties of tropical, sub-tropical, and temperate fruits, vegetables, and spices. It has a modest success in cultivating mandarin oranges, banana, pineapple, guava, pears, large cardamom, etc.

Animal Husbandry

Socio-economic life of the people of Upper Siang centres around livestock. Its role starts from birth of a baby or even earlier, and continues till death and has great significance. There are pre-birth formalities and post-death rites to be performed meticulously with the help of livestock. The fortunes are foretold with the help of writings on freshly cutout chicken's liver. Mithun (semi-domesticated), pig, cattle, goats, and poultry are common domesticated animals. These animals are mainly meant for meat, barter, sacrifice, payment of bride price, and discharge of social and religious obligations. The number of animals possessed by a person is considered as an index of wealth and is a prestige symbol.

Progress of IRDP and DWCRA

This district was formed in 1995-96 and, thus data were provided from 1996-97 only. During 1997-01 (five years period), DRDA assisted 1983 beneficiaries under IRDP (Table 4.5). Interestingly, 1281 women, and 702 men were given loan and subsidy during 1997-01. Similarly, on an average, Rs. 6098 were given as loan and subsidy in this district. Thus, the average assistance provided is relatively more and women out numbered men under IRDP in the district.

Table 4.5 : Progress of IRDP in Upper Siang, 1994-01

Year	*No. of schemes implemented*	*No. of beneficiaries*		*Subsidy (Rs. lakhs)*	*Bank loan (Rs. lakhs)*
		Men	*Women*		
1993-94	District was formed in 1995-96 only				
1994-95					
1995-96					
1996-97	602	255	347	22.55	1.46
1997-98	648	240	408	22.26	16.35
1998-99	550	105	345	20.56	12.36
1999-00	122	37	85	7.58	10.5
2000-01	161	65	96	5.32	2.00

Source: Records of the Project Director (DRDA).

As regards DWCRA, 33 groups were organised with a total membership of 184. The revolving money disbursed stood at Rs. 7.68 lakhs (Table 4.6). Weaving, knitting, piggery,

Table 4.6 : Progress of DWCRA Activities in Upper Siang, 1994-99

Year	*No. of groups*	*Membership*	*Amount sanctioned (Rs. lakhs)*	*Activities*	
1993-94	District was formed in 1995-96 only				
1994-95					
1995-96	Nil	Nil			
1996-97	7	41	1.75	Weaving	4
				Knitting	3
1997-98	11	61	2.75	Piggery	5
				Weaving	4
				Vegetable cultivation	2
1998-99	15	82	3.18	Piggery	6
				Vegetable cultivation	3
				Weaving	2
				Handloom	4

Source: Records of the Project Director (DRDA).

vegetable gardens, handloom, etc. were the activities covered under DWCRA in the district.

Lower Subansiri District

The district is named after river Subansiri that flows through Raga circle of this district. Till 1914, this area was a part of Lakhimpur district of Assam. The area covered by this district became a part of Lakhimpur Frontier Tract (LFT) of NEFT in 1914. During 1919, LFT alongwith western sector was renamed as Balipara Frontier Tract (BFT). Lower Subansiri area was carved out of BFT in 1946 and named as Subansiri area with headquarter at North Lakhimpur. This area was again renamed as Subansiri Frontier Division in 1954, and its headquarter was later shifted to Ziro. This division was once again renamed as Subansiri district in 1965. The district was bifurcated into Lower Subansiri and Upper Subansiri in 1980 (Daporijo sub-division was renamed as Upper Subansiri). Lower Subansiri district was once again bifurcated in 1992 into Lower Subansiri, and Papumpare.

It is located between 82°40′ to 94°21′ east longitudes, and 26°55′ to 28°21′ north latitudes. District is surrounded by China (Tibet), and parts of Upper Subansiri in the north, West Siang and parts of Upper Subansiri in the east, Papumpare and Assam in south, and East Kameng in west. The district has an area of 10135 sq. kms. which is mostly mountainous terrain. Hill ranges varies from 1000-1600 metres above sea level. Ziro, the district headquarters, is situated at 5000 feet on almost a level valley (Apatani plateau) enclosed on all sides by pine-clad low sloping hills. The Subansiri river, at one time famous for its gold dust, flows through the district and leaves at Dollungmukh circle of Lower Subansiri. Kamala, Khru, Panior, Kime, Panya, Selu, Pugo, Persen, Rein, Sipu, Pange, Kale, etc. are other rivers in the district.

The district has nine community development blocks with 595 villages. There are three major tribes in Lower Subansiri (Apatani, Nishi, and Hill-Miri). Total population of the district is 83167 with an average density of population of 8 persons/sq. km. Sex ratio of the district is 957 females/1000 males and the overall literacy rate is 24.24%.

Agriculture is the mainstay of this district. Paddy, maize, millets, potato, oilseeds, ginger, and vegetables are grown here. Both tropical (orange, pineapple, banana, lime, papaya, and jack fruit), and temperate (apple, pears, plum, and walnut) are grown in the district.

Paddy-cum-Fish Culture

This is an unique pisciculture activity in Lower Subansiri. This program was taken up in 1964-65 in Apatani Valley, Ziro on an experimental basis with 23 plots of paddy fields covering an area of 10 acres and was found remarkable success. This program was taken up intensively from 1968-69. Besides, attempts were also made to propagate the same at different areas of Lower Subansiri. As on 31st March, 2000, ha. 547 of paddy field was covered under this program. Advantages of this system are many: (1) rice and fish are cultivated simultaneously in the same water mass, (2) besides paddy, fish is obtained at low cost to offer food of animal protein, and (3) fish cultivation brings about a definite improvement in paddy crop by way of exercising an effective control on unwanted weeds, and mosquitoes.

Hydro-Electricity

Lower Subansiri district has vast power potentials for hydro electricity. The topography and climatic condition create innumerable perennial rivers and streams, which are capable of releasing hydel electric power for economic development. However, hydro-electric potential of the district has largely remained untapped. The first ever micro hydel of the district was commissioned in 1977 at Mai (phase-I) with an installed capacity of 2000 K.W. The Mai phase-II micro hydel was commissioned during 1984 with installed capacity of 1000 K.W. The Tago hydel project with installed capacity of 4510 K.W. was commissioned during March, 1992. The work of Ranganadi hydro electric project was also completed. The total installed capacity of electricity in the district is 7.782 M.W.

Progress IRDP and DWCRA

Data on progress of IRDP in Lower Subansiri is provided in Table 4.7. No trend is evident from the data. In all, 7004 beneficiaries were covered under IRDP during 1994-01 and

Table 4.7 : Progress of IRDP in Lower Subansiri, 1994-01					
Year	*No. of schemes implemented*	*No. of beneficiaries*		*Subsidy (Rs. lakhs)*	*Bank loan (Rs. lakhs)*
		Men	*Women*		
1993-94	856	581	275	32.54	10.50
1994-95	945	619	326	35.20	12.35
1995-96	764	519	245	30.48	8.43
1996-97	1054	715	339	27.50	9.55
1997-98	1235	810	425	26.48	10.44
1998-99	1105	654	451	32.55	7.58
1999-00	870	555	315	25.73	6.45
2000-01	175	80	95	12.43	8.87

Source: Records of the Project Director (DRDA).

women formed 35% of the total beneficiaries. An amount of Rs. 297.08 lakhs were made available as loan and subsidy under this program, providing on an average Rs. 4242/ beneficiary.

A total of 58 groups were organised under DWCRA in the district with a membership of 877. Revolving fund made available/participant worked out to be Rs. 1294 (Table 4.8). Discussions with the officials of DRDA revealed and that most of the groups are defunct and their impact on women is marginal.

West Kameng District

The name of the district is derived from Kameng river that flows through the district. This area was part of Darrang district of Assam till 1914. Area covered by this district became a part of the western section of NEFT in 1914 and was renamed as Balipara Frontier Tract in 1919 with headquarter at Charduar (Assam). This area was carved out of the Balipara Frontier Tract in 1919 and was named as Sela Sub-Agency in 1946 and the headquarter continued at Charduar. It was renamed as Kameng Frontier Division with headquarter at Bomdila in 1954, and once again renamed as Kameng district in 1965.[8] Kameng district was bifurcated into West and East Kamengs in 1980 (Seppa sub-division was named as East Kameng), and West Kameng district was further divided into West Kameng and Tawang districts in 1984 (Tawang sub-division was named as Tawang district).

West Kameng is located in the western part of Arunachal Pradesh and has an area of 7422 sq.kms. It lies between 91°.31′

Table 4.8 : Progress of DWCRA Activities in Lower Subansiri, 1994-99

Year	*No. of groups*	*Membership*	*Amount sanctioned (Rs. lakhs)*	*Activities*	
1993-94	15	246	2.28	Kitchen garden	3
				Fisheries	3
				Mushroom	2
				Knitting	2
				Weaving	3
				Piggery	2
1994-95	7	137	1.06	Kitchen garden	1
				Fisheries	1
				Mushroom	1
				Knitting	1
				Weaving	1
				Piggery	1
				Envelope and paper bags	1
1995-96	10	166	2.52	Kitchen garden	1
				Fisheries	1
				Mushroom	2
				Knitting	1
				Weaving	1
				Piggery	3
				Envelope and paper bags	1
1996-97	10	182	2.52	Kitchen garden	1
				Fisheries	1
				Mushroom	1
				Knitting	2
				Weaving	3
				Piggery	1
				Envelope and paper bags	1
1997-98	6	40	1.51	Sheep rearing	1
				Fisheries	2
				Weaving	1
				Piggery	2
1998-99	10	106	2.52	Goatery	1
				Handloom	1
				Ginger garden	1
				Fisheries	1
				Weaving	1
				Vegetable garden	1
				Grocery shop	2
				Sheep rearings	1
				Milch animals	1

Source: Records of the Project Director (DRDA).

to 92°.54′ east longitudes and 26°.54′ to 27°.53′ north latitudes. The altitudes of the district varies from 650 feet to 13714 feet. The district is surrounded by Tibet region of China in the north, Bhutan in the west, Tawang in the north-west, East Kameng in the east, and Sonitpur district of Assam in the south. Topography of the district is mostly mountainous. It has three mountain ranges (Sela range, Bomdila range, and foot hills range). Climate is hot and humid upto 4000 feet, temperate upto 7000 feet, and cold beyond it. Tenga, Bichom, and Dirang Chu are main tributaries of Kameng river which flows through the district.

The district has four community development blocks and 170 villages. Total population of the district is 56421 with a sex ratio of 822 females/1000 males. The percentage of literacy is 46.31 ranging between 55.03 and 35.22 for males and females respectively. Density of population of the district is 10/sq.km. The inhabitants of the district are Monpas, Miji, Sherdukpen, Aka, and Khawa (Bugun). Monpas are concentrated in Dirang, and Kalaktang circles while Mijis inhibit Nafra, and Akas in Thrizino circle. Khawas are in Wanghoo, Kaspi Singchung, and Tenga areas. Sherdukpens are located in Rupa, Jigaon, Shergaon, Thongre, and Doimara villages.

Initially there were no roads in this area and as a result priority was given to porter tracts and muleable tracts to supply essential commodities. Foothill to Bomdila road was opened to vehicular traffic in 1958 which was the first jeepable road in the district.

Agriculture and Horticulture

The climate is conducive to agriculture and horticulture. Wet rice cultivation is practiced in some pockets of Dirang, Thrizino, Kalaktang, and Nafra. Maize, millets, wheat, paddy, potato, and cabbage are grown in these areas. Jhumming is followed by Akas, Mijis, and Khawas. In order to educate farmers on modern agricultural practices a farmers' training centre was started at Salari in 1981. Both temperate (apple, pears, plum, and peaches) and sub-tropical (pineapple, orange, and grapes) fruits are grown in the district. A state horticultural farm was started at Shergaon in 1976-77 with a view to multiply good quality planting material and impart training on improved horticultural practices. There are about 75000 apple plants in Shergaon and Terizengaon. An apple plant on an average gives 100-150 kgs/year which is sold at Rs. 1220/kg. Cultivation of apple is taken as commercial activity in this region. Further, regional apple nursery was started at Dirang in 1977-78 to multiply temperate fruit plants. As the district is famous for orchids, Research and Training Centre has been functioning at Tipi. All these efforts helped in commercialization of agriculture.

Livestock

Due to availability of abundant green pasture, and heterogeneous climate, variety of animals are found here. They include cattle, yak, poultry, mithun, sheep, goat, donkey, pig, and dzo-dzomo. Foothills areas covering altitudes between 500-3000 feet are conducive for cattle, pig, poultry, and goats. Broad valley and plateau ranging from 3000 to 5000 feet are good for mithun, sheep, and poultry. Upper belt varying between 5000-10000 feet is good for sheep, yak, and dzo-dzomo. Regional sheep breeding farm was established at Sangti in 1975 to undertake work on sheep development. Further, regional temperate fodder seed production cum demonstration farm was organised at Dirang in 1986 to develop improved varieties of legume and non-legumenous fodders. A National Research Centre on Yak (ICAR) was established at Dirang in 1989. The objective of the centre is to improve productivity, husbandry conditions, and incorporate better germ plasam in existing population of yaks. Yaks are the major source of milk, wool, traction power, besides their limited use as a source of meat. It is considered as the only mammal which dwells in between 10000-18000 feet above the sea level.

Tourist Places

Bhalukpong, Tipi, Chandi Top, Bomdila, Kalaktang, and Dirang are worth visiting. A steep climb from Dirang through alpine landscape leads to Sela Pass (13700 feet). Paradise like rests in its crest. A little ahead is Nuranang Trout Hatchery where snow and rainbow trout are available.

Progress of the IRDP and DWCRA

The progress of IRDP in West Kameng district has been better than the other four districts studied in the state (Table 4.9). During the last 9 years (1993-01), 4493 beneficiaries of which

Table 4.9 : Progress of IRDP in West Kameng, 1993-01

Year	*No. of schemes implemented*	*No. of beneficiaries*		*Subsidy (Rs. lakhs)*	*Bank loan (Rs. lakhs)*
		Men	*Women*		
1992-93	518	403	115	42.82	5.75
1993-94	161	130	31	47.82	11.45
1994-95	1177	714	463	29.27	1.14
1995-96	396	135	261	31.45	5.55
1996-97	308	233	75	24.95	9.44
1997-98	755	415	340	35.92	10.80
1998-99	786	254	532	18.16	12.38
1999-00*	318	40	278	24.98	2.82
2000-01*	74	50	24	3.94	4.40

* SGSY.
Source: Records of the Project Director (DRDA).

2119 women were benefited through IRDP. On average, an amount of Rs. 7190 as loan and subsidy was provided. Of the total assistance provided subsidy outweighed the loan component.

The progress of DWCRA too is satisfactory. In all, 81 groups with a total membership of 810 women were organised (Table 4.10). An amount of Rs. 15.73 lakhs were provided as

Table 4.10 : Progress of DWCRA Activities in West Kameng, 1993-99

Year	*No. of groups*	*Membership*	*Amount sanctioned (Rs. lakhs)*	*Activities*	
1992-93	25	250	1.99	Fish farming	1
				Poultry	2
				Pineapple	7
				plantation	6
1993-94	25	250	2.16	Weaving	8
				Goatery	9
				Readymade garments	8
1994-95	Nil	00	2.89	Nil	
1995-96	07	70	2.00	Bhujia making	3
				Orange cum	2
				vegetable garden	2
				Knitting	
1996-97	05	50	1.61	Weaving	2
				Piggery	2
				Handicrafts	1
1997-98	07	70	1.76	Weaving	2
				Chilli cultivation	3
				Thenga weaving	2
1998-99	12	120	3.32	Goatery	4
				Knitting	3
				Weaving	2
				Cushion covers	3

Source: Records of the Project Director (DRDA).

Table 4.11 : Summary of Salient Features of Selected Districts

Particulars	*Lohit*	*Dibang Valley*	*Upper Siang*	*Lower Subansiri*	*West Kameng*
1. Headquarter	Tezu	Anini	Yingkiong	Ziro	Bomdila
2. Area (sq.kms.)	11402	13029	6188	10135	7422
3. Major rivers	Lohit, Kamlang, Noa- Dihing, Digaru	Dri,Mathu, Ethum, Embra, Talo, Ahi	Siang, Yamne, Nyigong	Rein, Kale, Pange, Kime, Panior, Persen, Khru (Kamala), Selu, Panya, Rugo, Sipu	Kameng (Bhorali), Tenga, Bichom, Gacham, Norgum, Dirang Chu, Jamiri (Dhonsiri) Rowta
4. CD blocks	5	3	4	9	3
5. Villages	487	238	72	595	170
6. Population	109706	43068	27779	83167	56421
Male	61043	24087	15248	42502	30966
Female	48663	18961	12531	40665	35455
7. Density of population (persons/sq.km.)	9	3	4	8	8
8. Sex ratio	797	787	822	957	822
9. Literacy rate(%)	49.21	46.88	35.33	24.24	36.48
Male	59.02	56.94	45.03	31.03	55.03
Female	36.21	33.27	23.66	17.15	35.22
10. Major tribes	Mishmis, (Taroan or Digaru, Kamans or Miju), Khamties, Singphoes	Idu Mishmi,Adi, Mushing	Adis (Pasi, Padam, Karko, Minyongs, Panggi, Shimong, Ashing, Tangam, Kimkar, Millang), Idu Mishmi, Khambas, Membas	Apatani, Nishi, (Nishangsor Dafla), Hill-Miri, Sulung	Monpa (Dirang Monpa, Boot Monpa, Lish Monpa, Kalaktang Monpa, Miji) , Sherdukpen, Aka, Begum (Khawa), Sulung

11. Festivals	Deori Reh-Di-Batai, Tamladu, Takka, Sanken	Reh, Sulung, Arang, Pime	Solung, Etor, Aran, Losar, Reh	Dree, Yapung, Myoko, Murung, Nyokum, Sirum, Booriboot, Wanyee	
12. Tourist places	Parasuram Kund, Empong, Faneng, Glow Lake, Hawa and Sewak Passes	Dri valley, Magawia, Bhishmaknagar, Rukmini Nati Mayodeo	Mariyang, Yingkiong, Tuting	Talle Valley, Ziro, Ranganadi Hydro Electric project	Rupa, Bomdila, Dirang, Sela Pass, Bhaukpong, Tippi, Chandi Top
13. Net area sown (ha.)	23904	13534	8520	33437	6542
14. Major crops	Paddy, oilseed Potato, ginger, maize, vegetables, sugarcane	Paddy, maize, millets, vegetables	Paddy, maize, millets, oranges, bananas, plum	Paddy, maize, millets, oilseeds, pulses, vegetables	Maize, potato, millets, cabbage, paddy
15. ICDS projects	3	3	3	2	9
16. Cooperatives					
LAMPS	4	3	1	3	3
Others	25	8	6	20	28
17. Entry and exit point	Sanpura, Dirak	Shantipur	Likabali, Oiramghat, Ruksin,	Kimin, North Lakhimpur	Bhalukpang

Source: Records of the Project Dir]ector (DRDA).

revolving fund to these groups. Fish farming, poultry, pineapple cultivation, weaving, goatary, orange cultivation, piggery, etc. are some of the activities financed under DWCRA.

An attempt is made in Table 4.11 to provide the salient features of the selected districts of Arunachal Pradesh. Proportion of rural population served by different districts are reported in Table 4.12. West Kameng district is better placed in all most all the facilities compared to rest of the districts covered in the study.

Table 4.12 : Proportion (%) of Rural Population Served by Different Amenities in Selected Districts

Amenity	*Lohit*	*Dibang Valley*	*Upper Siang*	*Lower Subansiri*	*West Kameng*
Education	62.5	59.0	92.9	75.3	61.7
Medical	31.5	26.6	22.9	32.5	46.4
Drinking water	100.0	100.0	100.0	100.0	100.0
Posts & telegraph	35.4	43.1	30.6	38.5	36.60
Market	20.5	8.5	18.6	20.5	35.7
Communication	38.5	41.9	31.3	40.7	50.8
Approach by pucca road	45.6	44.3	24.3	38.5	54.2
Power	39.5	48.6	41.3	45.6	63.6

Source: Sengupta (1996).

Summary

Topography, status of agriculture, horticulture, animal husbandry, fishery, and potential sectors for development in the selected districts are discussed in this Chapter. Progress of IRDP and DWCRA is also covered. All the districts are located in high attitudes with little scope for terraced or wet rice cultivation. Jhumming is the life line followed by dependence on forests. Produce from jhumming is adequate for 3-4 months of the year. There is hardly any scope for industrial development. Communication and transport facilities are in nascent stage. On an average, 1/3 of the beneficiaries from both IRDP and SGSY are women. The impact of DWCRA is less than marginal. West Kameng district is better placed compared to rest of the selected districts.

NOTES

1. The Mishmis who stay on the banks of Lohit tell a charming story on the origin of river Lohit. Once upon a time, there were two deities, Khrane and Matai. Together they created sun, moon, and earth. Having made all these, they felt that there should be some creatures on earth so that the earth could look more beautiful. Khrane made a model that Matai tried to copy. But he could not. So they called Khrane's model a woman and Matai's model a man. Then they wanted to make more creatures. Matai made a model of small human hand and called it 'Sang-Khran'. They had created a crab. The crab bore a whole in the ground and lo and behold water came splurging on to the ground. The crab then moved a little distance away and bore another hole and another spring sprouted. Khrane and Matai told the water to take their own course and one of them was Lohit, born, as it were, of a crab. The river in old Bodo diallet is known as Luhit. Later, it was sanskritized to read as Lauhitya which is later known as Lohit. Another school of thought says that the name Lohit has sanskrit origins and actually means red river due to a mithological story colours it so (Sen, 2001).
2. Kahoo is the last village in Kibithoo circle of Walong sector. Chinese invasion of India in Lohit Valley commenced with attack on McMahon ridge north of Kibithoo at 11.45 p.m. on October 21, 1962. Kibithoo was being held by our troops as temporary position. Chinese contacted Walong defences at Namti Plain, 7 kms. from Walong, at the dawn of October 25, 1962. Indian troops stopped invading Chinese for 27 days here. Indian 11 infantry brigade was kept defending Walong under numerous handicaps. There being no road beyond Tezu, which is 230 kms. to south. There was a severe shortage of artillery, rations, ammunitions, winter clothing, and defence stores at Walong. On November 14, 1962, Chinese occupied high feature, Tri Junction, which was not held by Indian troops. 11 infantry brigade was ordered to withdraw on November 16, 1962. Chinese suffered 4000 causalities and for unable to advance any further towards Tezu.
3. Parasurama killed his mother Renuka with an axe at the behest of his father Jamadagni. As a result, the axe got stuck to his hands. He roamed all over India visiting holy places to atone for his sins. Ultimately, he came to Brahma Kund, now in Lohit district, on the advice of some sages. He took a dip in the holy water of the Kund and the axe immediately became unstuck and fell from his hands. Parasurama picked up the axe and threw it as far as he could into the mountains. The axe split the mountains, and the spot where it fell became the source of Lohit river (Nath, 2001). It was thus this Kund was known as Parasuram Kund and now it is one of the many revered holy spots in the country. The blood he washed off his hands is said to have made the water red and so the name Lauhitya. Actual distance between Tezu, and Parasuram Kund is only 25 km. to the north east of Tezu, and 15 kms to the east of Wakro. Due to non-availability of motarable road, one has to travel 100 kms. by crossing four unpredictable rivers to reach this holly place. Mr. J Bedford has mentioned the Kund as about 70 feet long and 30 feet wide in the Government Gazette of September 21,

1826. But due to topographical changes through centuries particularly so during the earthquake of 1950, original site and structure of the Kund have damaged and changed very much.

4. Bhishmaknagar is a magnificent fort made of brick dates back to 9th-10th centuries of the Chutiya dynasty. It is situated 29 km. away from Roing. Popular legend associated the place with the epical character king Bhishmak. It is believed that Sri Krishna came to Bhishmaknagar and took away Rukmini, the daughter of the Bhishmak as his spouse. The site was excavated in 1969-70 and revealed a brick structure of a fort measuring 1860.52 metres of plinth area. The structure is enclosed by a rectangular ramport wall made of stone. It has two impressive brick built in the eastern and western directions.
5. Mayodeo is located at an altitude of 9000 feet from the sea level. It is 52 kms. from Roing and presents a very magnificent spectacle with snow capped mountains all around. It also provides an enchanting view of the bluish and limitless expanse of the vast plain down south. Besides picturesque scenic beauty of the place, Mayodeo is a abound with rare birds and animals which make the place a very potential picnic spot.
6. Siang is a tributary of Tsanpo in Tibet region of China, where it is originated. It is known as Siyum in upper region of the district.
7. A mention about my visit to Yingkiong is interesting and thrilling. I proposed to reach Yingkiong by helicopter and accordingly booked the ticket from Naharlagun. It is once a weekly service and on the scheduled day pilot took off from Naharlagun airfield. By the time we reached Mohanbari, it was heavily raining and helicopter reached Pasighat with great difficulty. As I was the only passenger to Yingkiong, the pilot waited for 2 hours expecting weather to be clear. As there was no chance, pilot told me either to come back to Naharlagun or get dropped at Pasighat. As my programme to Upper Siang and Lower Subansiri were planned long back, I decided to go by road. On reaching Pasighat, to add to my nervousness, I was told that there were heavy landslides between Pasighat and Yingkiong. It took a day to clear the road and I started by a Tata Sumo the next evening to Yingkiong. As the condition of the road was bad, passengers were asked to walk at three places for a distance of 4 kms enabling the Tata Sumo to cross the bad road safely. Finally, I reached Yingkiong (250 kms) in about 12 hours.
8. The administration was under the overall incharge of Ministry of External Affairs of the Government of India during 1954-65 and Ministry of Home Affairs took charge in 1965.

5

MARTIAL AND ECONOMIC STATUS OF WOMEN

Introduction

An attempt is made in this chapter to describe martial and economic status of women. It includes information on education, marriage, family incomes, etc. Such an information is essential to have a close understanding about the target group.

Age of Respondents

As mentioned earlier, sample respondents represent five major tribes (Miju Mishmis, Idu Mishmis, Adis, Nyishi/ Nishis, and Monpas) of Arunachal Pradesh. Table 5.1 provides frequency distribution of respondents by age. It can be seen from table that over 50% of participants have more than 30 years of age. This is true across the districts. About

Table 5.1 : Frequency Distribution of Respondents' by Age

Age (years)	*Lohit*	*Dibang Valley*	*Upper Siang*	*Lower Subansiri*	*West Kameng*	*Total*
< 21.0	6 (15.0)	8 (20.0)	6 (15.0)	9 (22.5)	15 (37.5)	44 (22.0)
21.1-30.0	15 (37.5)	16 (40.0)	10 (25.0)	12 (30.0)	12 (30.0)	65 (32.5)
30.1-45.0	11 (27.5)	9 (22.5)	18 (45.0)	14 (35.0)	7 (17.5)	59 (29.5)
> 45.0	8 (20.0)	7 (17.5)	6 (15.0)	5 (12.5)	6 (15.0)	32 (16.0)
Total	40 (100.0)	40 (100.0)	40 (100.0)	40 (100.0)	40 (100.0)	200 (100.0)

Source: Field study.

45% of the respondents in Upper Siang belong to the age group of 30.1-45 years. Thus, selected respondents are young and can be used as change agents in development process.

Level of Education

Education is an important variable in the process of development. It has been said, time and again, that there is a positive co-relation between education, and development. Respondents are grouped in to four categories (illiterate, 1-5 classes, 6-10 classes, and more than 10 classes) and data are presented in Table 5.2. According to the level of education, respondents of Lower Subansiri have highest number of illiterates followed by Upper Siang, Lohit, Dibang Valley, and West Kameng. This finding is in tune with the observations made by Duarah (1998), and Directorate of Census of

Table 5.2 : Frequency Distribution of Respondents' by Level of Education

Years of schooling	*West Kameng*	*Dibang Valley*	*Lohit*	*Upper Siang*	*Lower Subansiri*	*Total*
0	12 (30.0)	15 (37.5)	16 (40.0)	18 (45.0)	24 (60.0)	85 (42.5)
1-5	14 (35.0)	15 (37.5)	16 (40.0)	11 (27.5)	12 (30.0)	68 (34.0)
6-10	11 (27.5)	9 (22.5)	7 (17.5)	10 (25.0)	4 (10.0)	41 (20.5)
> 10	3 (7.5)	1 (2.5)	1 (2.5)	1 (2.5)	0 (0.0)	6 (3.0)
Total	40 (100.0)	40 (100.0)	40 (100.0)	40 (100.0)	40 (100.0)	200 (100.0)

Source: Field study.

Operations (2001). Thus, West Kameng district reported highest literacy. These tribes have no written language and there are wide variations in their dialects. Such variations are mainly due to topography and the same are presented in Table 5.3. This is a fact which prohibited various tribes from interacting with each other. Innumerable number of rivers, streams, high mountains, deep forests, and variations in climate led to such differences. This inturn forced them to develop a regional dialect. As a result, when people from different tribes meet, they communicate either in hindi or english. Developing a common language would go a long way in this direction.

Table 5.3 : Variations in Dialects Across Selected Tribes

Relation	*Miju Mishmis*	*Idu Mishmis*	*Adis*	*Nyishi/ Nishis*	*Monpas*
Mother	Anu	Nani	Ane	Ann	Ama
Father	Apa	Naba	Abu	Abh	Apa
Elder brother	Kyok	Amy-Apiya	Bibing	Abwe	Atta
Younger brother	Kyok-Kshik	Amy-Aliya	Ani	Borre	Kota
Elder sister		Athi-Apiya	Mimi	Anyie	Ana
Younger sister		Athi-Aliya		Berme	Nunu
Mother-in-law		Ayu	Ayo	Aai	Ani
Father-in-law		Abra	Ato	Ath	Ayang
Grand mother		Naya	Ane mine	Aai	Abi
Grand father		Nata	Abu Mizing	Ath	Mami
Brother-in-law		Eyu	Makbo	Rhiyo	Khotken
Sister-in-law		Ena	Nyaments	Rehm	Mathang
Maternal uncle		Nayu	Kite/Kiye	Khyi	Aku
Maternal aunty		Nani-Aliya	Amo	Mhyi	Atung
Father's sister		Nani-Aliya	Nanyi	Aatte	Ani
Father's brother		Naba-Aliya/ Apiya	Pai	Achi-Pai	Apchi
Husband		Echi	Milo	Nyol	Yongpha
Wife		Yaku	Mime	Nyehii	Niza
Son		Amya	Ao	Kho Niga	Za
Daughter		Aaya	Ome	Kho Nem	Jamin
Niece		Aaya	Ome	Kho	Chimin
Nephew		Amya	Ao	Kho	Makpa

Source: Compiled by the author.

Marriage

Marriage is an important and universal social institution of society. As a social institution, it provides a recognised form for entering into relatively enduring heterosexual relationship for bearing and rearing of children. It is thus primarily a way of regulating human reproduction. This reproduction, however, also has a sociological dimension. The right of sexual relationship, that universally accompanies marriage, provides legitimization to children born in wedlock; this legitimacy is of great importance in the matters of inheritance and succession. Besides, through marriage there comes into existence the family, a relatively stable social group, that is responsible for care and training of children. The age at marriage varies with region, caste, and tribe. Child marriages are not allowed and in fact there is minimum prescribed age for marriage for both boys and girls. Minimum age prescriptions have advantages for overall development of the society. Frequency distribution of respondents by age at marriage is given in Table 5.4.

Table 5.4 : Frequency Distribution of Respondents' by Age at Marriage

Years	*Lohit*	*Dibang Valley*	*Upper Siang*	*Lower Subansiri*	*West Kameng*	*Total*
< 15	8 (20.0)	7 (17.5)	11 (27.5)	125 (62.5)	6 (3.0)	57 (28.5)
16	15 (37.5)	12 (30.0)	14 (35.0)	8 (20.0)	10 (25.0)	5 (29.5)
17	7 (17.5)	10 (25.0)	8 (20.0)	4 (10.0)	13 (44.5)	42 (21.0)
18	5 (12.5)	4 (10.0)	4 (10.0)	2 (5.0)	5 (12.5)	20 (10.0)
19	4 (10.0)	4 (10.0)	3 (7.5)	1 (2.5)	4 (10.0)	16 (8.0)
20 and more	1 (2.5)	3 (7.5)	0 (0.0)	0 (0.0)	2 (5.0)	6 (3.0)
Total	40 (100.0)	40 (100.0)	40 (100.0)	40 (100.0)	40 (100.0)	200 (100.0)

Source: Field study.

It can be seen from table that as may as 62.5% are reported to have got married at less than 15 years in Lower Subansiri. The percentage of respondents who have got married below 15 years are less in rest of the districts studied. In fact, only 3% of the respondents in West Kameng reported to have got married at less than 15 years of age. As mentioned earlier, marriages at childhood is not in the interest of society. However, due to certain traditions, beliefs, and existing social systems, Nishings prefer childhood marriages. Thus, as regards age at marriage, district administration is not in a position to implement rules prescribed in the law. Maximum number of women got married either at the age of 16 or 17. On an average, about 13% got married at the age of 16 followed by 21% at 17 years. Thus, majority of the respondents (50.5%) are getting married at the age of 16-17 years. A close observation of Tables 5.2 and 5.4 indicate that districts with higher level of education reported relatively higher age at marriage.

Forms of Marriage

Marriage has a large variety of forms. These forms can be identified on the basis of number of partners and rules governing who can marry whom. In terms of number of partners that can legitimately enter into matrimony, we have two forms of marriage (monogamy, and polygamy). Monogamy restricts individuals to one spouse at a time. Under this system, at any given time a man can have only one wife, and a women can have only one husband. In many societies individuals are permitted to marry again often on the death of the first spouse or after divorce. Such monogamous marriage is termed as serial monogamy. Polygamy denotes marriage to more than one mate at one time and takes the form of either polygyny (one husband with two or more wives) or polyandry (one wife with two or more husbands). In certain situations males marry the wife's sisters, and females their husband's brothers. Such marriages are termed as sororal polygyny, and fraternal polyandry respectively. Though pre-martial relationships among tribes are tolerated, and self selection is permitted, all regular marriages are parent arranged. Irregular marriages are effected through elopement, intrusion or forcible application of vermilion, all of which are eventually accepted by the parents and families concerned, as signifying wedlock. Various forms of mate selection (selection by purchase and service, youth dormitories, selection by capture, and selection by trial) are prevalent in some of these tribes.

We come across a variety of forms of marriages in Arunachal Pradesh and it varies from tribe to tribe and some times within the tribe (Pandey (1997), Mishra (1991), Banthia (2001), Deuri (1986), Dutta (1975), Mitkong (1996), Parul (1976), Shukla (2000), and Srutikar (1990)). We found arranged, love, love and arranged, elopement, and second marriage among the respondents. Love and arranged marriages are common (39%) in the study area (Table 5.5). It is followed by arranged marriages (32.5%), second marriage (11%), love marriage (10%), and elopement (7.5%). Arranged marriages are prominent in Lower Subansiri while West Kameng and Dibang Valley reported love and arranged

Table 5.5 : Frequency Distribution Respondents by Forms of Marriage

Nature of marriage	*Lohit*	*Dibang Valley*	*Upper Siang*	*Lower Subansiri*	*West Kameng*	*Total*
Arranged	11 (27.5)	12 (30.0)	9 (22.5)	23 (57.5)	10 (25.00)	65 (32.5)
Love	3 (7.5)	5 (12.5)	5 (12.5)	4 (10.0)	3 (7.5)	20 (10.0)
Love and arranged	16 (40.0)	18 (45.0)	17 (42.5)	9 (22.5)	18 (45.00)	78 (39.0)
Elopement	6 (15.0)	3 (7.5)	3 (7.5)	1 (2.5)	2 (5.00)	15 (7.5)
Second marriage	4 (10.0)	2 (5.0)	6 (15.0)	3 (7.5)	7 (17.5)	22 (11.0)
Total	40 (100.0)	40 (100.0)	40 (100.0)	40 (100.0)	40 (100.0)	200 (100.0)

Source: Field study.

marriages (45%). Lohit district too reported that 40% of the women had love and arranged marriages.

Nishings of Lower Subansiri are war like people. Living in far flung areas, as mentioned earlier, they followed child marriages. In all these cases bride prices are common and a must. Bride price[1] is paid in the form of mithuns, ornaments and beads, bells, clothes, meat, dry fish, rice beer, dao, and various other locally available materials. There is no formal marriage ritual but when the couple has sex and lives together and there is no objection from community then such a union is recognised as that of husband and wife. They form family and raise their children. Generally such unions are formed between members of neighboring territories but care is taken to avoid such relatives with whom sex relations are prohibited[2]. In most of cases opinion of girl is not taken and marriage takes place after a prolonged bargaining. Mediators are used for mate selection.

Woman who spends her life time with a single husband is appreciated. Married women have to change their attitudes towards male members after being married. They keep their standard of styles simple after marriages. These women have no marks of being married for identification. A married woman can be known from her way of behavior and degree of style she does. One of the important aspects of female status is that she has to join the married group after she gets married, whether young or aged. Fearing that adultery may happen with her, a women is not allowed to do too much warm behavior and cut jokes with other men after she gets married.

Respondents are asked to express preferred qualities of a prospective husband and the same are presented in Table 5.6. On an average about 24% of women reported that 'husband should have only one wife'. This finding has significance in the sense that polygyny has been common in all these tribes. Though men provide a variety of reasons for having more number of wives, women feel the burden and troublesome to have co-wives.

Table 5.6 : Frequency Distribution of Respondents Opinion on Preferred Qualities of a Husband

Quality	*Lohit*	*Dibang Valley*	*Upper Siang*	*Lower Subansiri*	*West Kameng*	*Total*
1. Earning enough to take care of daily needs	7 (17.5)	7 (17.5)	10 (25.0)	6 (15.0)	15 (37.5)	(22.5) (22.5)
2. Good looking and faithful	1 (2.5)	4 (10.0)	1 (2.5)	2 (5.0)	2 (5.0)	10 (5.0)
3. Having lot of jhum lands	4 (10.0)	5 (12.5)	5 (12.5)	9 (22.5)	4 (10.0)	27 (13.5)
4. Take opinion of wife	2 (5.0)	3 (7.5)	3 (7.5)	1 (2.5)	5 (12.5)	14 (7.0)
5. Does not drink and beat	2 (5.0)	2 (5.0)	1 (2.5)	2 (5.0)	1 (2.5)	8 (4.0)
6. Should have only one wife	14 (35.0)	9 (22.5)	8 (20.0)	12 (30.0)	5 (12.5)	48 (24.0)
7. Educated	2 (5.0)	4 (10.0)	4 (10.0)	3 (7.5)	2 (5.0)	15 (7.5)
8. Should have government job	5 (12.5)	3 (7.5)	3 (7.5)	1 (2.5)	2 (5.0)	14 (7.0)
9. Should be settled in city	1 (2.5)	2 (5.0)	3 (7.5)	2 (5.0)	3 (7.5)	11 (5.5)
10. Good character and manners	2 (5.0)	1 (2.5)	2 (5.0)	2 (5.0)	1 (2.5)	8 (4.0)
Total	40 (100.0)	40 (100.0)	40 (100.0)	40 (100.0)	40 (100.0)	200 (100.0)

Source: Field study.

Parents give their daughters to a person who has more than one wife because they get heavy bride price on such occasions. Women do not like to share their husband with an another woman and that happens in almost all societies. Under these circumstances, woman is under tremendous amount of tension because a man lives with the newly married wife for some time and when she is out of his looks he searches for a new wife. This makes woman try to be young and beautiful so as to be in good looks of husband. Today's woman says that 'we are like a cane basket; when it wears out, it is unceremoniously discarded'.

Earning enough to take care of daily needs is another quality of the prospective husband. As many as 22.5% have mentioned this as a quality which is justifiable. Further, having lot of jhum lands is mentioned by as many as 13.5% of the respondents. Ownership of jhum land was considered as a status symbol in traditional and primitive societies. However, due to changes in the out look and civilization, it is no more a prized possession. Other qualities of prospective husband, as mentioned by the respondents, are taking opinion of wife, education, should be settled in city, good looking and faithful, does not drink and beat, and good character and manners. These are the qualities as opined by the respondents. These qualities may or may not be valid in other parts of the country.

Size of the Family

Status of living and expired children among respondents is provided in Table 5.7. Once again, Lower Subansiri reported highest number of both living and expired children. On an

Table 5.7 : Average Living and Expired Children and Family Planning Measures Adopted in the Study Area

District	*Living*	*Expired*	*Underwent Tubectomy*
Lohit	3.3	2.6	13
Dibang Valley	3.0	2.5	15
Upper Siang	3.8	2.9	12
Lower Subansiri	4.0	3.1	4
West Kameng	3.5	1.7	1
Total	3.5	2.6	45

Source: Field study.

average, women in this district have four living children and 3.1 expired. Thus they had, on an average, seven deliveries which is on a high side at any standard. At the state level, women have 3.5 living children and 2.6 expired. As regards family planning measures adopted by women, only 45 (20%) out of 200 underwent tubectomy. Some of women also reported about using Saheli tablets, and Nirodh. However, they are very few in number and it is difficult to get information on such delicate issues.

The people in this part of the country believe controlling population is against law of nature. Further, they believed in the saying that 'more the children more the prosperity'. Persons with many children got respect in the society too. The number helps during inter and intra tribal quarrels and that inhabits women in going for tubectomy. However, such wars are history now. But it is a herculean task to convince both men and women in this regard. Further, tubectomy needs rest which they can not afford. However, due to education and penetration of non-locals/christianity, some of them are now going for family planning measures. Slowly women are now realizing advantages of small family. The tribal society follows patrilineal descent system in which a boy at birth becomes a member of his descent group, and a coparcener in a joint family. A girl, by contrast, is only a residual member of her natal group; at marriage she is incorporated into her husband's descent group and ultimately offered worship by their male descendants. Residence is patrilocal. Taken together, it is a patriarchal society. It has patrilineal descent, patrilocal residence, inheritance from father to son, and authority in the hands of seniors, as against juniors, and males as against females. A number of social practices testify to the fact that a woman's only legitimate roles are those of wife and mother.

Jhum Cultivation

As mentioned elsewhere in the report, jhum cultivation is predominant in Arunachal Pradesh. Jhum cycle varies from 3 to 10 years depending upon the availability of vacant lands/ forests, and pressure of population. There is little scope for wet rice cultivation here. Exceptions to this are found in some places of Lohit, Changlang, and Lower Subansiri. There is no cadastal survey and people are not habituated to measure the lands. It's not yet a marketable commodity. They are aware of only the number of plots owned by them and not the area. Accordingly, frequency distribution of jhum lands owned by respondents is given in Table 5.8. Majority of the respondents (81.5%) have plots ranging between 1-4. This observation is true across all the selected districts. Only three respondents from Dibang Valley and Upper Siang have reported having plots between 9-10.

Table 5.8 : Frequency Distribution of Jhum Lands Owned by Respondents

Number	*Lohit*	*Dibang Valley*	*Upper Siang*	*Lower Subansiri*	*West Kameng*	*Total*
0	3 (7.5)	0 (0.0)	0 (0.0)	2 (5.0)	2 (5.0)	7 (3.5)
1-2	15 (37.5)	22 (55.0)	22 (55.0)	20 (50.0)	18 (45.0)	97 (48.5)
3-4	16 (40.0)	12 (30.0)	10 (25.0)	12 (30.0)	16 (40.0)	66 (33.0)
5-6	5 (12.5)	5 (12.5)	4 (10.0)	3 (7.5)	3 (7.5)	20 (10.0)
7-8	1 (2.5)	0 (0.0)	2 (5.0)	3 (7.5)	1 (2.5)	7 (3.5)
9-10	0 (0.0)	1 (2.5)	2 (5.0)	0 (0.0)	0 (0.0)	3 (1.5)
Total	40 (100.0)	40 (100.0)	40 (100.0)	40 (100.0)	40 (100.0)	200 (100.0)

Source: Field study.

Preparations for jhum cultivation start from March/April. Forest clearing and cleaning is undertaking by men folk with help of women during these months. As jhum cultivation depends upon monsoon rains sowing through broad casting or dibbling is done during the months of June/July. It is to be mentioned here that locals are not used to ploughing and topography do not allow it. Thus, there is no need for animal power in agriculture in the study area. Soon after sowing, fencing is prepared followed by regular weeding, and watch and ward. Men generally do not attend activities associated with agriculture and it is the sole responsibility of women to take care of entire life cycle of the crop. Some facts about jhum cultivation are given in Table 5.9. Only 33 out of 200 respondents used purchased inputs and it was fertilizer. This' input is supplied by the department of agriculture on subsidy basis. When asked about expectations from department of agriculture, they mentioned that regular supply of good quality seeds, saplings, fertilizer, and advise on agriculture should be ensured. Vast majority to them belong to this category.

Table 5.9 : Some Facts About Jhum Cultivation Among Respondents

Number	*Lohit*	*Dibang Valley*	*Upper Siang*	*Lower Subansiri*	*West Kameng*	*Total*
Average jhum holdings (plots)	3.0	3.2	3.2	2.6	2.2	2.9
Busy agricultural months						
(a)	March	April	March	March	April	
(b)	June	May June	June	June	June	
(c)	November	November December	November	November	December	
Agriculture operations in those months						
(a)	Cleaning	Cleaning	Cleaning	Cleaning	Cleaning	
(b)	Sowing	Sowing	Sowing	Sowing	Sowing	
(c)	Harvesting	Harvesting	Harvesting	Harvesting	Harvesting	
Crops grown						
(a) Paddy	15	52	25	26	38	
(b) Maize	25	22	25	36	30	
(c) Bajra	15	28	30	15	12	
(d) Local pulses	10	30	19	29	15	
(e) Vegetables	25	18	25	25	20	
(f) Horticulture	18	10	8	10	15	
Use of purchased inputs						
(a) Yes	4	2	4	15	8	33
b) No	36	38	36	25	32	167
Expectation from department of agriculture						
a) Seeds	35	33	30	35	38	171
b) Fertilizers	30	28	25	34	38	155
(c) Saplings	4	5	2	0	40	51
(d) Advice	31	28	27	38	40	164

Source: Field study.

Apart from lands, these households posses a variety of animals and they include mithuns, yaks, cows, sheep, goat, pigs, and poultry. The importance of mithuns and chicken in the social and religious life of Arunachalis was described earlier in the report. Mithun is a prestigious animal mostly given as bride price. The importance of chicken is everywhere starting from ceremonies associated with birth and it continues till the last rites of a person. Thus, society revolves around these two animals. Frequency distribution of these animals owned by the households is given in Table 5.10. As expected, only 11 households out of 200 do not process either of these animals. As many as 58% of respondents have 1 to 4 animals. Respondents in Dibang Valley, and Lohit districts have more number of animals compared to rest of the districts. Animals are exclusively for social and religious purposes and locals are non-vegetarian by core.

Table 5.10 : Frequency Distribution of Possession of Yaks/Mithuns/ Cows Among Respondents

Number	*Lohit*	*Dibang Valley*	*Upper Siang*	*Lower Subansiri*	*West Kameng*	*Total*
0	6 (15.0)	2 (5.0)	1 (2.5)	2 (5.0)	0 (0.0)	11 (5.5)
1-2	13 (32.5)	12 (30.0)	15 (37.5)	12 (30.0)	16 (40.0)	68 (34.0)
3-4	7 (17.5)	10 (25.0)	8 (20.0)	10 (25.0)	12 (30.0)	47 (23.5)
5-6	5 (12.5)	5 (12.5)	6 (15.0)	9 (22.5)	7 (17.5)	32 (16.0)
7-8	4 (10.0)	4 (10.0)	6 (15.0)	5 (12.5)	3 (7.5)	22 (11.0)
9-10	3 (7.5)	2 (5.0)	3 (7.5)	2 (5.0)	2 (5.0)	12 (6.0)
> 10	2 (5.0)	5 (12.5)	1 (2.5)	0 (0.0)	0 (0.0)	8 (4.0)
Total	40 (100.0)	40 (100.0)	40 (100.0)	40 (100.0)	40 (100.0)	200 (100.0)

Source: Field study.

Household Income

Income of household decides about status of household in a society. This income can be derived from agriculture, animal husbandry, trade, service or any other avocation. However, income from off-farm is negligible in this part of the country. Some of Arunachalis are involved in doing contracts, supplies to government departments, and very few in trade. Some of them are also working in government departments. A frequency distribution of sum total of income derived from above sources is given in Table 5.11. As many as 17.5% of them have less than Rs. 15000 of income/annum. About 48% of them have reported to have incomes ranging between Rs. 15001-25000/annum. Thus, majority of them fall in this category. They are on border of the poverty line, a minor shift from this level will either make them above or below the poverty line. It is essential to have concerted efforts to provide necessary infrastructure, inputs, and guidance to bring them into the main stream/above poverty line. Any lethargy in this regard on the part of government will spoil efforts so far made in the development of locals. About 21% of respondents are in the annual income group of Rs. 25001-35000. This category belongs to either salaried or involved in contracts and trade. Only 12% of respondents have income above Rs. 45000. The percentage of respondents falling in the income bracket of Rs. 15001-25000 are more in Upper Siang and Lower Subansiri. More or less similar pattern is observed in the rest income brackets.

Table 5.11 : Frequency Distribution of Annual Family Income of the Respondents

Annual income (Rs.)	*Upper Siang*	*Dibang Valley*	*Lohit*	*Lower Subansiri*	*West Kameng*	*Total*
< 15000	8 (20.0)	10 (25.0)	7 (17.5)	6 (15.0)	4 (10.0)	35 (17.5)
15001-25000	22 (55.0)	18 (45.0)	17 (42.5)	20 (50.0)	19 (47.5)	96 (48.0)
25001-35000	6 (15.0)	7 (17.5)	10 (25.0)	9 (22.5)	10 (25.0)	42 (21.0)
35001-45000	2 (5.0)	2 (5.0)	5 (12.5)	2 (5.0)	4 (10.0)	1 5 (7.5)
45001-55000	1 (2.5)	2 (5.0)	1 (2.5)	2 (5.0)	2 (5.0)	8 (4.0)
55001 and above	1 (2.5)	1 (2.5)	0 (0.0)	1 (2.5)	1 (2.5.)	4 (2.0)
Total	40 (100.0)	40 (100.0)	40 (100.0)	40 (100.0)	40 (100.0)	200 (100.0)

Source: Field study.

Usage of Iodized Salt

Salt is an important ingredient of respondents in the study area. They are habituated to boiled non-vegetarian food with negligible oil, chilly powder, and other spices[3]. The only ingredient required alongwith their food is salt. The advantages of iodized salt is known to the readers. The area is endemic to iodine deficiency. Keeping in view of this fact, respondents are asked to provide details on use of salt and the same are presented in Table 5.12.

Table 5.12 : Responses on Type of Salt Purchased

District	*Loose*	*Packed*		*Total*
		Powder	*Rock salt*	
Lohit	10	15	15	40
Dibang Valley	8	18	14	40
Upper Siang	12	18	10	40
Lower Subansiri	4	20	16	40
West Kameng	8	23	9	40
Total	42	94	64	200

Source: Field study.

Large proportion of respondents are either using packed powder salt or packed rock salt. This finding suggest that respondents have realised the importance of packed items, particularly salt. However, 1/3rd of respondents are still using rock salt which is not iodized. There is need to educate the people and bring awareness about the advantages of iodized salt.

When asked about the frequency of purchase of salt by respondents (Table 5.13), it was revealed that nearly 50% of the respondents purchasing salt once in a fortnight. As many as 65 respondents (32.5%) reported purchases once in a week. Thus, 82% reported purchasing salt within a fortnight Across districts, respondents of West Kameng purchased salt frequently compared to other four districts covered. Quantity of salt purchased varies with number of persons in the household, and number of mithuns owned by the respondents. About 78% of the respondents are purchasing

Table 5.13 : Frequency of Purchase of Salt by Respondents				
District	*Once a week*	*Once a fortnight*	*Once a month*	*Total*
Lohit	18 (45.0)	15 (37.5)	7 (17.5)	40 (100.0)
Dibang Valley	10 (25.0)	22 (55.0)	8 (20.0)	40 (100.0)
Upper Siang	12 (30.0)	25 (62.5)	3 (7.5)	40 (100.0)
Lower Subansiri	9 (22.5)	20 (50.0)	11 (27.5)	40 (100.0)
West Kameng	16 (40.0)	17 (42.5)	7 (17.5)	40 (100.0)
Total	65 (32.5)	99 (49.5)	36 (18.0)	200 (100.0)

Source: Field study.

more than 3 kgs. of salt/month (Table 5.14). As many as 44 respondents have demand for 1-2 kgs. of salt/month. Thus, majority of respondents consume any where between 3-10 kgs of salt/month. As regards usage of iodized salt, 106

Table 5.14 : Quantity of Salt Purchased (kgs/month) by Respondents				
District	*1-2 kgs*	*3-5 kgs*	*6-10 kgs*	*Total*
Lohit	7 (17.5)	20 (50.0)	13 (32.5)	40 (100.0)
Dibang Valley	10 (25.0)	15 (37.5)	15 (37.5)	40 (100.0)
Upper Siang	9 (22.5)	18 (45.0)	13 (32.5)	40 (100.0)
Lower Subansiri	10 (25.0)	13 (32.5)	17 (42.5)	40 (100.0)
West Kameng	8 (20.0)	18 (45.0)	14 (35.0)	40 (100.0)
Total	44 (22.0)	84 (42.0)	72 (36.0)	200 (100.0)

Source: Field study.

respondents revealed that they are not aware of iodized salt (Table 5.15). The percentage of respondents 'not familiar with iodized salt' are more in Lohit district followed by Dibang Valley, and Upper Siang.

The source of purchase also varied across districts. On the whole, 35 (37%) respondents out of 94 who used iodized

Table 5.15 : Respondents Opinion Regarding Usage of Iodized Salt

District	*Yes*	*No*	*Total*
Lohit	15 (37.5)	25 (62.5)	40 (100.0)
Dibang Valley	18 (45.0)	22 (55.0)	40 (100.0)
Upper Siang	18 (45.0)	22 (55.0)	40 (100.0)
Lower Subansiri	20 (50.0)	20 (50.0)	40 (100.0)
West Kameng	23 (57.5)	17 (42.5)	40 (100.0)
Total	94 (47.0)	106 (53.0)	200 (100.0)

Source: Field study.

salt purchased it from nearby village while as may as 41 (74%) had it from the same village (Table 5.16). It is clear from the above tables that though they are aware of advantages of iodized salt, some of them are not opting for it. Respondents were asked to express constraints in not purchasing iodized salt and results are presented in Table 5.17. Price of iodized salt is costly and hence most of them (57%) are not using. Other reasons mentioned by respondents are non-availability, and change in taste of food. The district administration should ensure supplying iodized salt on regular basis through cooperative societies at reasonable rate. Such an effort would ensure people going for iodized salt.

Table 5.16 : Point of Purchase of Iodized Salt Among Respondents

District	*Village*	*Nearby village*	*Nearby town*	*Total*
Lohit	8 (51.3)	5 (31.3)	2 (17.4)	15 (100.0)
Dibang Valley	3 (16.7)	10 (55.6)	5 (27.7)	18 (100.0)
Upper Siang	9 (50.0)	5 (27.7)	4 (22.3)	18 (100.0)
Lower Subansiri	11 (55.0)	5 (25.0)	4 (20.0)	20 (100.0)
West Kameng	10 (43.5)	10 (43.5)	3 (13.0)	23 (100.0)
Total	41 (43.7)	35 (37.0)	18 (19.3)	94 (100.0)

Source: Field study.

Table 5.17 : Reasons for not Using Iodized Salt				
District	*Non availability*	*Expensive*	*Change in taste of food*	*Total*
Lohit	6	10	9	25
Dibang Valley	3	13	6	22
Upper Siang	5	12	5	22
Lower Subansiri	2	15	3	20
West Kameng	5	9	3	17
Total	21	59	26	106

Source: Field study.

Sanitation

Water is life and all civilizations have grown around water bodies. Water is essential not only for drinking but also for irrigation and industries. Clean drinking water is a prerequisite for a healthy life. Respondents mentioned various sources of water namely tap, bore well, spring, and river. Though there are many rivers and streams in this part of country, their usage for locals is negligible. As a result district administration has been making efforts to supply clean drinking water though bore wells and taps. At the state level, as many as 77.5% of the respondents reported taps and borewells as the source of drinking water leaving only 22.5% who are dependent on springs and rivers (Table 5.18). Thus, there is need for administration to extend this facility to far off areas as well.

Table 5.18 : Source of Water Among Respondents						
Particulars	*Lohit*	*Dibang Valley*	*Upper Siang*	*Lower Subansiri*	*West Kameng*	*Total*
Tap	15 (37.5)	15 (37.5)	25 (62.5)	25 (62.5)	15 (37.5)	95 (47.5)
Borewell	10 (25.0)	15 (37.5)	10 (25.0)	10 (25.0)	15 (37.5)	60 (30.0)
Spring	10 (25.0)	5 (12.5)	5 (12.5)	5 (12.5)	5 (12.5)	30 (15.0)
River	5 (12.5)	5 (12.5)	0 (0.0)	0 (0.0)	5 (12.5)	15 (7.5)
Total	40 (100.0)	40 (100.0)	40 (100.0)	40 (100.0)	40 (100.0)	200 (100.0)

Source: Field study.

Cleanliness and sanitation are pre-requisites for a healthy life. However, weather and climate is hostile in this state and terrain is uneven. Under these circumstances it is difficult to get regular supply of clean water. Respondents were asked to indicate frequency of taking bath/week. Only 13% of respondents reported taking bath daily while as many as 36% reported thrice a week (Table 5.19). Percentage of respondents taking bath once a week is at 17. Thus, majority of them are not taking bath daily. As mentioned earlier, it is not only the negligence but also the climate which obstructs taking bath daily. However, they need to be educated about advantage of taking regular bath. Respondents are asked about number of pairs of dresses owned by them (Table 5.20). Majority of respondents (66%) mentioned owning 5-8 pairs of dresses while 17.5% have 9-10 pairs.

Table 5.19 : Pairs of Dresses Owned by Respondents

District	*3-4 pairs*	*5-6 pairs*	*7-8 pairs*	*9-10 pairs*	*Total*
Lohit	8 (20.0)	12 (30.0)	15 (37.5)	5 (12.5)	40 (100.0)
Dibang Valley	5 (12.5)	10 (25.0)	19 (47.5)	6 (15.0)	40 (100.0)
Upper Siang	10 (25.0)	15 (37.5)	11 (27.5)	4 (10.0)	40 (100.0)
Lower Subansiri	7 (17.5)	18 (45.0)	10 (25.0)	5 (12.5)	40 (100.0)
West Kameng	3 (7.5)	10 (25.0)	12 (30.0)	15 (37.5)	40 (100.0)
Total	33 (16.5)	65 (32.5)	67 (33.5)	35 (17.5)	200 (100.0)

Source: Field study.

Summary

An analysis of Chapter 5 revealed that selected respondents are young and majority of them are in the age group of less than 30 years. According to level of education, respondents of Lower Subansiri have highest number of illiterates followed by Upper Siang, Lohit, Dibang Valley, and West Kameng. These tribes have no written language and there are wide variations in their dialects. Districts with higher levels of education reported relatively higher ages at marriage. A variety of forms of marriages (arranged, love, love and arranged, elopement, and second marriage) are noticed in the study area. Nishi community preferred child marriages. Among preferred qualities of a prospective husband, majority of them reported that husband should have only one wife. On an average, women have 3.5 living children and 2.6 expired, and 20% of them reported following family planning measures. It is a patriarchal society. Jhum cultivation is predominant in the study area and majority of respondents have plots ranging between 1-4. Almost all the respondents have some form of animals (mithun, yaks, cows, sheep, goat, pigs, and poultry). They fall in the income category of Rs. 15001-25000/annum. The percentage of respondents falling in this income bracket are more in Upper Siang, and Lower Subansiri. A large proportion of respondents are either purchasing packed powder salt or packed rock salt and 78% of them are purchasing more than 3 kgs. of salt/month. The percentage of respondents 'not familiar with iodized salt' are more in Lohit district. As many as 77.5% of respondents reported taps and borewells as the source of drinking water.

NOTES

1. The idea behind bride price is that: (a) it ensures permanency of relationship between two families and lineages, (b) it is a kind of compensation to the girl's parents who had brought her up, and (c) it is a status symbol for the boy's parents to bring a new member into the family by paying price. The amount of bride price depends on: (a) capacity of boy's parents, (b) number of immediate relatives on girl's side, and (c) the image, beauty, household quality, and capability of the bride.
2. Cross cousin marriages are preferred in Monpas while village exogamy is preferred among Mishims. Adis and Nishis choose in between Monpas and Mishmis.
3. There has been a gradual shift in the consumption pattern. Youth, salaried, and business class are now slowly shifting towards oily and fried foods. By now, number of processed foods too penetrated in to this land. The average consumption of oil is about a kilo/ household/ month in the study area. However, there are variations across tribes.

6

WORKLOAD AND PARTICIPATION IN DECISION-MAKING

Introduction

An attempt is made in this chapter to analysis workload pattern and participation in decision making process by sample respondents. Such an attempt would help us to understand the contribution of workforce via-a-vis levels of participation in day to day decision making.

Women's Work

According to anthropologists and some historians, women were the major producers of food, textile, and handicrafts throughout human history and continue to provide a major labour input where production is still in small scale subsistence sector. Most of the women's work is either not visible or is only partially accounted for in the data on workforce participation. The components of women's work include housework, paid and unpaid work related to home based craft activities, family enterprise or business, and paid work outside home. The kind of work women attend is determined by women's position in the society, and family's location in the social hierarchy. Women's work also differ according to age, gender, income, occupational group, location (rural/urban), size, and structure of the family. As women's work is mostly for self consumption, much of the work that they do is not recognised as 'work' in the national income statistics. In the tribal areas women are engaged in cooking, housekeeping, childcare, fetching fuel wood, and water, collection of forest produce, care of livestock, house repair and maintenance, storing grains, preparation and preservation of foods, etc. Much of the work which is important for the maintenance of families, is largely done by these women. Thus, conventional definition of 'work' does not include activities which are of *use value* and do not have *exchange value.*

Distribution of Work Load

An attempt is made in following pages to analyse workloads of respondents (Table 6.1) At the aggregate level, 35.5% of respondents reported 10-12 hours of workload/day i.e. more than 1/3rd of respondents are putting in 10-12 hours of work/day. Similarly, 58 out of 200 respondents (29%) reported to have workloads between 8-10 hours/day. Thus, about 2/3rd of the respondents have workloads ranging between 8-12 hours/day. Percentage of women having workloads less than 6 hours/day, and more than 14 hours/day are 6% and 3% respectively. Thus, majority of respondents are putting in, on an average, 8-12 hours of work/day. Percentage of respondents reporting higher workloads are found in Dibang Valley followed by Lohit, and West Kameng.

Table 6.1 : Frequency Distribution of Work Load (hours/day) of Respondents

Hours/ day	*Lohit*	*Dibang Valley*	*Upper Siang*	*Lower Subansiri*	*West Kameng*	*Total*
< 6	1 (2.5)	2 (5.0)	1 (2.5)	5 (12.5)	3 (7.5)	12 (6.0)
6.1-8.0	4 (10.0)	3 (7.5)	7 (17.5)	11 (27.5)	7 (17.5)	32 (16.0)
8.1-10.0	8 (20.0)	7 (17.5)	18 (45.0)	13 (32.5)	12 (30.0)	58 (29.0)
10.1-12.0	19 (47.5)	22 (55.0)	10 (25.0)	7 (17.5)	13 (32.5)	71 (35.5)
12.1-14.0	7 (17.5)	5 (12.5)	2 (5.0)	3 (7.5)	4 (10.0)	21 (10.5)
> 14.0	1 (2.5)	1 (2.5)	2 (5.0)	1 (2.5)	1 (2.5)	6 (3.0)
Total	40 (100.0)	40 (100.0)	40 (100.0)	40 (100.0)	40 (100.0)	200 (100.0)

Source: Field study.

As mentioned above, women attend vide variety of activities in their day to day life. These activities are identified as cooking, fetching water, washing clothes, upkeep of house, collecting fire wood, collection of vegetables and fruits from forest, caring children, agriculture, feeding animals, handicrafts, preparation of rice beer, and social visits. The data on activity-wise and district-wise distribution of workload among respondents are presented in Table 6.2. Interestingly, average workload (hours/day) of respondents hovered around 12 hours/day. Minor variations across districts can be noticed in Lohit, and Lower Subansiri. These districts reported higher workload hours compared to rest of the districts. Across activities, agriculture took as much as 3 hours in Upper Siang, Lohit, and West Kameng, while women allocated only 1 hour and 45 minutes/day on this activity in Dibang Valley. Interior locations might have contributed to this phenomena. On an average, women worked for about 2 hours and 48 minutes/day on agriculture at the state level.

Table 6.2 : Activity-wise Distribution of Work Load (hours/day) Among Respondents

Quality	*Lohit*	*Dibang Valley*	*Upper Siang*	*Lower Subansiri*	*West Kameng*	*Total*
1. Cooking	1.00	1.15	1.00	0.45	1.00	1.00
2. Fetching water	0.45	0.45	0.15	0.15	0.15	0.27
3. Washing clothes	0.45	1.00	0.45	0.30	0.30	0.42
4. Upkeep of house	1.00	0.45	1.00	1.00	0.45	0.54
5. Collecting firewood	2.00	2.30	1.30	2.00	1.30	1.54
6. Collection of vegetables and fruits from forest	1.00	1.00	0.45	1.30	1.00	1.00
7. Caring children	0.30	0.45	1.00	1.00	1.00	0.51
8. Agriculture	3.00	1.45	3.15	3.00	3.00	2.48
9. Feeding animals (poultry/mithun/yak/pigs)	1.30	1.15	2.00	1.30	1.30	1.33
10. Handicrafts	0.15	1.15	0.15	0.15	0.15	0.15
11. Preparation of rice beer	0.15	0.30	0.30	0.15	0.30	0.24
12. Social visits	0.15	0.15	0.15	0.15	0.15	0.15
13. Total	12.15	12.00	11.30	12.15	11.30	11.45

Source: Field study.

Next major activity of women is collecting fire wood from forests. At the aggregate level, this activity consumed as much 1 hour and 54 minutes/day of women. This is due to location of households away from forest and is a daily routine. In fact this activity made them strong and fit in the hostile environment. Feeding animals (poultry, mithuns, yaks, pigs, and cows) is another activity of women. In the case of poultry and pigs, feeding is done twice a day while mithun comes to take salt once a week. Cows and sheep require day to day management. This activity consumed, on an average, 1 hour and 33 minutes/day. Cooking, and collection of vegetables and fruits from forest are other activities in the order of priority. These, again, are the sole responsibilities of women and society feel that men should not participate in these activities.

Rice beer is an important item of the tribal life. It is called differently among tribes, but is an important item among them A tribal household require approximately 30-35 kgs. of rice/month for preparation of rice beer. Surprisingly, equal quantity is required for food consumption. There is a belief among them that 'women in dirty periods are not supposed to prepare this' which is offered to guests, and relatives. Based on the ingredients used (rice, millets, etc.), there are many varieties of rice beers. Offering unlimited rice beer on festivals and feasts is a custom among these tribes. Both men and women, including children, take rice beer without hesitation. The culture required for preparation of rice beer is made by old women after their menopause. This activity takes about 24 minutes of a woman/day.

On the whole, women enjoys freedom in attending household duties. She does her work without much interference from husband and other family members, and most of her works are considered as feminine jobs. Normally, her daily routine starts right from the dawn. She gets up early and kindle the fire. Then she starts cooking and prepares lunch. Side by side, she does grinding of cereals assisted by daughters, if any, and also feeds pigs, and poultry. When everything is ready, she serves the members. By then, it is time to go to field. She works in field throughout the day and returns home with firewood, fruits, vegetables, leaves, and roots by evening. On reaching home, she again starts preparing dinner, rice beer, and serves the members. Thus, she is the first to get up in the morning, and the last to go to bed in the late night.

Exchange Labour

Jhum cultivation, like wet rice cultivation, has three important operations namely, sowing, weeding, and harvesting. These activities takes place at a specified point of time for all households in a given area. As most of respondents have many jhum plots, family labour is inadequate for these operations. As a result, they depend upon labour from neighborhood which is known as exchange labour in economics. About 83% of respondents reported the need for exchange labour (Table 6.3). Since almost all of them depend on exchange labour, priorities among households are arranged. Neighbours are informed about number of labour, and date on which it is required. Hence, these requirements

Table 6.3 : Some Facts on Exchange Labour Among Respondents

Particulars	*Lohit*	*Dibang Valley*	*Upper Siang*	*Lower Subansiri*	*West Kameng*	*Total*
Dependence on exchange labour						
(a) Yes	37	35	36	28	30	166
(b) No	3	5	4	12	10	34
Purpose of exchange labour						
(a) Cleaning	15	18	16	2	0	51
(b) Sowing	8	9	7	10	12	46
(c) Harvesting	14	8	13	16	14	65
Advanced notice required (days)	4.2	3.4	3.3	6.2	5.5	4.5
Items to be given						
(a) Food	37	35	36	25	30	163
(b) Meat/fish	37	35	36	25	34	157
(c) Tobacco	37	35	36	25	34	157
(d) Rice beer	37	35	36	28	30	166
Difficulty in getting exchange labour						
(a) Yes	31	30	31	12	15	119
(b) No	6	5	5	16	15	47

Source: Field study.

are to be informed in advance so as to carry out operations smoothly. On an average, 4.5 days of advance notice is required for getting exchange labour. This time period is more in Lower Subansiri, and West Kameng because there is wet rice, and off-seasonal vegetable cultivation in the area. Hence, demand for labour is more, and accordingly longer advance noticed is required for getting labour.

Labour on wages is not available in the study area, it is yet to be monitized. However, owner is required to provide food, preferably non-vegetarian. In addition to non-vegetarian food, labourers are also to be given unlimited rice beer and tobacco. Majority of the respondents from Lohit, Upper Siang, Dibang Valley, and West Kameng reported these observations. The percentage of respondents reporting 'items to be given for exchange labour' is low in Lower Subansiri. Because the concept of wage labour is already prevalent in this district. They are facing problems in getting exchange labour due to change in their perceptions towards agriculture, changing professions, literacy, loss of community feeling, etc.

Factors Affecting Levels of Workload

With a view to study impact of various factors on level of workload, linear equations are estimated. Total man days worked by respondents/day is taken as dependant variable. Independent variables included in the equation are number of jhum plots (X_1), number of animals (X_2), years of schooling (X_3), and index of awareness (X_4). Awareness index is prepared by clubbing respondents' views on cooperatives, primary health centre, anganwadi centre, school, bank, loan repayment, and self-help groups. The results of linear equations are presented in Table 6.4. It is observed that adjusted co-efficient of multiple determination ranged between 0.56-0.87, thereby indicating 56-87% of variation in workload is associated with variables included in the equations. The pooled function gave a $R^{-2}$of 0.68. All the five F-values are significant at 1% level. Baring few, all variables in equations turned to be significant at various levels, thereby indicating their importance in the workload of selected respondents.

Table 6.4 : District-wise Employment Functions

S.No.	*Intercept*	*Regression coefficients of*				*R2*	*Observ-ation*	*F-value*
		No. of animals	*Jhum plots*	*Years of schooling*	*Index of awareness*			
Lohit	8.7405 (12.59)	0.0911** (2.52)	0.4711* (2.06)	0.1850** (3.69)	0.0072** (5.06)	0.76	40	32.0
Dibang Valley	9.3270 (8.44)	0.0264** (3.25)	0.2662** (4.21)	0.2906** (2.63)	0.0417** (5.24)	0.56	40	13.4
Upper Siang	6.9890 (10.44)	0.6463** (3.46)	0.1382** (4.92)	0.0963** (3.68)	0.0950** (4.62)	0.82	40	44.4
Lower Subansiri	5.3888 (6.26)	0.8750** (4.58)	0.2394* (1.88)	0.1339* (1.96)	0.1287 (1.64)	0.80	40	41.1
West Kameng	6.9498 (8.51)	0.0417** (2.28)	0.6788** (3.47)	0.2623** (4.34)	-0.0205 (1.19)	0.87	40	64.3
Pooled	7.0936 (19.71)	0.1158* (2.05)	0.4433** (4.94)	0.2140** (4.72)	0.1432 (3.57)	0.68	200	109.1

Figures in parenthesis are t-values.
** Significant at 1% level of significance.
* Significant at 5% level of significance.
Source: Estimated.

The negative co-efficient of index of awareness in West Kameng is mainly due to relatively higher levels of exposure in the district. Years of schooling has a positive and significant relationship in all the functions. It is to be mentioned here that the level of education in the state among women is relatively low compared to rest of the country and hence continues to show positive relationship with the workload. The positive and significant relationships between number of jhum plots and number of animals owned, and workload is self explanatory.

Decision-Making

The family's decision-making process is implicit in all its distribution of responsibilities and resources. The most powerful family member is determined by prevailing cultural values, such as those attached to old age, sex, and the relative importance attached to men's and women's productive role (Charlton, 1984). Further, level of education, exposure to developmental activities, media, etc. will also be counted. In a society like ours, women are generally not expected to be self-supporting, have few opportunities to earn significant incomes, and in general cannot inherit land or other immovable property. It is said that 'failure to involve women in decision making about new technologies meant that several factors crucial to the usefulness of technology were overlooked'.

While considering the process of decision making, an attempt is made to study nature and power achieved or authority exercised by women (Table 6.5). Authority, as defined by Leacock (1986), is influenced and exerted through recognised channels. Operationalization of decision making is done through women's perception as to who mainly decides and controls the family in particular activity.

A close observation of Table 6.5 reveals interesting results. Women took decisions related to child care, children's education, type of feast to be prepared, purchase of utensils and clothes, and agricultural activities. Thus, decisions related to major issues are taken by husbands, while decisions on activities within the house are dominated by women. Men dominated in taking decisions on number of children to bear, arranging children's marriage, taking/given loans, sale/purchase of animals, settlement of disputes, social visits, and to some extent voting. Child care is essentially a female activity. Liberty to women spending money is, nevertheless, limited to domestic purposes. Thus, controlling and decision making in important activities is decided by the husbands. In other words, where there is social prestige men dominated, while decisions associated with responsibility and duties of use value are left to women.

There is a positive relationship between levels of education and decision making by 'self', and there is positive change among women. For example, at the aggregate level, 22% of the respondents took decisions in voting which shows their awareness, freedom, and forward looking nature. They are now taking decisions in disputes settlement also.

Summary

An analysis of workload and participation in decision making process by women revealed that majority of respondents are putting in, on an average, 8-12 hours of work/day. Women attended activities like cooking, fetching water, washing clothes, upkeep of house, collecting fire wood, collection of vegetables and fruits from forest, caring children, agriculture,

Table 6.5 : Decision Makers in Household Activities Among Selected Districts

Decision	*Lohit*				*Dibang Valley*			
	Self	*Husband*	*Both*	*Total*	*Self*	*Husband*	*Both*	*Total*
(a) Number of children	0 (0.0)	27 (67.5)	13 (32.5)	40 (100.0)	0 (0.0)	28 (70.0)	12 (30.0)	40 (100.0
(b) Child care	23 (57.5)	0 (0.0)	17 (42.5)	40 (100.0)	25 (62.5)	0 (0.0)	15 (37.5)	40 (100.0)
(c) Children's education	15 (37.5)	6 (15.0)	19 (47.5)	40 (100.0)	10 (25.0)	17 (42.5)	13 (32.5)	40 (100.0)
(d) Children's marriage	0 (0.0)	25 (62.5)	15 (37.5)	40 (100.0)	0 (0.0)	20 (50.0)	20 (50.0)	40 (100.0)
(e) Type of feast	18 (45.0)	7 (17.5)	15 (37.5)	40 (100.0)	21 (52.5)	6 (15.0)	13 (32.5	40 (100.0)
(f) Purchase of utensils	25 (62.5)	3 (7.5)	12 (30.0)	40 (100.0)	30 (75.0)	5 (12.5)	5 (12.5)	10 (100.0)
(g) Purchase of clothes	22 (55.0)	2 (5.0)	16 (40.0)	40 (100.0)	8 (20.0)	12 (30.0)	20 (50.0)	40 (100.0)
(h) Taking/giving loans	10 (25.0)	15 (37.5)	15 (37.5)	40 (100.0)	4 (10.0)	26 (65.0)	10 (25.0)	40 (100.0)
(i) Sale/purchase of animals	3 (7.5)	25 (62.5)	12 (30.0)	40 (100.0)	17 (42.5)	8 (20.0)	15 (37.5)	40 (100.0)
(j) Agricultural activities	15 (37.5)	10 (25.0)	15 (37.5)	40 (100.0)	12 (30.0)	18 (45.0)	10 (25.0)	40 (100.0)
(k) Voting	10 (25.0)	20 (50.0)	10 (25.0)	40 (100.0)	0 (0.0)	20 (50.0)	20 (50.0)	40 (100.0)
(l) Disputes	0 (0.0)	25 (62.5)	15 (37.5)	40 (100.0)	4 (10.0)	19 (47.5)	17 (42.5)	40 (100.0)
(m) Social visits	5 (12.5)	18 (45.0)	17 (42.5)	40 (100.0)	0 (0.0)	20 (50.0)	20 (50.0)	40 (100.0)

(Contd...)

Table 6.5 : *Contd...*

Decision	*Upper Siang*				*Lower Subansiri*			
	Self	*Husband*	*Both*	*Total*	*Self*	*Husband*	*Both*	*Total*
(a) Number of children	0 (0.0)	26 (65.0)	14 (35.0)	40 (100.0)	1 (2.5)	19 (47.5)	20 (50.0)	40 (100.0)
(b) Child care	27 (67.5)	0 (0.0)	13 (32.5)	40 (100.0)	25 (62.5)	0 (0.0)	15 (37.5)	40 (100.0)
(c) Children's education	12 (30.0)	13 (32.5)	15 (37.5)	40 (100.0)	18 (45.0)	7 (17.5)	15 (37.5)	40 (100.0)
(d) Children's marriage	0 (0.0)	26 (65.0)	14 (35.0)	40 (100.0)	0 (0.0)	22 (55.0)	18 (45.0)	40 (100.0)
(e) Type of feast	23 (57.5)	4 (10.0)	13 (32.5)	40 (100.0)	25 (62.5)	2 (5.0)	13 (32.5)	40 (100.0)
(f) Purchase of utensils	24 (60.0)	5 (12.5)	11 (27.5)	40 (100.0)	21 (52.5)	7 (17.5)	12 (30.0)	40 (100.0)
(g) Purchase of cloths	25 (62.5)	5 (12.5)	10 (25.0)	40 (100.0)	20 (50.0)	8 (20.0)	12 (30.0)	4 (100.0)
(h) Taking /giving loans	10 (25.0)	15 (37.5)	15 (37.5)	40 (100.0)	2 (5.0)	27 67.5)	11 (27.5)	40 (100.0)
(i) Sale/purchase of animals	0 (0.0)	28 (70.0)	12 (30.0)	40 (100.0)	5 (12.5)	28 (70.0)	7 (17.5)	40 (100.0)
(j) Agricultural activities	20 (50.0)	8 (20.0)	12 (30.0)	40 (100.0)	20 (50.0)	10 (25.0)	10 (25.0)	40 (100.0)
(k) Voting	8 (20.0)	22 (55.0)	10 (25.0)	40 (100.0)	6 (15.0)	21 (52.5)	13 (32.5)	40 (100.0)
(l) Disputes	0 (0.0)	24 (60.0)	16 (40.0)	40 (100.0)	5 (12.5)	25 (62.5)	10 (25.0)	40 (100.0)
(m) Social visits	5 (12.5)	20 (50.0)	15 (37.5)	40 (100.0)	8 (20.0)	22 (55.0)	10 (25.0)	40 (100.0)

(Contd...)

Table 6.5 : *Contd...*

Decision	*West Kameng*				*Grand total*			
	Self	*Husband*	*Both*	*Total*	*Self*	*Husband*	*Both*	*Total*
(a) Number of children	2 (5.0)	13 (32.5)	25 (62.5)	40 (100.0)	3 (1.5)	113 (56.5)	84 (42.0)	20 (100.0)
(b) Child care	14 (35.0)	0 (0.0)	26 (65.0)	40 (100.0)	114 (57.0)	0 (0.0)	86 (43.0)	200 (100.0)
(c) Children's education	17 (42.5)	5 (12.5)	18 (45.0)	40 (100.0)	72 (36.0)	48 (24.0)	80 (40.0)	200 (100.0)
(d) Children's marriage	3 (7.5)	12 (30.0)	25 62.5)	40 (100.0)	3 (1.5)	105 (52.5)	92 (46.0)	200 (100.0)
(e) Type of feast	27 (67.5)	6 (15.0)	7 (17.5)	40 (100.0)	114 (57.0)	25 (12.5)	61 (30.5)	200 (100.0)
(f) Purchase of utensils	23 (57.5)	3 (7.5)	14 (35.0)	40 (100.0)	123 (61.5)	23 (11.5)	54 (27.0)	200 (100.0)
(g) Purchase of cloths	27 (67.5)	2 (5.0)	11 (27.5)	40 (100.0)	102 (51.0)	29 (14.5)	69 (34.5)	200 (100.0)
(h) Taking /giving loans	15 (37.5)	10 (25.0)	15 (37.5)	40 (100.0)	45 (22.5)	79 (39.5)	76 (38.0)	200 (100.0)
(i) Sale/purchase of animals	11 (27.5)	20 (50.0)	9 (22.5)	40 (100.0)	23 (11.5)	127 (63.5)	50 (25.0)	200 (100.0)
(j) Agricultural activities	15 (37.5)	15 (37.5)	10 (25.0)	40 (100.0)	87 (43.5)	51 (25.5)	62 (31.0)	200 (100.0)
(k) Voting	20 (50.0)	8 (20.0)	12 (30.0)	40 (100.0)	44 (22.0)	91 (45.5)	65 (32.5)	200 (100.0)
(l) Disputes	12 (30.0)	15 (37.5)	13 (32.5)	40 (100.0)	17 (8.5)	109 (54.5)	74 (37.0)	200 (100.0)
(m) Social visits	13 (32.5)	16 (40.0)	11 (27.5)	40 (100.0)	31 (15.5)	96 (48.0	73 (36.5)	200 (100.0)

Source: Field study.

feeding animals, preparation of rice beer, and social visits. Average workload (hours/day) of respondents hovered around 12 hours/day. There are minor variations in workloads across districts. As regards exchange labour, majority of respondents reported that there is a need for it. On an average, 4.5 days of advance notice is required for getting such labour. Factors like number of jhum plots, number of animals, years of schooling, and index of awareness are found to be positive and significant. Decision making in important activities are decided by husbands, while decisions associated with responsibility and duties of use value are left to women. There is a positive change among younger generations and are actively participating in making variety of decisions.

7

AWARENESS ABOUT LOCAL ORGANISATIONS

Introduction

This chapter concerns awareness of the respondents about local organisations like cooperatives, primary health centre, anganwadi centre, and loans availed under various developmental programmes. Awareness is consciousness about something. Such level of awareness helps in understanding participatory role of target group in various activities of their life.

Respondents' Visits to Selected Places

Table 7.1 provides data on various places visited by respondents. They include bank, post office, panchayat, town, and cinema hall. On the whole, number of respondents visiting these organisations are more in West Kameng followed by Lower Subansiri. As mentioned earlier, levels of literacy is more in West Kameng while Lower Subansiri is close to plains with developed communication facilities. Thus,

Table 7.1 : Respondents' Visits to Selected Places

Place	*Lohit*	*Dibang Valley*	*Upper Siang*	*Lower Subansiri*	*West Kameng*	*Total*
Bank	8	5	4	12	18	47
Post office	10	7	5	15	12	49
Panchayat	3	3	2	5	5	18
Town	12	10	8	25	30	85
Cinema hall	7	10	8	18	25	68

Source: Field study.

respondents of these districts reported higher levels of participation. From among the places visited, town happens to be the most frequent place visited followed by cinema hall, post office, bank, and panchayat. Number of respondents reported visiting panchayat is as low as 18 out of 200. It is to be, once again, mentioned here that role of woman is restricted to house and she is not allowed into institutions like panchayat. Almost all the 18 members who reporting visiting panchayats had disputes due to family affairs and hence were called to panchayat.

Awareness About Cooperatives

Status of cooperatives in the state is provided in Chapter 2. Cooperatives are lifelines of Arunachalis. They were the first to bring essential commodities from plains and provided in far flung areas. They continue to do so till today. Further, they are second largest employment provider in the state. The contribution of cooperatives to Arunachalis is beyond imagination. Though women are main users of services of these cooperatives, their involvement in planning and management of cooperatives is far from satisfactory. On an average, 23 out of 40 respondents reported knowledge about cooperatives (Table 7.2). This is, once again, more in West Kameng, Dibang Valley, and Lohit districts. The average distance of a cooperative from respondents household is 7.1 kms. This distance is the lowest (4.4 kms.) in Lower Subansiri, and highest (10.6 kms.) in Upper Siang. Though, there are minor variations across districts, one-fifth of respondents are reported to be members of these cooperatives. Women visited society at least twice a month.

Sugar, rice, salt, and pulses are available at these cooperatives. Card holders of below poverty line gets 25 kgs. of rice/month at subsidies rates. Though other consumable items are available at cooperatives, they are not provided on card. Thus, consumers are to purchase them at higher prices. Majority of the respondents (44%) reported unsatisfactory quality of goods provided. Thus, they are not happy either with price or quality of goods provided by cooperatives. Respondents also requested for items like utensils, stationery, kerosene, and clothes to be made available through

Table 7.2 : Some Facts About CGS, LAMP, and Other Cooperatives by Respondents

Particular	*Lohit*	*Dibang Valley*	*Upper Siang*	*Lower Subansiri*	*West Kameng*	*Total*
Awareness	21	25	18	16	34	23
Distance from village (kms)	6.4	8.5	10.6	4.4	5.7	7.1
Membership	8	10	6	4	12	8
Frequency of visits to cooperative	2.5	3.0	2.2	2.0	2.0	2.3
Items available						
(a) Sugar	24	28	20	18	31	121
(b) Rice	15	25	16	20	32	108
(c) Salt	12	15	10	12	17	66
(d) Pulses	7	10	8	5	6	36
Opinion on quality						
(a) Good	12	10	11	15	10	58
(b) Satisfactory	15	13	10	8	8	54
(c) Unsatisfactory	13	17	19	17	22	88
Opinion on price						
(a) Low	8	10	10	10	12	50
(b) Same	10	12	10	15	10	57
(c) High	22	18	20	15	18	93
Items required to be kept in cooperative						
(a) Clothes	10	12	10	7	9	48
(b) Utensils	8	7	4	5	7	31
(c) Stationery	5	6	8	8	7	34
(d) Kerosene	17	15	18	20	17	87
Behavior of staff						
(a) Good	10	12	8	14	11	55
(b) Satisfactory	13	15	10	15	12	65
(c) Unsatisfactory	17	13	22	11	17	80

Source: Field study.

cooperatives. When asked about the behavior of staff of cooperatives, respondents reported that they are not happy. The cooperatives may look into these aspects and try to be user friendly.

Respondents were requested to suggest ways and means to improve working of cooperatives, and the results are provide in Table 7.3. Major suggestions revolved around reasonable price, good quality, adequate quantity, and timely availability. These four factors are crucial in the business and cooperative must adhere to it. Any deviation from these core factors would erode members loyalty and confidence. Such a failure on the part of cooperatives would only encourage emergence of private traders. Thus, respondents have rationality in expressing opinions towards cooperatives. Other suggestions include convenient timings, open membership to women in the society[1], representation of women on the committees of societies, and improvement in buildings, and premises.

Table 7.3 : Suggestions to Improve Working of Cooperative

Suggestion	*Lohit*	*Dibang Valley*	*Upper Siang*	*Lower Subansiri*	*West Kameng*	*Total*
1. Good quality	8 (20.0)	7 (17.5)	8 (20.0)	7 (17.5)	7 (17.5)	37 (18.5)
2. Reasonable Price	10 (25.0)	12 (30.0)	11 (27.5)	13 (32.5)	14 (35.0)	60 (30.0)
3. Adequate Quantity	7 (17.5)	6 (15.0)	7 (17.5)	6 (15.0)	6 (15.0)	32 (16.0)
4. Timely Availability	6 (15.0)	5 (12.5)	6 (15.0)	6 (15.0)	4 (10.0)	27 (13.5)
5. Convenient timings	4 (10.0)	6 (15.0)	5 (12.5)	4 (10.0)	3 (7.5)	22 (11.0)
6. Membership to women in the society	2 (5.0)	2 (5.0)	3 (7.5)	2 (5.0)	2 (5.0)	11 (5.5)
7. Women on the board	2 (5.0)	1 (2.5)	0 (0.0)	0 (0.0)	3 (7.5)	6 (3.0)
8. Improvement in Buildings	1 (2.5)	1 (2.5)	0 (0.0)	2 (5.0)	1 (2.5)	5 (2.5)
9. Total	40 (100.0)	40 (100.0)	40 (100.0)	40 (100.0)	40 (100.0)	200 (100.0)

Source: Field study.

Awareness About Health Care Centre

To take care of health care requirements of the people, state government has been establishing number of primary health centers, dispensaries, and district level hospitals in the state. Some facts about health care among respondents are provided in Table 7.4. In majority of the cases, health care centers are not located in villages studied. The average distance of health care centre is about 12 kms. Though *dais* are posted in villages, their utility is negligible. They neither have required expertise nor adequate medicines at their disposal. As a result, locals are to travel long distances to get health care facilities. When asked about the number of visits to these centres during the last year, it was reported that respondents, on an average, made 3.4 visits. About 114 (57%) respondents out of 200 had prenatal checkups. Most of them (77.5%) had deliveries at husbands' residence while only 22.5% had deliveries in hospitals. Further, 41% of the respondents reported having postnatal checkups too. With regard to facilities at health care centre, respondents gave a mixed response. One third of them reported that the facilities are good.

Table 7.4 : Some Facts About Health Care Among Respondents

Particular	*Lohit*	*Dibang Valley*	*Upper Siang*	*Lower Subansiri*	*West Kameng*	*Total*
Health care centre (kms)	8.5	12.0	10.0	16.5	12.8	12.00
No. of visits to centre during last year	3.2	2.3	2.0	4.0	5.2	3.4
Prenatal checkups	25	20	24	15	30	114
Place of delivery						
(a) Residence	28	30	35	38	24	155
(b) Hospital	12	10	5	2	16	45
(c) Post natal checkups	20	14	15	12	21	82
Facilities at PHC						
(a) Good	12	10	15	11	19	67
(b) Satisfactory	18	18	10	17	10	73
(c) Unsatisfactory	10	12	15	12	11	60

Source: Field study.

Locals are habituated to traditional methods of curing diseases and personal problems. Almost all tribes have belief [2] in spirits and depend upon priest for redressal. Priest is indispensable for an Arunachali, no matter whether he/she is literate or illiterate. The priest is known with different names among the tribes. Mishmis call him as igu while

Monpas as Lama. Priest is a mediator between person and spirit, and their belief is that diseases are caused due to spirits. The role of priest is to please/appease the spirit. For example, Mishmis believe in *Amu wu yahon* (where their ancestors from different clans met first time), *Iduba* and *Innisamra* (a cluster of trees where their priest tests the soul for its deeds and a slippery rock beyond *Iduba* from where their priest takes the souls of unnatural deaths), and *Bun li yahn* (a cluster of eight mountains where a soul rests for a while *en rote* to heaven). All persons cannot become priests, and it is believed that they have certain super natural powers. Among Adis, priest decides auspicious day as also reasons for certain causes by looking at liver of a chicken. Due to various historical and religious regions, locals heavily depend upon priest. Frequency of visits to these priests by respondents is given in Table 7.5.

Table 7.5 : Frequency of Visits/Year to Shamans/igu/lama by Respondents

District	*0*	*1-2*	*3-4*	*5-6*	*Total*
Lohit	1 (2.5)	17 (42.5)	19 (47.5)	3 (7.5)	40 (100.0)
Dibang Valley	0 (0.0)	15 (37.5)	20 (50.0)	5 (12.5.)	40 (100.0)
Upper Siang	0 (0.0)	19 (47.5)	18 (45.0)	3 (7.5)	40 (100.0)
Lower Subansiri	0 (0.0)	20 (50.0)	17 (42.5)	3 (7.5)	40 (100.0)
West Kameng	2 (5.0)	15 (37.5)	20 (50.0)	3 (7.5)	40 (100.0)
Total	3 (1.5)	86 (43.0)	94 (47.0)	17 (8.5)	200 (100.0)

Source: Field study.

About 98.5% of the total respondents mentioned that they visit priest every year. Respondents visiting priest 1-4 times/year are of the order of 90%. Two respondents from West Kameng and one from Lohit reported not visiting priests. They belong to relatively better off sections of the society whose husbands are working in government departments. As many as 17 respondents visited 5-6 times/year. Thus, it is clear from Tables 7.4 and 7.5 that respondents consult both doctor and priest. When asked about the preference towards them, as many as 40% mentioned that priest is better than doctor while 35.5% mentioned other way round. About 22% of respondents preferred both. General practice is that for any minor ailments and issues related to spirits, for good crops, and prosperity, locals depend upon priest first. They turn towards qualified doctors and hospitals when the problem is acute. Respondents with literacy, having educated husbands, and close to town have preferred doctors over priests. However, priest comes next. On the other hand, illiterate women of the far flung areas preferred priest over doctor.

Table 7.6 : Respondents Preference Towards Doctor and igu/lama

District	*Doctor*	*Igu*	*Both*	*None*	*Total*
Lohit	14 (35.0)	15 (37.5)	10 (25.0)	1 (2.5)	40 (100.0)
Dibang Valley	15 (37.5)	16 (40.0)	7 (27.5)	2 (5.0)	40 (100.0)
Upper Siang	12 (30.0)	18 (45.0)	10 (25.0)	0 (0.0)	40 (100.0)
Lower Subansiri	10 (25.0)	19 (47.5)	8 (20.0)	3 (7.5)	40 (100.0)
West Kameng	20 (50.0)	12 (30.0)	8 (20.0)	0 (0.0)	40 (100.0)
Total	71 (35.5)	80 (40.0)	43 (21.5)	6 (3.0)	200 (100.0)

Source: Field study.

Table 7.7 : Respondents Awareness About Presence of Anganwadi Centre in the Village

District	*Yes*	*No*	*No idea*	*Total*
Lohit	18 (45.0)	10 (25.0)	12 (30.0)	40 (100.0)
Dibang Valley	21 (52.5)	8 (20.0)	11 (27.5)	40 (100.0)
Upper Siang	16 (40.0)	6 (15.0)	18 (45.0)	40 (100.0)
Lower Subansiri	15 (37.5)	15 (37.5)	10 (25.0)	40 (100.0)
West Kameng	24 (60.0)	8 (20.0)	8 (20.0)	40 (100.0)
Total	94 (47.0)	47 (23.5)	59 (29.5)	200 (100.0)

Source: Field study.

Awareness About Anganwadi Centre

Particulars on ICDS scheme and anganwadi centres are provided in Chapter 3. Anganwadi centre is base level institution for implementing ICDS. It is managed by a health worker/helper who are trained by the department of social welfare, and women and child development. Government of India provides pre and post natal checkups for women, and nutritious food to children under this scheme. Locally they are known as *channa badam schools* and these centres are familiar in villages. Respondents were asked about their awareness with regard to presence of anganwadi centres. On the whole, 47% of them are aware of anganwadi centre while 29.5% mentioned as 'no idea'. Thus, majority of them are familiar with anganwadi centres.

Activities of anganwadi centre and members responses are presented in Table 7.8. According to 45% of respondents, major activity of anganwadi centre is supply of nutritious foods to children. As many as 25.5% mentioned it as supply

Table 7.8 : Awareness of Respondents About Activities of Anganwadi Centre

Activity	*Lohit*	*Dibang Valley*	*Upper Siang*	*Lower Subansiri*	*West Kameng*	*Total*
1. Supply of nutritious foods to children	15 (37.5)	18 (45.0)	22 (55.0)	20 (50.0)	15 (37.5)	90 (45.0)
2. Supply of medicines	10 (25.0)	12 (30.0)	8 (20.0)	9 (22.5)	12 (30.0)	51 (25.5)
3. Immunization for both children and mothers	7 (17.5)	4 (10.0)	8 (20.0)	5 (12.5.)	5 (12.5.)	29 (14.5)
4. Health care for pregnant women	3 (7.5)	2 (5.0)	1 (2.5)	2 (5.0)	2 (5.0)	10 (5.0)
5. Education to children	2 (5.0)	1 (2.5)	1 (2.5)	2 (5.0)	2 (5.0)	8 (4.0)
6. Imparting discipline among children	1 (2.5)	1 (2.5)	0 (0.0)	2 (5.0)	2 (5.0)	6 (3.0)
7. Eradication of malnutrition	2 (5.0)	2 (5.0)	0 (0.0)	0 (0.0)	2 (5.0)	6 (3.0)
Total	40 (100.0)	40 (100.0)	40 (100.0)	40 (100.0)	40 (100.0)	200 (100.0)

Source: Field study.

of medicines. Other activities as mentioned by respondents are immunization for both children and mothers, health care for pregnant women, education to children, imparting discipline among children, and eradication of malnutrition.

Though there are variations across districts, about 3/4th of respondents reported either good or satisfactory about working of anganwadi centre (Table 7.9). A vast majority (90%) of respondents from Upper Siang reported that they

Table 7.9 : Opinion Regarding Working of Anganwadi Centre

District	*Good*	*Satisfactory*	*Unsatisfactory*	*Total*
Lohit	15 (37.5)	13 (32.5)	12 (30.0)	40 (100.0)
Dibang Valley	18 (45.0)	16 (40.0)	6 (15.0)	40 (100.0)
Upper Siang	22 (55.0)	14 (35.0)	4 (10.0)	40 (100.0)
Lower Subansiri	15 (37.5)	14 (35.0)	11 (27.5)	40 (100.0)
West Kameng	18 (45.0)	12 (30.0)	10 (25.0)	40 (100.0)
Total	88 (44.0)	69 (34.5)	43 (21.5)	200 (100.0)

Source: Field study.

are doing well. Similar pattern was also noticed in Dibang Valley. Respondents were also asked about sincerity and integrity of anganwadi worker/helper (Table 7.10). In majority of cases they are happy. Percentage of respondents unhappy with anganwadi worker are more in Dibang Valley.

Table 7.10 : Respondents Opinion About Sincerity of Anganwadi Worker/Helper

District	*Good*	*Satisfactory*	*Unsatisfactory*	*Total*
Lohit	13	17	10	40
Dibang Valley	21	14	5	40
Upper Siang	19	15	6	40
Lower Subansiri	12	17	11	40
West Kameng	20	11	9	40
Total	85	74	41	200

Source: Field study.

At one point or other, all women respondents were beneficiaries of anganwadi centre (Table 7.11). However, benefits availed varied from respondent to respondent, and across districts. On an average, 40.5% of women reported that their children got education from the centre. On the other hand, 26.5% of respondents opined that their children got nutritious foods. Thus, 2/3rd of the respondents mentioned

Table 7.11 : Opinion Regarding Benefits Availed from Anganwadi Centre

Benefit	*Lohit*	*Dibang Valley*	*Upper Siang*	*Lower Subansiri*	*West Kameng*	*Total*
1. Nutritious foods to children	10 (25.0)	10 (25.0)	12 (30.0)	13 (32.5)	8 (20.0)	53 (26.5)
2. Education to children	13 (32.5)	17 (42.5)	16 (40.0)	15 (37.5)	20 (50.0)	81 (40.5)
3. Pre & postal natal checkups	5 (12.5)	7 (17.5)	6 (15.0)	8 (20.0)	10 (25.0)	36 (18.0)
4. Awareness about health care and sanitation	5 (12.5)	3 (7.5)	0 (0.0)	2 (10.0)	1 (2.0)	11 (5.5)
5. Awareness about family planning	2 (5.0)	2 (5.0)	4 (10.0)	2 (10.0)	1 (2.5)	11 (5.5)
6. Education to self	5 (12.5)	1 (2.5)	2 (5.0)	0 (0.0)	0 (0.0)	8 (4.0)
Total	40 (100.0)	40 (100.0)	40 (100.0)	40 (100.0)	40 (100.0)	200 (100.0)

Source: Field study.

either their children receiving nutritious foods or education from the centre. A sizeable percentage (18) of respondents also reported receiving pre and post natal checkups. Other facilities availed from the centre are awareness about healthcare and sanitation, family planning, and education to self. Thus, it is evident from above tables that contribution of the centre towards women and children is substantial. Keeping in view of this, women were asked to suggest additional requirements of anganwadi centre in their respective villages (Table 7.12). As many as 12 requirements were suggested and timely and adequate supply of medicines stood first in this category. About 29% of respondents requested this facility. Other requirements in the order of

Table 7.12 : Respondents Opinion About Requirements of Anganwadi Centre

Requirement	*Lohit*	*Dibang Valley*	*Upper Siang*	*Lower Subansiri*	*West Kameng*	*Total*
1. Own building	5 (12.5)	6 (15.0)	2 (5.0)	3 (7.5)	7 (17.5)	23 (11.5)
2. Supply of electricity	0 (0.0)	0 (0.0)	0 (0.0)	1 (2.5)	1 (2.5)	2 (1.0)
3. Supply of water connection	0 (0.0)	1 (2.5)	0 (0.0)	1 (2.5)	1 (2.5)	3 (1.5)
4. Timely and adequate supply of medicines	10 (25.0)	13 (32.5)	15 (37.5)	12 (30.0)	8 (20.0)	58 (29.0)
5. Timely and adequate supply of nutritious foods	10 (25.0)	6 (15.0)	8 (20.0)	7 (17.5)	7 (17.5)	38 (19.0)
6. Health care camps	3 (7.5)	4 (10.0)	2 (5.0)	2 (5.0)	5 (10.0)	16 (8.0)
7. Training to worker/helper	2 (5.0)	1 (2.5)	1 (2.5)	3 (7.5)	2 (5.0)	9 (4.5)
8. Visits by CDPOs	2 (5.0)	0 (0.0)	0 (0.0)	3 (7.5)	0 (0.0)	5 (2.5)
9. Increasing the age of children to 8 years	2 (5.0)	2 (5.0)	1 (2.5)	1 (2.5)	1 (2.5)	7 (3.5)
10. Enhancement in the house rent	1 (2.5)	1 (2.5)	2 (5.0)	0 (0.0)	0 (0.0)	4 (2.0)
11. Enhancement of honorarium of worker/helper	2 (5.0)	2 (5.0)	4 (10.0)	1 (2.5)	5 (10.0)	14 (7.0)
12. Supply of furniture and play materials	3 (7.5)	4 (10.0)	5 (12.5)	6 (15.0)	3 (7.5)	21 (10.5)
Total	40 (100.0)	40 (100.0)	40 (100.0)	40 (100.0)	40 (100.0)	200 (100.0)

Source: Field study.

priority are timely and adequate supply of nutritious foods (19%), own building[3] (11.5%), supply of furniture, and play material (10.5%), and organising regular healthcare camps (8%). Respondents also mentioned about training to workers, enhancement of honorarium of worker/helper, enhancement in the house rent, etc. A close look at suggestions made by respondents reveal that their involvement and concern for the centre.

As mentioned elsewhere in the report, gramsevika has to visit the centre regularly. Frequency of visits depends on number of centres under her control, mode of transport available, and spread of the centres. About 1/3rd of the respondents mentioned that gramsevika visiting centre once a month while 26% reported once in two months (Table 7.13). On the other hand, about 27.5% of the respondents either mentioned gramsevika never visiting society or about their ignorance.

An observation of Tables 7.7 to 7.13 reveals that majority of respondents are aware of activities of anganwadi centers. They are also familiar with their working and behavior of anganwadi worker/helper. Women have high expectations from the centre and demanded additional facilities for it's effective functioning.

Table 7.13 : Frequency of Visits by Gramsevika to Anganwadi Centre

Frequency of visits	*Lohit*	*Dibang Valley*	*Upper Siang*	*Lower Subansiri*	*West Kameng*	*Total*
1. Never visited	5 (12.5)	8 (20.0)	10 (25.0)	7 (17.5)	8 (20.0)	38 (19.0)
2. Once a month	10 (25.0)	12 (30.0)	11 (27.5)	16 (40.0)	17 (42.5)	66 (33.0)
3. Once in two months	15 (37.5)	5 (12.5)	10 (25.0)	10 (25.0)	12 (30.0)	52 (26.0)
4. Once in three months	5 (12.5)	10 (25.0)	5 (12.5)	4 (10.0)	3 (7.5)	27 (13.5)
5. No idea	5 (12.5)	5 (12.5)	4 (10.0)	3 (7.5)	0 (0.0)	17 (8.5)
Total	40 (100.0)	40 (100.0)	40 (100.0)	40 (100.0)	40 (100.0)	200 (100.0)

Source: Field study.

Awareness About Government Loans

State government has been implementing IRDP and DWCRA for quite some time. There has been a provision for 30% of loans to women under IRDP/SGSY. Despite these provisions, 88 out of 200 respondents had not availed loan so far in their life time (Table 7.14). When probed about factors against availing loan, respondents gave reasons like unfamiliarity with government procedures, no avenues to repay loans, taking loan against tribal custom, delays and bribes involved in

Table 7.14 : Factors Against Availing a Loan						
Frequency of visits	*Lohit*	*Dibang Valley*	*Upper Siang*	*Lower Subansiri*	*West Kameng*	*Total*
1. Not familiar with procedures	2	5	1	2	3	13
2. No avenue to repay loan	6	3	3	2	1	15
3. Taking loan against our custom	2	0	0	3	2	7
4. Delays and bribes involved in getting loan	4	3	2	3	7	19
5. Less scope for productive investment	3	5	7	1	4	20
6. No banking facility nearby	1	5	4	4	0	14
Total	18	21	17	15	17	88

Source: field study

getting loan, less scope for productive investment, and no banking facility nearby. Number of respondents failed to get a loan so far are more in Dibang Valley, followed by Lohit, Upper Siang, West Kameng, Lower Subansiri. Of the 88 respondents who had not availed loans so far, 20 of them mentioned the reason as 'less scope for productive investment'. The other inhabiting factor is delays and bribes involved in getting loan.

Remaining respondents (112) were asked about the performance of assets purchased with government loan (Table 7.15). About 50% of respondents mentioned that asset's performance is satisfactory while 22.3% mentioned as unsatisfactory. The percentage of respondents availed loan

Table 7.15 : Respondents' Opinion About Performance of Assets				
District	*Good*	*Satisfactory*	*Unsatisfactory*	*Total*
Lohit	5	10	7	22
Dibang Valley	3	12	4	19
Upper Siang	7	11	5	23
Lower Subansiri	6	13	6	25
West Kameng	10	10	3	23
Total	31	56	25	112

Source: Field study.

are more in Lower Subansiri followed by West Kameng, Upper Siang, Lohit, and Dibang Valley. As regards repayment of loan, 20.5% of them repaid fully, and 23.5% partly. Thus, about 40% have not repaid at all (Table 7.16). The percentage of defaulters are the highest in Lower Subansiri followed by Upper Siang. Major reason for defaulting is under performance of the asset purchased. Members were given no choice in selection of scheme, and place to purchase asset. As they were not involved in the process, percentage of failures are more. On the contrary, percentage of respondents fully paid are more in Lohit.

Table 7.16 : Repayment of Loan by Respondents

District	*Fully*	*Partly*	*Not at all*	*Total*
Lohit	6	7	9	22
Dibang Valley	3	8	8	19
Upper Siang	5	8	10	23
Lower Subansiri	5	8	12	25
West Kameng	4	11	8	23
Total	23	42	47	112

Source: Field study.

Members were asked to give their option to avail a new loan (Table 7.17). Half the respondents conveyed their willingness to this while balance either mentioned 'no' or 'no opinion'. Percentage of respondents opted for loan are more in West Kameng followed by Lower Subansiri while

Table 7.17 : Respondents' Opinion About Preference to Avail a New Loan

District	*Yes*	*No*	*No opinion*	*Total*
Lohit	18 (45.0)	15 (37.5)	7 (17.5)	40 (100.0)
Dibang Valley	20 (50.0)	12 (30.0)	8 (20.0)	40 (100.0)
Upper Siang	17 (42.5)	15 (37.5)	8 (20.0)	40 (100.0)
Lower Subansiri	22 (55.0)	9 (22.5)	9 (22.5)	40 (100.0)
West Kameng	23 (57.5)	7 (17.5)	10 (25.0)	40 (100.0)
Total	100 (50.0)	58 (29.0)	42 (21.0)	200 (100.0)

Source: Field study.

percentage of respondents declined loan are more in Upper Siang and Lohit. Some facts about individual loan requirements are given in Table 7.18. Depending upon availability of local resources, skills, and market for the final product, respondents opted for activities like horticulture, fish ponds, vegetable cultivation, and weaving. Of the 100 respondents who opted for loan, 49% gave option for horticulture. In all, Rs. 10.07 lakhs is required for these schemes. Across districts, respondents of West Kameng made a demand for Rs. 2.64 lakhs while respondents of Lohit asked Rs. 1.25 lakhs. Across activities, horticulture accounted for 65% of the total loan demanded and majority of them have expressed their willingness to repay loan promptly.

Table 7.18 : Some Facts on Individual Loan Requirement

Quality	*Lohit*	*Dibang Valley*	*Upper Siang*	*Lower Subansiri*	*West Kameng*	*Total*
Purpose						
(a) Horticulture	7	10	6	15	11	49
(b) Fish ponds	6	4	2	3	3	18
(c) Vegetable cultivation	3	4	4	1	4	16
(d) Weaving	2	2	5	3	5	17
Amount required						
(a) Horticulture (Rs)	8500	12500	12000	15500	16000	64500
(b) Fish ponds	5500	7200	7500	8000	7500	35700
(c) Vegetable cultivation	6000	6000	6500	7500	7200	33200
(d) Weaving	7050	7000	7500	7200	7300	36050
Willingness to repay						
(a) Yes	12	10	8	12	12	54
(b) No	6	10	9	10	11	46
(c) Total	18	20	17	22	23	100

Source: Field study.

Summary

An observation of Chapter 7 reveals that women started slowly visiting number of institutions like bank, post office, panchayat, town, and cinema hall. Though most of women are not members of cooperatives, they have been utilizing its services. Respondents of below poverty line got a monthly ration of 25 kgs. of rice at subsidized prices. Women are not happy with quality and price of items available at cooperatives. They felt that items of daily necessity with good quality should be supplied through cooperatives regularly at reasonable price. In majority of the cases, health care centres are not located in villages studied. Due to non availability, and socio- religious reasons, women depended both on doctor and priests. Respondents with literacy, educated husbands, and close to town have preferred doctors over priests. On the other hand, illiterate women from far flung areas preferred priest. Respondents are familiar with anganwadi centres and their activities. According to them, supply of nutritious food to children is the core activity of anganwadi centre. Almost all of them are beneficiaries of these centres. As many 12 suggestions were made to improve efficiency of anganwadi centre. About 44% of women had not availed any government loan during their life time. As regards repayment of loan, 20.5% of them repaid fully, 23.5% partly, and half of the respondents are averse to avail a new loan. Depending upon availability of local resources, skills, and market for final product, respondents opted for activities like horticulture, fish ponds, vegetable cultivation, and weaving. In all an amount of Rs. 10.07 lakhs is required to implement to these schemes.

NOTES

1. The state government has reserved 33% seats in Panchayati Raj system for women. However, not many women are coming forward to participate in this process. Patriarchal nature of society, illiteracy, and taboos are coming in the way of women entering Panchayat Raj system.
2. All the tribes have a number of beliefs/superstitions. Adis believe in crow's arrival as a bad omen. Mishmis consider strongly cat coming on the way as bad sign. I am a witness to one such incident. During my visit to Anini (Anini is perched strategically on Chinese border, Government pays Rs. 50 for each kilo of rice made available to locals, and buying a bag to cement can set you back by Rs. 1000), we started for village on a rainy day. The condition of road in this region is far from satisfactory. Two CDPOs and supervisor accompanied me during this trip. With great difficulty we reached the village and completed field work. We left the village at about 5 p.m. (it gets dark by 5 p.m. in this part of the country.), and we had no torch light. Further, it was raining too and the road was slippery. Added to it, vehicle developed trouble on the way. Knowing that it will take sometime to start the vehicle, we all got down. There was complete darkness all around and

no settlement in about 12 kms. distance. Three beautiful ladies accompanying me suggested, after sometime, that we should walk down. Subsequently, we walked for about a kilometer in the rain on a muddy road. By this time, it appears that the ladies got tired. They started telling about an accident which took place there three years ago. Five senior army officers and a driver were killed in that accident. According to local belief, as it was an accidental death, their souls are wandering in this area. These spirits talk to passers-by and keep their hands on passengers during nights. Thus, according to these women we should not go further. I had no option but to follow them and was afraid of wild animals.

Since we failed to reach Anini before 10 p.m., one of the CDPO's husband reached us by jeep. We were relieved on seeing jeep and went back to get the other vehicle. Both drivers repaired vehicle, and finally we reached Anini by 11.30 p.m. On reaching home, one of the ladies was telling that entire episode is due to cat which came across road in the beginning of our journey.

3. As per the Government of India regulations, building for housing a anganwadi centre is to be provided by villagers through pooling their resources. This sends a signal about their commitment towards the centre. However, it is to be mentioned here that most of the target group in this region are below poverty line with little awareness about health care. As a result, they find it difficult to make contributions towards construction of a building. There is a provision for house rent of Rs. 25/month in such cases but it is too low in an expensive area like this. When asked about 50% contribution towards construction of house, majority of them readily agreed to this suggestion.

8

SELF-HELP GROUPS IN STUDY AREA

Introduction

This chapter explains about status of self-help groups (SHGs) in study area. Respondents perceptions and expectations from such SHGs is also dealt with in this chapter. Experience has shown that many of poverty alleviation programmes through institutional credit channels have not achieved desired success. It has been observed that in respect of financing poverty alleviation programmes and creation of employment in rural areas, there are a number of factors, such as lack of awareness among participants in respect of development through credit and thereby making proper use of it, which prevent small borrowers and poor people from securing adequate credit from formal agencies. This situation reveals that rural poor require small but regular urgent loans whereas their options are restricted to programmes designed and approved by government which do not cater to their needs. Hence, to bridge gap between demand for and supply of funds in lower rungs of the rural economy micro-finance schemes promoted by NABARD and other government and non-government agencies have made a smooth foray into rural economy and generating self-reliance, and self-sufficiency in Indian rural scenario.

Self-help Groups

SHGs comprise members who are poor, having low savings capacity, and also who depend on money lenders or private sources for meeting their consumption needs. A typical SHG will comprise of like-minded persons who volunteer to save small amounts of money in a common pool out of which need based loans are given to members for meeting their urgent credit requirements based on priorities decided by the group. Group members take collective decisions on all matters including those relating to terms of credit (purpose, size, rate of interest, and repayment period). They exercise close supervision on utilization of loans and exert peer and moral pressure on members to continue savings and repay loans promptly. In other words, SHG can be referred to as a group of persons who own, manage, and control a micro bank of their own.

A SHG offers a range of benefits much beyond savings and credit facilities. SHG extends to its members a sense of critical self-awareness and give a feeling of self-confidence, solidarity, and social security which are preconditions for an empowerment process. Management of common funds by SHGs create distinct capabilities in financial management, develops business acumen, respect for collective decision making, and enforcement among their members. The collective initiatives of poor also enhances in them risk taking ability, appreciation of micro-enterprise management, and market survival strategies.

As mentioned earlier, a number of agencies (domestic and international, and governmental and non-governmental) are involved in promoting SHGs. NABARD is in the forefront among them. It has been promoting SHGs since 1992 and a special department, Micro Credit Innovation Department, was created to look after promotion and refinancing these SHGs. Rashtriya Mahila Kosh and voluntary agencies too are contributing their might in promoting SHGs. A close observation of Table 8.1 reveals that SHGs linked to bank, loan availed, and refinance by banks have increased substantially during 1993-01.

SHGs in Arunachal Pradesh

Though a number of DWCRA groups are working in the state, the concept of SHG is still new here. It is mainly due to poverty, illiteracy, and patriarchal nature of the society. Efforts are being made by a number of NGOs to organise

Table 8.1 : Progress in SHGs Credit Linkage, 1993-01

Year	*SHGs linked*	*Bank loan (Rs. crores)*	*Refinance (Rs. crores)*
1992-93	255	0.29	0.27
1993-94	620	0.65	0.46
1994-95	2122	2.44	2.13
1995-96	4757	6.06	5.66
1996-97	8598	11.84	10.65
1997-98	14317	23.76	21.39
1998-99	32995	57.07	52.09
1999-00	94645	192.98	150.13
2000-01	213213	480.87	400.74

Source: NABARD (2001).

SHGs in the state. One such NGO is Gyanodaya located at Itanagar. Mr. Vijay Swamy, a teacher at the Vivekananda Kendriya Vidyalaya started this NGO and has been trying to sensitize women to form SHGs. Gyanodaya, so far, organised nine SHGs in the state. A list of these SHGs is given in Table 8.2. An attempt is made in the following sections to describe one of the SHGs organised by Gyanodaya.

Table 8.2 : Status of SHGs Promoted by Gyanodaya in Arunachal Pradesh

Sr. No.	*Name of the SHG*	*Location*	*Membership*
1.	AKEYAA	Roing, Dibang Valley	20
2.	AMEYA	Mayu, Dibang Valley	16
3.	KARMA	Enjuno, Dibang Valley	12
4.	PODHEM	Popu, Papumpare	11
5.	NAHSA	Ziro, Lower Subansiri	12
6.	SRADHA	Hija, Lower Subansiri	14
7.	AKASHH	Lembia, Lower Subansiri	12
8.	RUPA	Rupa, Lower Subansiri	12
9.	MANJUSHRI	Tawang, Tawang	13
	TOTAL		122

Source: Field study

AKEYAA SHG

Alombro Enjuno Koronu Yakuchi Ame Akhamu (AKEYAA) SHG was formed in Roing (Dibang Valley) in 1999. Enjuno and Koronu are twin villages situated at the foothills of high Himalayan ranges of Arunachal Pradesh. Surrounded by thick forest with all wilderness, these are inhabited by Idu Mishmis. The tribe is mainly depend upon minor contracts, forest resources, and agriculture (wet rice cultivation). Heavy rainfall and unchecked rivers carry much of the year's labour of tribals and the rest is eaten away by wild elephants.

Even for the smallest thing, people of these two villages have to come to Roing, the nearest small town after walking around 22 km. As mentioned elsewhere in the report, Roing is located in a plain area as entry point to Anini. It is situated at 339 metres above the sea level and by now farmers are exposed to all commercial crops. It is 110 kms. away from Tinsukia (Assam), and the journey takes 7 to 8 hours due to turbulent Brahmaputra. Off the road and crossing two rivers, which become unmanageable during rainy seasons, locals face lot of difficulty in getting essential commodities and avenues for employment. Due to lack of education and earning resources, their economic condition is far from satisfactory.

Because of the polygamy, women are the main earning members in the family. They have to work hard in fields, attend household chores, rear children, and take care of the house. Education among girls is quite low here. Traditionally, people consume locally made rice beer. Many of the women adopted selling 'apung' a local rice beer, as a means of earning livelihood, even though it gives very little income.

Seeing the situation, Gyanodaya, a NGO, decided to mobilize women for formation of self-help group. The first meeting of village women was convened in July 1999, which was attended by 42 women. The meeting was chaired by Mrs. Savitri Khampti, Child Development Project Officer (ICDS) who hails from the same community. Elderly persons of the community and bank officers from Roing were also present in the meeting. The women were informed about concept of SHG, advantages, and mechanics involved. That encouraged women to come together for self development through group approach.

Accordingly, the first SHG with 20 women was formed with a contribution of Rs. 20/month, and linked with the

Arunachal Pradesh State Cooperative Apex Bank Ltd. (Roing). The name of the group AKEYAA was coined by the group itself. It is a short form of 'Alombro Enjuno Koronu Yakuchi Ame Akhamu' whose literary meaning is 'all Enjuno Koronu women's money saving'. The group consisted ten housewives, a widow, and nine unmarried girls. The group organised meetings with regular intervals under the guidance of social workers of Gyanodaya. For the first six months, during every meeting, SHG members discussed activities they will be able to take up.

They surveyed Roing town and found that there are around 200-300 school-going girls and there is no ladies undergarments shop managed by the ladies. The school going girls and women in the area have to go to gents shop to purchase these items. This was a problem of their own society. Therefore, group hit upon the first idea, to open a ladies undergarments shop.

The group approached the Apex Bank (Roing) to provide a loan. Seeing enthusiasm of the group, bank provided an individual loan of Rs. 30000 to three members, with an interest of Rs. 14%/annum. A shop was offered by an elderly person of the community with a rent of Rs. 800/month. The group decided that even though loan is individual, business will be done under one roof by all three put together. The shop was named as Maselo Garments. Purchases were done from Tinsukia, the nearest wholesale market. The shop was inaugurated on October 20, 1999. Initially, furniture and fixtures worth of Rs. 25000, and garments of Rs. 65000 were brought to start the business.

They did a turnover of Rs. 1.85 lakhs during 1999-00, with a working capital of Rs. 65000. Daily sales proceeds were deposited in bank regularly. The members decided not to take any money from sales for their daily expenditure. They decided to bring food from their home till loan is repaid. They have been following such procedure till today. Out of the total turnover, Rs. 20000 was kept as fixed deposit in a joint account of three members.

Turnover increased to Rs. 2.50 lakhs in 2000-01. Seeing the success of the first two years, the DRDA decided to extend SGSY scheme so as to expand the business. In April 2001, the group received an assistance of Rs. 3.00 lakhs under the scheme, through Apex Bank, which includes Rs. 1.00 lakh subsidy and Rs. 2.00 lakhs as loan. With the enhanced capital and moral support, group expanded the shop. The school uniform of nearby schools, sweaters, bed sheets, etc. were also kept in the shop. It was quite surprising that from April to October 2001, group achieved a sale worth Rs. 2.42 lakhs, and the same was regularly deposited in the bank.

Seeing the positive response and demand, group hit upon another idea to start a tailoring shop. Another five members were trained for six months in tailoring with their own money. They approached the bank again for loan and all the five got a bank loan of Rs. 30000 each. They established AKEYAA tailoring shop under one roof in October 2000 just adjacent to Maselo Garments. During the last year they undertook around 250 school uniforms and sold cloth worth Rs. 60000. Both the units have been depositing sales proceeds daily in bank and paying loan installments regularly.

The group hit upon another idea. They surveyed Roing town and found that consumers were facing difficulty in carrying gas cylinders from gas dealer to their homes. The group decided to enter into this service sector (transporting gas cylinders). They approached for a bank loan to purchase an auto rickshaw. The bank could not entertain them as 15 of the members were covered under a loan (no formal rules to cater to a group of 15 who are dynamic and enthusiastic). One of the members approached private money lender and borrowed Rs. 50000. She purchased an auto rickshaw on credit by paying the loan amount as part payment. She gave an advertisement saying that if anybody wants a cylinder 'just give a ring on given telephone number, the cylinder will reach at your home' for a payment of Rs. 20 for the service. She has employed a driver, and earns around Rs. 3000/month.

Presently the group has two shops, Maselo Garments, and AKEYAA tailoring shop. As mentioned above a member of the group owns a auto rickshaw too. The group also has Rs. 30000 in bank of their own for internal lending. All this suggests that it's a materialistic development, but there is personality development too here.

The village girls who were sitting idle at home, who were selling local rice beer, and women who were not knowing anything other than household chores, are now dealing with lakhs of rupees successfully. Those who were shy and never entered any of the office, are now meeting Additional Deputy Commissioner, Project Director, BDO, Bank Officers, etc. What to tell, the group could impress upon and invite Hon'ble Chief Minister of Arunachal Pradesh, Shri Mukut Mithi to inaugurate their second venture, the tailoring shop. Initially, they were taught how to select saleable material, how to purchase, how to fix the price etc., now everything is done by them. Those who have studied up to class four are now able to maintain daily cash book.

The story does not end here. When the Apex Bank sponsored a motivational programme for women for formation of SHGs in collaboration with Gyanodaya, the Secretary of the group Miss Kichili Mena went along with the resource persons in five districts of Arunachal Pradesh and delivered their success story to other women. The women in the area are getting encouraged seeing the model set by their own sisters. Looking at the success, four women SHGs have come up in the area and getting guidance from them. I hope, this SHG will surely become a catalyst to make it women's movement in this remote part of the state.

Respondents Preference Towards SHGs

Gyanodaya has been making efforts to popularise the concept of SHGs in this state. However, due to socio, religious, and ecological factors, many of them are not aware of SHGs. Respondents were asked to indicate their awareness about SHGs (Table 8.3). On the whole, 29% of respondents gave a positive answer. The percentage of women having familiarity with SHGs are more in Dibang Valley, West Kameng, and Lower Subansiri. About 1/3rd of the respondents in these districts have heard about SHGs. With a view to organise SHGs in the study area, women were asked to indicate their willingness to form a SHG in their village (Table 8.4). Interestingly, 57.5% of women conveyed their willingness to organise a SHG. As expected, 3/4th of women from Dibang Valley came forward for this. Excellent response received from Dibang Valley is mainly due to awareness created by

Table 8.3 : Respondents Awareness About Self-help Groups

District	*Yes*	*No*	*Total*
Lohit	7 (17.5)	33 (82.5)	40 (100.0)
Dibang Valley	15 (37.5)	25 (62.5)	40 (100.0)
Upper Siang	8 (20.0)	32 (80.0)	40 (100.0)
Lower Subansiri	13 (32.5)	27 (67.5)	40 (100.0)
West Kameng	15 (37.5)	25 (62.5)	40 (100.0)
Total	58 (29.0)	142 (71.0)	200 (100.0)

Source: Field study.

Table 8.4 : Respondents Willingness to form a Self-help Group

District	*Yes*	*No*	*Total*
Lohit	22 (55.0)	18 (45.0)	40 (100.0)
Dibang Valley	30 (75.0)	10 (25.0)	40 (100.0)
Upper Siang	15 (37.5)	25 (62.5)	40 (100.0)
Lower Subansiri	23 (57.5)	17 (42.5)	40 (100.0)
West Kameng	25 (62.5)	15 (37.5)	40 (100.0)
Total	115 (57.5)	85 (42.5)	200 (100.0)

Source: Field study

Gyanodaya through organising group meetings. Success of SHGs in Tezu also contributed to this overwhelming response from Dibang Valley. Similarly, level of education in West Kameng is more and hence 2/3rd of them conveyed their willingness. Not only women are willing to form but also confident (45.5%) of their ability to organise SHGs (Table 8.5). Percentage of respondents who are confident of organising SHGs are more in Dibang Valley followed by West Kameng.

They were informed about need for regular savings, meetings, and record keeping. Women expressed willingness

Table 8.5 : Respondents Confidence About Organising Self-help Group			
District	*Yes*	*No*	*Total*
Lohit	15 (37.5)	25 (62.5)	40 (100.0)
Dibang Valley	26 (65.0)	14 (35.0)	40 (100.0)
Upper Siang	12 (30.0)	28 (70.0)	40 (100.0)
Lower Subansiri	18 (45.0)	22 (55.0)	40 (100.0)
West Kameng	20 (50.0)	20 (50.0)	40 (100.0)
Total	91 (45.5)	109 (54.5)	200 (100.0)

Source: Field study.

and eager to start, and have bank account in the name of the group. They also suggested few names for proposed groups.

Women opted for activities like fish ponds, vegetable cultivation, horticulture, garment shop, petty trade, weaving, and breeding mithuns to be taken up under SHGs. In all, women from 23 out of 40 villages opted for these schemes under SHGs (Table 8.6). These 23 schemes would require as much as Rs. 40.00 lakhs[1]. The Ministry of Social Justice and Empowerment, Government of India may take up these schemes on pilot basis for promoting SHGs in the study area. Department of social welfare, women and child development of the Government of Arunachal Pradesh may be given responsibility to implement these schemes. As mentioned

Table 8.6 : Opinion on Activities to be Organised by Through Self-help Groups						
Activity	*Lohit*	*Dibang Valley*	*Upper Siang*	*Lower Subansiri*	*West Kameng*	*Total*
1. Fish ponds	5	5	5	2	3	20
2. Vegetable cultivation	0	5	2	3	3	13
3. Horticulture	5	5	0	5	12	27
4. Garment shop	0	1	0	2	0	3
5. Petty trade	0	0	0	0	2	2
6. Weaving	5	5	5	2	0	17
7. Breeding mithuns	0	5	0	4	0	9
Total	15	26	12	18	20	91

Source: Field study.

elsewhere, this department has a wide network of projects in the length and breadth of the state and have close contact with women in the rural areas. Hence, they may be entrusted with this responsibility.

Though there are 9 SHGs operating in the state, there is no common platform to discuss about problems and experiences of these groups. There is an urgent need to have a centrally located office to cater to this requirement. The proposed office would serve as a transit camp for women, help in conducting meetings, and sharing common problems/ strategies. It is hoped that by seeing this common place, many more such women can get inspiration to come together. They would form groups which will ultimately emerge as a women's movement for boosting rural economy. Thus, an office of semi-Assamese structure is proposed with a cost Rs. 5.00 lakhs. This proposed amount would also be sufficient to purchase furniture, and computer for day to day work. Thus, Rs. 45.00 lakhs would be required to take up SHGs on a experimental basis in this state. Depending upon the success, this can be extended to other parts of the state with the help of various ministries of Government of India. Regular savings, meetings, maintenance of records, internal loaning, linkage with bank, and continuity should be taken as indicators of success.

When asked about the training required for managing SHGs, 68 out of 91 conveyed their willingness, thus, 75% of them are in favour under going training (Table 8.7). January to April are the leisure months for undergoing training (Table 8.8).

Table 8.7 : Respondents Opinion to Undergo Training Managing of Self-help Groups

District	*Yes*	*No*	*Total*
Lohit	13	2	15
Dibang Valley	20	6	26
Upper Siang	7	5	12
Lower Subansiri	12	6	18
West Kameng	16	4	20
Total	68	24	91

Source: Field study.

Table 8.8 : Respondents Opinion Regarding Leisure Months for Training on Self-help Groups

District	*January*	*February*	*March*	*April*	*Total*
Lohit	5 (33.3)	5 (33.3)	5 (33.3)	0 (0.0)	15 (100.0)
Dibang Valley	13 (50.0)	8 (30.8)	4 (15.4)	1 (3.8)	26 (100.0)
Upper Siang	5 (41.7)	5 (41.7)	1 (8.3)	1 (8.3)	12 (100.0)
Lower Subansiri	9 (50.0)	8 (44.4)	1 (5.6)	0 (0.0)	18 (100.0)
West Kameng	10 (50.0)	8 (40.0)	1 (5.0)	1 (5.0)	20 (100.0)
Total	42 (46.1)	34 (37.4)	12 (13.2)	3 (3.3)	91 (100)

Source: Field study.

Summary

A close observation of Chapter 8 revealed that there are 9 SHGs working in the state. Women respondents are in favour of organizing SHGs. They are willing to have regular savings, meetings, and internal loaning. Women opted for schemes like, fish ponds, vegetable cultivation, horticulture, garment shop, petty trade, weaving, and breeding mithuns to be taken up through SHGs. An amount of Rs. 45.00 lakhs would be required to implement these schemes on an experimental basis which would go a long way in improving socio-economic status these women.

NOTE

1. A project cost of Rs. 1.00 lakh/fish pond, Rs. 1.25 lakhs/vegetable cultivation, Rs. 2.50 lakhs/horticulture, Rs. 1.00 lakh/garment shop, Rs. 1.50 lakhs/petty trade, Rs. 1.50 lakh/weaving, and Rs. 2.00 lakhs/breeding mithun is made.

9

CASE STUDIES

Introduction

An attempt in made in this chapter to document individual profiles of selected respondents. These women were selected on the basis of cooperation extended, responses provided, and extensive interviews I had with them. In all 10 women, representing two each from five tribes studied, were selected. The researcher, with prior appointment, stayed 24 hours/each in their houses and thus had close interaction with them. They are typical in nature, and provide insights in to lives of these women.

Premadan Tulang[1]

Ms. Tulang is 70 years old and belong to Miju Mishmi tribe. The village is located[2] on the banks of pristine river Lohit, and situated about 30 kms from international border (Kahoo) in Lohit sector. Further, it is 200 kms. away from district headquarters, Tezu. Her husband expired in 1990, and has been staying with elder son who has five sons and two daughters. When asked about her schooling, she smiled and said that 'where were the facilities in those days for schooling? These children are fortunate enough because government has been providing many facilities now'. She had maize, local beans, and sprouted vegetables on the day of my visit to her house. She has two sons and three daughters and equal number expired in their childhood. Ms. Tulang had an arranged marriage at the age of 14. She still remembers bride price (10 mithuns, 15 pigs, 20 chickens, 2 beads, and some cloth) given by her husband. She goes to forest regularly and helps her daughter-in-law in household chores.

She has been getting old age pension and has no other fixed assets. When asked about the Indo-China war of 1962, she informed that she was about 30 years old and narrated few instances about the war. 'I saw Chinese army who stayed in our house. An Indian soldier was hit by bullet while he was eating a maize cob near our house. We provided necessary help but he died ultimately. Chinese army has not harassed us, they also wanted help from us!. We provided food to Indian soldiers'. She had five children at that stage and were all staying in the same house along with her co-wife who had no issues.

Currently, she has a mithun, 4 pigs, and 14 chicken. Further, she has two silver earrings which she wanted to have them on her graveyard. According to her they are very costly. Since she is staying with her elder son, most of the decisions are taken by daughter-in-law and son. However, she enjoyed full freedom during her family life. Her husband was cooperative and family purse was maintained by Premadan Tulang. She visited Sadiya, Tezu, and Dholaghat when she was a child. It took some 12 days to visit Tezu from Hawai, her natal village, in those days. When asked about her knowledge about Britishers she mentioned that she talked to a British Officer (Nimprai) who was at Hawai. She is not happy with functioning of village cooperative, health care centre, and anganwadi centre. According to her 'anganwadi worker is careless'. Premadan Tulang believes in priest (Gokhani) than doctor. As she was ill, recently performed a pooja, paid Rs. 100, and sacrificed 3 pigs, and 4 chickens. She remembers of availing a loan for fish pond, however she is not sure about amount received.

In Miju Mishmi society, a women has absolute right over her earnings before marriage. But after the marriage, ownership of her property is shared by husband. A married daughter has no right to inherit properties of her parents. However, she can inherit properties of her deceased husband. In this regard, Ms. Tulang is appreciative of her husband who gave a free hand to her. Cooking, entertaining guests, preparation of rice beer, feeding domestic animals and birds, and taking care of agriculture are jobs of females in Mishmis. At the time of delivery a woman is segregated in house. The mother is not supposed to touch anything except her belongings and she can't cook for others. She is also not allowed to go out of house for nine days in case of a female child and ten days in case of a male child. Mrs. Premadan Tulang is happy about facilities being provided by government and would like to visit Dibrugarh.

Akhalu Kri

Young (24 years), energetic, and cheerful Mrs. Akhalu Kri hails from Quibang of Lohit district. She is an illiterate and got married at the age of 16/17. When enquired about her marriage, she happily narrated the entire episode. She met her husband in a nearby weekly market and got fancy to each other. Subsequently, they eloped to a nearby village. Some of her husband's relatives came to know about this and started negotiations with Kri's parents. The bride price was settled as 12 mithuns, 15 pigs, and 20 chickens. Since bride price was not readily available with them, they both worked hard for payment. They had two children (son and a daughter) and two more expired during this period. Finally, they settled bride price after five years of family life. Thus, her husband entered Kri's parents house (*ghar ghusna*) after a long period leading to a formal marriage. According to her, it is the duty of the husband to pay in the form of money, mithuns, pigs, rice beer, dry meat, etc, to in-laws as and when required. Thus, bride price is a continuous process and not one time payment.

Kri's husband is working as peon in education department and getting Rs. 4500/month and her widowed father-in-law is also staying with them. According to her, 'husband should earn enough to take care of basic needs of family and this is the criteria she followed in selecting husband'. At the moment she has no co-wives and when asked about the possibility of husband bringing another wife she philosophically mentioned that 'till now he has not brought but he might bring at any time. Neither I can stop him bringing a co-wife nor he is going to consult me at that time'. According to her, 'being born as man is good because he has all freedom with little responsibilities'.

Apart from a kacha house, Mrs. Kri has four jhum plots,

two mithuns, 6 pigs, 16 chicken, a radio, and a cycle. Activity-wise, average number of hours spent by her/day is given in Table in 9.1. It is clear from Table 9.1 that, on an average, Mrs. Kri is working for about 10 hours and 45 minutes/day. Work related to agriculture, collection of firewood, upkeep of house, cooking, and collection of minor forest produce are activities consuming about 70% of her workload. She has been exercising her decision on issues like childcare, preparation of feast, purchase of utensils, sending children to school, and agricultural activities. Husband is the final authority in rest of the activities.

Table 9.1 : Activity-wise Average Working Hours/day by Kri

No.	*Activity*	*Time spent (hours)*
1.	Cooking	1.00
2.	Collecting firewood	2.15
3.	Caring children	0.30
4.	Tending animals	0.30
5.	Attending agriculture	2.30
6.	Upkeep of house	1.00
7.	Fetching water	0.30
8.	Washing clothes	0.30
9.	Collecting MFP	1.00
10.	Handicrafts	0.30
11.	Preparation of rice beer	0.15
12.	Social visits	0.15
	Total	10.45

Source: Field study.

As regards her awareness towards village institutions, Mrs. Kri is familiar with cooperatives, primary health care, and anganwadi centres. She liked concept of anganwadi centre and requested strengthening centre by providing more facilities and funds. As regards primary health centre she informed that though services are free patients are to purchase the medicines from outside. She felt that medicines also need to be provided by the government. Apart from visiting PHC she also performs pooja 3 to 4 times a year. This year she sacrificed a mithun, four pigs, and a cow and paid Rs. 200 to priest. She is of the opinion that 'productivity of jhum plots is very low. Produce is sufficient for 3-4 months only. Government should give improved seeds and fertilisers so that production can be increased'.

She neither availed a loan from the government nor willing to have one. As her income is low, she felt that she cannot repay the loan. However, she liked the idea of organising a self-help group in their village and conveyed willingness to be part of it.

Ngasi Umpo

Ngasi Umpo belongs to Idu Mishmi tribe and hails from Ryalin of Upper Dibang Valley. Her village falls on the Roing-Anini main road. She got married at the age of 17. It was a love marriage, and was later arranged by elders. When asked about preferred marriage in Idu Mishmis she mentioned that 'in our society, practice of levirate marriage (permitting a man to marry a widow of his brothers), and surrorate marriage (a younger sister marries widowed husband of her deceased elder sister) is allowed. However, monogyny is good for society.'

Her husband was a political interpreter and expired in 2000 due to paralyses. She had two elder co-wives of which one is surviving at the moment. She has two sons and two daughters who are married. Her eldest son left school at the age of seven, her youngest had never seen the inside of one, and to keep family on its feet, she scrounges for work everywhere. On probing she mentioned that jhum cultivation, hunting, collection from forests, supplies to government departments, and contracts are the sources of income in this part of the country. Master hunters look for musk deers. Musk is a substance with a strong smell produced from certain glands of male deers. It is used in making perfumes and has medicinal value. These musk deers are found in high altitude and comes out for mating during winter. Hunters kill them indiscriminately for getting musk. The government has declared it as a endangered animal. On being told about musk deer, Ngasi Umpo sarcastically mentioned that 'if we don't hunt them we will be endangered species'.

Her first co-wife expired in 1985, and second co-wife got

command over husbands assets (jhum lands, pukka house at Roing, and money). Thus, second co-wife is well-off now and is staying in Roing. Eldest co-wife has a son and two daughters and son is working as a doctor at Hunli dispensary. He has been supporting Mrs. Ngasi Umpo also by providing timely financial support. He also helped her in getting a fair price shop which is the main source of her income.

Her husband paid two mithuns, and one thousand rupees as bride price at the time of marriage. She being the youngest enjoyed the privilege and affection of her husband. When asked about gender-wise distribution of work she opined that 'basic things like cooking, washing, cleaning, caring children, etc. are seen as prerogative of women. Infact, a man would be considered effeminate if he were to do these things or would be mocked by others as henpecked', and hence she felt that being born as man is better than woman in a tribal society. When asked about her opinion about status of women in their society she mentioned that 'parents think that their daughter is a property which can be encashed. Husband expresses a strong sense of possessiveness over her. She is considered as a person who is purchased as a commodity. It is in this respect that she is expected to perform all kinds of work. And if he decides to give her divorce, he is required only to pay back bride price he paid to her parents. On the contrary, it she takes fancy to some other man, her lover is obliged to pay bride price which her present husband had paid to her parents'.

One has to climb a ladder having six steps and bend his/ her head to enter into her house. Ngasi Umpo has few fixed assets including a bank account with a balance of Rs. 2500. On an average, she spends around 12 hours/day to earn a measly income of Rs. 1800/month.

She feels that women should be educated and get employment. Ngasi Umpo is proud of her elder co-wive's daughter-in-law who is working as CDPO. As of marriage she opined that 'men sought after independent women because of economic compulsions. Educated women are outgoing, independent, dominating, and know what they are doing. Men are undoubtedly attracted to them'.

She visited Dibrugarh and Tinsukia with her husband and believes in spirits. She performs pooja thrice a year mostly for health and good harvest. She visited health centre once in her life time because of problems related to urinary bladder. However, she is not happy with the treatment. She is a member of cooperative society as also familiar with anganwadi centre. She never availed loan from government but interested in organising a self-help group. She expects to get tin sheets from government for constructing a pukka house. Idu Mishmis of Anini now have communication centre. 'I know of such a centre, which I have never been there', she admits. Little education and less awareness keep information away from those who need it most. Umpo felt that government should distribute improved seeds and fertilisers on free of cost so that tribals can fend round the year

Semeri Mihu

Semeri Mihu is very active, and cheerful at the age of 70. She belongs to Anini and got married at Hunli. It was an arranged marriage. Mihu is aware of 1952 earthquake as also 1962 Indo-China War. It took about a month to reach Sadiya by walk in those days. They used to carry handlooms, handicrafts, chicken, etc. and brought rice and salt from Sadiya. According to her some Tibetians came to Anini and Roing in 1962 but locals forced them to go to Tezu where they are settled in refugee camps. She is an expert in preparing brooms, and clothes with cotton as also fibre. Further, she is also familiar with dyeing activities. These goods were also sold in Sadiya market. There was neither electricity nor water nor roads nor health care facilities in those days.

She is proud of Mishmi dress which is distinct from other Arunachalis. Mishmi women wear a coloured cloth fastened loosely round the waist which reaches to the knees and a scanty bodice. The hairdo held by bandeau of a think silver plate, broad over the forehead and tapering to about half an inch inside the over the ears, thence continued round the back of the head by a chain of small shells is extremely attractive. The hair are turned up and gathered in a knot and secured by a bodkin.

When asked about negotiations in Idu Mishmi marriages, she happily narrated following details. A young Mishmi man may decide to marry as and when he likes and he exercises free personal choice in selecting a bride. A female go-between ascertains girl's feeling for no girl is married against her will. The bride price is heavy and sometimes horrible to a common man to pay. Marriage, in most cases, involves material as well as non-material transactions between bride giver, and bride taker. Bride price or payment in cash and kind to bride's father by groom's father reflects transfer of authority over bride from her father to groom and his family. The idea of compensation for loss of a productive worker is also implicit in it. The bride's family loses a productive worker when a girl get married and leaves her natal home. The girl is a source of wealth, and prestige to her natal family, family in which she is born. In this sense, transaction implies transfer of all that the girl stands for.

Her husband expired in 1985 and since then staying with her son. Remaining three sons and two daughters also got married and all of them are settled around Hunli. Her husband had many jhum plots. When asked about fixing boundaries of jhum plots she interestingly mentioned that 'jhum lands are clearly demarcated on four sides with help of big stones. People are afraid of touching them or shifting them. Further, elders too punish such people who dares to shift these stones. Some trees are also grown as a mark of demarcation'. Her son is having few wet rice cultivation plots and undertakes contracts. According to her, 'though I attended all activities and a major income earner, I was never considered as head of the household. It was husband who controlled family when he was alive and it is the turn of son now. Thus, there is no status for women in our society'. She is proud to be an Indian but not happy with facilities being extended by the government. Semeri Mihu is aware of primary health care, and anganwadi centres but never had been there. However, she visited cooperative number of times.

Kiptak Modi

Kiptak Modi has a beautiful thick black hair falling till her waist and belong to Upper Siang. Siang districts (East, West, and Upper Siangs) are inhibited by Abors (unruly) who are independent by nature. Initially, they resented outside interference, and were suspicious of strangers. There is lot of change now. They are now known as Adis covering Minyongs, Padams, Gallongs, etc.

The village has 67 households with 182 females and 176 males. Since it is close to Mariyong, almost all facilities are available in the village. Ms. Modi studied 9th standard and got married at the age of 17 to a contractor who did his LLB from Pune. Her husband is a district BJP secretary and most of the time stays in Delhi. She is living in a joint family with 3 married brother-in-laws and 2 unmarried sister-in-laws. Ms. Modi has a son and four daughters and is interested in providing education to them. She would like to see them as doctors and engineers. When asked about her preference towards son and daughter, she opined that 'no such value is attached to the birth of a son in our society. No doubt, birth of a son is a welcome addition to a tribal family. But he does not provide any assurance for salvation. On the other hand, birth of daughter is an occasion for joy. When she grows up and is married she brings bride price. More the birth of daughters in a family more there is pumping of money'.

They have 10 jhum plots, big house, 50 mithuns, 10 pigs, 15 chicken, radio, motorcycle, and jeep. Ms. Modi mostly attends household work and supervises agricultural operations. Since her husband is mostly staying away, almost all decisions are taken by her, of course under the overall supervision of her father-in-law. On an average, she works for about 7-8 hours a day. She is an active member of the anganwadi centre and according to her many pregnant women were reluctant to accept medicines and get health care facilities from the anganwadi centre. There was a misunderstanding among mothers that medicines supplied to pregnant women were meant for birth control. However, there is a lot of change in perceptions of women in these days. Many women are now availing facilities provided by anganwadi centre. According to Modi love marriage is the commonest practice in their tribe. Girls have right to choose their life partner yet it is the custom that boys should approach girls for marriage first. As girls enjoy rights to love and marriage, unmarried girls are free to do so as they like. Consequently they marry at early ages.

The traditional marriage system is very simple. In the first stage, two life partners (boy and girl) contact for marriage or their relative for marriage. In the second step, two families of boy and girl agree for marriage. In the third stage, parents of boy send a pair of smoked squirrels along with other food items like rice beer and ginger paste to girl's house as a token of gift and confirmation. In the fourth stage, boy goes to girl's house as Makboo (son-in-law) and sleeps there every night till girl comes to his house. He can continue to be at girl's house normally up to four years if the girl's parents do not agree to send her to his house. During such period, boy and his parents helps in-laws and supply foodstuffs as bride price. Lastly, bride goes to boy's house on an appointed day. On this day, parents and other relatives of bride give her cereal seeds for future production, pigs, fowls, necklaces, bracelets, emuls (bell metal), etc. as marriage gifts. The parents of bridegroom offer pork, rice beer, etc. to parents of bride. There is no provision for a bride to bring valuables to bridegroom's house. Similarly, girl's parents too do not claim valuables as bride price.

When asked about problems being faced by women she mentioned that 'I think women are the best agents of change and not all of them realise their potential. Young and educated women have to bring about a difference. Roads, infrastructure, telecommunications, polygyny, environmental issues, health, sanitation, forestry, and welfare of the poorest of poor are mandatory issues before women. There is need to discuss women's problems, and unfortunately, society does not recognise this as important issue'.

She has a bank balance of Rs. 10000 and visited Delhi and Bombay. Though she is not having BPL and ration card she is familiar with facilities being provided by cooperative society. She has belief in doctor than priest but for good harvest and prosperity she performs pooja. She had the opportunity to attend a program on self-help groups and keen to organise one such group in the village.

Oming Apang

Oming Apang belongs to Minyong Adi tribe of Upper Siang. It is 8 kms. from Yingkiong, district headquarters. The bridge on Siang river, which was inaugurated by Mr. Deve Gowda, Ex-Prime Minister of India, was washed away due to torrential floods and as a result one has to cross a suspension bridge (popularly known as Indira bridge) of 400 metres to reach this village. The condition of the bridge is far from satisfactory and a minor slip will take him/her into dead cold waters of Siang at a depth of 250-300 metres. People like me can only walk with closed eyes with the help of fellow passengers.

She hails from Jengging which is 40 km from her husband's place. Apang studied upto 10th standard and now working as a anganwadi worker. The local MLA helped her to get this job. She got married at the age of 16 and it was a love and arranged marriage. Husband is an influential person in the village having both wet rice, and jhum cultivation. They have a very big house with many facilities. Further, she has 10 orange plants fetching an annual income of Rs. 1500. Her family income (Rs. 80900), source-wise, is provided in Table 9.2. Her husband has two brothers and three sisters who are now staying separately. Though she has a married life of 11 years, she has no children. As she is barren, she is worried that her husband might bring a co-wife which she doesn't like. She gets no help from her husband in agriculture and house maintenance. Thus, she has to attend anganwadi centre as also household chores, and cultivation. She felt that government should supply improved seeds and fertilizers so as to bring tribal people above poverty line.

Table 9.2 : Average Annual Income of Oming Apang

Sr. No	*Source*	*Income (Rs./annum)*
1.	Jhum cultivation	24000
2.	Horticulture	1500
3.	Salary	5400
4.	Contracts	50000
	Total	80900

Source: Field study.

She works for about 4 hours/day in anganwadi centre for which she is paid a measly monthly salary of Rs. 450. She complained about problems involved in transportation of SNP items, expenditure on monthly meetings, etc. and suggested that some of educated and senior anganwadi workers should be absorbed as gramsevikas. Apang also felt that 'we have to cross Siang river by a treacherous suspension bridge and then climb for about 5 kms to reach the village. It will be a tedious journey during monsoon and unsafe to travel'. Further, she also opined that 'anganwadi centres should be provided with tables, benches, chairs, black board, play material, and utensils'.

When asked about her religion she said that 'Adis, like other tribes of Arunachal, are believers in a world of spirits. They believe that many of numerous spirits or demons bring evil to community and are, therefore, to be appeased by various ritual practices. Priests entrusted with this function are persons of considerable authority who are also vested with secular responsibilities such as allocation of fields for cultivation and decision regarding auspicious time for sowing, and harvesting operations. By observing liver of a chicken, they can predict reasons for ailment, sacrifices to be made, auspicious occasions, culprits, etc'.

Further, she also mentioned that we (Adis) are followers of Dinyin Polo who worship forces of nature (sun and moon) and have rich folklore and mythologies. Christianity has already taken inroads in this district. Most of the marriages are arranged, and love marriages are becoming popular and accepted. Marriages are largely exogamous and polygyny is not unknown. Families are patriarchal.

As Apang is educated and working as anganwadi worker, she is familiar with functioning of primary health care centre, cooperative, and school. She visits health care centre as and when required. She has belief in both doctor and traditional priest. Oming Apang has so far not availed any loan from government but interested to organising a self help group.

Biku Yapap

Biku hails from Raga circle of Lower Subansiri. Her father,

who is no more, was political interpreter. He got her admitted in a boarding school at Raga. While she was in 8th standard she got fancy to her husband and later betrothed at the age of 15. Her parents visited Raga and saw omen that favoured the proposal.

Her father-in-law is an ex-MLA who is also staying in the same village. She has a provision shop and takes active part in social and cultural activities. Biku has 3 sons and a daughter and all of them are studying in a convent school near Raga. She spends around Rs. 1.5 lakh/annum on their education. However, she is happy because her two sons are getting scholarships partly meeting their expenses.

They have motorcycle, jeep, TV, refrigerator, and are considered rich in the near by villages. On the basis of above description I thought that their income must be around Rs. 3 lakhs/year (she gave no estimate). Though Nishis (Lower and Upper Subansiris) prefer boiled food using bamboo shoots, salt, laisa (leafy green vegetables), and Yardak and Chilli (plucked after it is red), Biku's family developed taste for fried and spicy foods. Meat is either boiled or dried. A popular drink called Apang is made from fermenting rice or millet.

She has leadership qualities, and mobilized women to organise a poultry cooperative society under DWCRA. They invited the ex-CM to inaugurate the function. However, due to diseases and lack of timely health care, most of the birds died. Subsequently, she organised a handloom weavers' cooperative for women. There are 30 women in this society. She is familiar with the primary health centre, and anganwadi centre and has belief in both doctor and priest. Biku is also interested in organising a SHG.

She has a bank account in Apex bank at Raga with a balance of Rs. 10000. She is also depositing Rs. 500/month in a recurring deposit on her daughter's name.

Her father had 5 wives and she experienced tensions and misunderstandings among co-wives. She decided not to marry a man who already had one. Accordingly, she was successful in getting a husband who is caring and affectionate. They both visited Bombay and New Delhi and would like to visit Bangalore and Chennai. Husband has taken up a big contract of constructing a hydro electricity project. She took us to show the tunnel under construction. According to her 'women with a large social circle are actually less content with their lives than those with a smaller group of friends. Smaller is the circle, less is the complication and problems. This holds true in tribal and non-tribal women also. The problem is acute with illiterate women who got married to political leaders and employed. In order to be in good looks of their husbands now they are following all western habits, thus spoiling tribal culture'.

When asked about child marriages among Nishis she mentioned that 'it is a custom that has been going on for centuries in Nishis. Villagers see no reason why it should end now. We are taking all efforts to put an end to this practice, but social customs take time to change. Women are now coming together to fight these social evils. These problems had to encountered by spreading education, social awareness and economic upliftment'.

Payment of bride price plays a major role in the marriage of Nishis. It binds parents of a girl in a single direction for, once payment is made girl's parents cannot think otherwise of their daughter's marriage without repaying price paid for. Further, if girl dies before her coming to husband's house or without any issue, it is customary that husband may claim back bride price already paid or demand one of the sisters of the deceased, if any. If the girl runs away due to one reason or other, it is the responsibility of girl's parents to help their son-in-law in bringing back the daughter.

Nishi society is patriarchal, patrilineal and patrilocal in character. Under these circumstances female interferences in decision making is not appreciated. Further, birth of a female child does not receive happiness. Biku mentioned that there is no difference in attitude when a daughter is born at the first instance. But if woman repeats such deliveries husband feels bad and gets disappointed. A pregnant mother is, thus, generally worried about the sex of the prospective child.

A Nishi women enjoys freedom in attending household duties. She does her work without much interference from husband and other family members. Normally her daily routine starts right from the dawn. She is the first to get up in the house and also last to go to bed. Thus, she is mostly confined within the house and agricultural fields. She also rear pigs and poultry for domestic purposes.

Nara Yashi

Nara Yashi is born in Lower Talo near Yachuli. She was sold to her present husband at the age of 7. She is the third wife to her husband. He paid 12 mithuns, and 10 pigs as bride price. She was brought to her husbands house at the age of 13. By that time, her husband had 4 children from her 2 elder co-wives. Her average income is around Rs. 25000/annum. She has 3 sons and equal number of daughters and none of them attended school. Further, three children expired in their childhood. When asked as to why she has this many children Nara said that 'children are god's gift, family planning/norms has never been taken seriously in this area. Tribal families, for reasons of backwardness, illiteracy, topography, nature, and lack of proper healthcare facilities, go ahead and have upto 10-12.children/family'. When I further posed the same question, she smilingly said that ' ask my husband why he did this'? In all her husband has 16 children now.

They live in a long house where a separate compartment is provided to a wife. The family centers around mother who owns few jhum lands, mithuns, poultry, pigs, etc. She has 4 jhum plots, 3 mithuns and a pig. She goes to forest regularly for getting fuelwood as also vegetables and roots. On an average she spends 10-12 hrs/day in attending all these works. She is of the opinion that 'women should be treated on par with men, however men are not going to realise until and unless there is a change in their attitude. Educated women will be able to bring this change'. She once visited Itanagar for medical check-up. Nara believes in priest and performs pooja 1-2 times/year depending upon requirement. Recently she sacrificed a mithun and two pigs and paid Rs. 200 to the priest. Nara got a bank loan for a fish pond in 1995. However, due to inadequate rains all fish died and there were no returns from the investment. She has not returned even a single rupee. However, she is interested in availing a new loan.

Most of these villagers are now converting into Christianity. Nara is also a Christian and goes to church on Sundays. She is appreciative of the 'father' who has been providing help both in kind and cash. There is a practice of wives making arrangements for husbands education in Nishi society. Soon after marriage wife and husband work hard and husband goes for higher education. However, Nara is not in favour of such arrangements. There are 6 such families in her village. One boy who is studying at Dibrugarh fell in love with an educated girl and left his wife. Later the issue was taken up by village elders and settled after a protracted negotiations. Bridegroom's father repaid twice the original bride price paid by him. Nara is neither familiar with cooperative nor health centre nor any other village institution.

For all practical purposes she is head of the household. The husband is given rice beer and food as and when he pays a visit to her chamber. Decision making with regard to arranging marriages to children, giving or taking big loans, disputes, etc. are taken by husband while the rest are left to wife. In case co-wives are cooperative they may share both happiness and sorrows and if they are not, it becomes difficult for them to manage lives. Husband plays a major role in bringing a compromise among co-wives. There are cases where a husband has 8-9 wives, and there are also instances where elder wive's son got fancy to the youngest wife.

Tsering

Mrs. Tsering is 37 years old charming lady in her Monpa dress[3] and appears to be in her youth. She came to know about our visit to anganwadi centre and reached just before we were about to leave the village. Tsering invited us to her house. Encouraged by her innocent look, I readily agreed. On reaching home, she pleaded to drink locally prepared maize beer or cereal beer which I politely declined. She later boiled 3 eggs and offered to us with respect which the accompanying CDPO took while I conveyed my regrets for this too.

While coming from the forest on a cloudy day, Mrs. Tsering met with an accident. As a result, her right eye had damaged, there was bandage and water was oozing out of it. On inquiry, she broke and started crying. Myself and CDPO consoled her and Mrs. Tsering started her story.

Tawang is her natal village, while her uncle was living in a refugee camp at Mysore and encouraged her to study there. Thus, she studied up to 7th standard in a Central School at Mysore. On completion of 7th standard, Tsering's parents called her back and arranged a marriage with her maternal uncle. She was 17 years old then. During this time, Tsering fell in love with a person belonging to other tribe and in the process they had two children, son and daughter. However, this marriage was not recognised by the society. As her mother was not happy with the inter tribe marriage and was interested in arranging with her cousin, Tsering was forced to divorce from the first husband. Monpas prefer cross cousin marriages. In case such marriages are not performed, bride's parents are to give compensation in terms of cloth, rice beer, yak, sheep, goat, and poultry to the aggrieved. There was compulsion from her brothers side either to arrange marriage or to pay compensation.

Thus, after four years of their happy love marriage, Tsering's mother forcibly brought her home and arranged marriage with one of Tsering's maternal uncle. Unfortunately by this time Tsering underwent vasectomy operation which took place in 1985. The ex-husband took children and kept them in a school at Tezpur. Since she is barren, her second husband (maternal uncle) has been ill-treating her. He beats her daily and insults saying that 'go with this fellow or that fellow, they will provide all items required for your maintenance'. She feels that her life has been spoiled and has no meaning. Her only hope is on son/daughter but they are not calling her as mother. Despite this she is in process of constructing a house for her son in Dirang.

Tsering's mother expired in 1998 and since then her problems have increased manifold. Soon after her mother's death, father married a Mishmi and shifted to Tezu. He visited Tsering's house thrice during the last two years and advised her to divorce this husband too. Father also encouraged to come and stay with him. However, Tsering is of the opinion that 'how many times I marry and divorce, am I a toy/commodity'? Tsering feels that 'as long as girls are young, beautiful, and working hard there won't be much problem. But the moment we loose these qualities, husbands get attracted to other women, and there starts problems. Except as workers we have no place in husbands minds'. Her elder sister married a person from Adi tribe and they are leading a happy life at Pasighat. Her sister too asked to desert husband. But she feels that it's not going to solve the problem.

Tsering's day starts at 4.30 in the morning. Since it is bamboo house not much sweeping is carried out, she prepares food, feeds yak, two sheep, and eight chickens. Soon after this, Tsering bring water from a nearby tap. There are not many vessels either for cooking or storing water. She will have her lunch at around 9.30 a.m. and goes to forest at 10.30. Tsering has three jhum plots located at 2.5 kms from house. She attends almost all works in the field (cleaning the forest, fencing, sowing, weeding, harvesting, bringing produce from the fields, and preservation of grains). During her visits to forest she also collect fire wood, vegetables, roots, tubers, fruits, honey, etc. for household consumption. She is back to house by 4.00 p.m., cleans utensils, and prepares dinner. Then she fetches water, feeds animals, serves husband, and finally go to bed at 7.00 p.m. Thus, she works for about 14.30 hours/ day. This way her contribution to the maintenance of the house is substantial which is not recognised by her husband. Most of the time he drinks and play cards with neighbours. And on the top of it he beats and harass her. According to her yield from jhum plots is inadequate to maintain a family. Government should come forward to supply seeds and fertilizers for sufficient production. This would enable tribals to be self sufficient.

The accompanying CDPO promised to provide some help and asked Tsering to visit CDPO's office. We both told her to have faith in god and be bold (what else can we do?).

Lang Droma

Lang Droma is 69 years old whose husband expired in 1992 and hence staying with youngest son. She had 9 children (4 sons and 5 daughters) and all married. Most of her children are staying outside the village and they all meet on festival occasions once a year. Even at this age, she regularly goes to forest to collect vegetables, leaves, honey, etc. for her consumption (her youngest son has 4 jhum plots). Lang Droma also helps daughter-in-law in agricultural, and household chores. When asked about her feelings towards past and present, Lang Droma felt that 'these days are good because government has been providing number of facilities like health care, education, mid-day meals, roads, electricity, loans, etc'. She is happy with services being provided by the government of India. According to her, except religious teachings at Tawang monastery, there was no school in the entire region those days. She felt that 'girls should study and get employment in government and other offices'. She loves daughter-in-law who is educated and has been taking care of her for the last couple of years.

Her natal village is about 7 kms. away and during youth a number of a boys were behind her. She was treated as a mini-queen those days. She felt that 'unmarried girl is happy because she has liberty with no responsibilities'. She remembered having walked up to Tawang (160 kms.) in 5 days to get salt from Tibetan traders. She visited hospital only at the age of 60 for getting a proof of age so as to enable her to get old age pension. As a result, she has been getting Rs. 1800/year. She remembers Indo-China war of 1962. Her husband participated as a porter to Indian soldiers and was paid heavily. In all, 23 men from their village died in the war and most of them worked as porters. Since she was not familiar with nationalities, she provided food to both Indian and Chinese soldiers when they entered their village. One of the Chinese soldiers gave a silver chain which she has even today.

She has a BPL ration card and has been getting 25 kgs. of rice/month. However, she wanted 35 kgs. alongwith salt, wheat, and kerosene to be supplied on card at a subsidized price. She is happy with the functioning of anganwadi centre and its contribution to village.

She has few silver items and two beads necklaces which were given by mother at the time of marriage. It appeared that she is happy with limited resources and requirements. She has no complaints, other than the once mentioned above, against anybody. When mentioned about my identity, she felt happy to talk to a person from plains. During her life time I am the only fellow who had come from that far off to their village.

Summary

An observation of individual case studies revealed that all tribes studied belong to patriarchal, patrilineal, and patrilocal societies. Barring Nishis women from other tribes got married in the age varying between 14-18 years. In majority of the cases, they have freedom in selection of spouse. Though arranged marriages were practised in olden days love marriages and love and arranged marriages are accepted and followed now. Bride price is compulsory in almost all the tribes. But the form and amount is changing fast due to increased education. Infant mortality is very high and women prefer to have sons over daughters. However, neither daughters are ill treated nor there is any female infanticide. Women have full freedom in household and agricultural activities while they have little role in decision making pertaining to outside the household. More number of women are now visiting health care centres, and the role played by priest is relatively declining. Slowly and steadily women have started realising importance of education, family planning, health, and sanitation. They are participating in village cooperatives and anganwadi centres and demanding more facilities for their well being. Educated women also started bringing pressure against polygyny, and bride price. Due to all weather roads, and improved communication facilities women started moving out of their homesteads and as a result their outlook is broadening. Jhum lands, and mithuns as assets of prestige are loosing ground to well furnished houses in towns, bank balances, government jobs, consumer durables, etc. In majority of the cases income from jhum plots is sufficient only for 3-4 months. Women are also entering into business, contracts, self-employment, service, etc.

NOTES

1. Unlike women from plains, Arunachalis do not include their husband's name after marriage. They keep their identity as such. Married tribal

women do not keep mangalsutra, bindi, bangles, etc. Thus, it would be difficult to differentiate between a married and unmarried woman. One can only guess on the basis of their behaviour and peer group.

2. Dang village is situated on the right bank of Lohit river and is just 8 kms. from her village. It is the first to get sun rays in India. One has to travel 7 kms. by foot to reach this village. It has two houses with a population of 16. The state government made elaborate arrangements for a view of sunrise on January 1, 2000 and a helipad was also constructed to enable visitors to reach this remote place.

3. The picturesque Tawang gridled by lofty hills is the home of Monpas. They are of mangoloid descent. Monpas live in a cozy double storied houses, constructed of stone with plank floor, often carved doors and window frames. Monogamy is the rule, and marriage by negotiation is general practice. Cross-cousin marriage is preferred. Levirate form of marriage is also practised. Ladies dress consists of a red coloured gown with white stripes covering body right from shoulders to knee level (shingka) and is gridled at waist by a sash. A flat rectangular piece of wooden cloth is worn at rear of waist. The upper garments consists of lavishly embroidered endi shirt with opening in front (Kyanchen Thoe-thung). They have a variety of dishes (Memo, Zan, Khura, Gyapa-Khazi, Thupka, etc.). Thupka is the common dish of Monpas. It consists of noodles with soup minced meat. This kind of Thupka is called Dre-thuk. Thupka made of maize, meat and bean is called Ashum thukpa, Gyapa Khatzi made of rice and fermented cheese. Bak-tze is another kind of thupka made of same style as that of noodles with difference that instead of noodles, flat rectangular shape of dough is used. Vegetables are also added to it. Favourite ornaments of Monpa women are silver bangles (nyondup), earrings (along), finger rings (soldop), and breast-pins, silver necklaces with lockets (yugau). Weaving among Monpas is exclusively woman's work. Normally, it is practiced for their own purpose.

10

SUMMARY AND RECOMMENDATIONS

Introduction

Arunachal Pradesh has not many written records. The area covered under present Arunachal got entity only in 1873 through an inner line regulation. There are 25 major tribes, and over 100 sub-tribes inhabiting this pristine land. Diaries of early explorers, British administrators, and writings of Verrier Elwin help understanding status of Arunachal Pradesh till 1950. These tribes were considered as unruly and it was a non-regulated area during British regime. As it is located in hilly area with undulated topography, it has a wide variety of climates. Jhum cultivation (slash and burn), hunting, and forests are major sources of income to locals.

It is strategically located with 1630 kms of international border. As it is situated on fragile eastern Himalayas, state is increasingly facing problem of landslides. Massive deforestation has led to degradation of top soil. Coupled with mercurial Himalayan rivers that often change their courses, the result is flash floods. Land slides, snowfall, and heavy rains cut off most part of the state, and washing away of bridges have become common phenomenon. Interestingly, 80% of the discharge of Brahmaputra is contributed by rivers of Arunachal. At the time of independence it was thought to be maintained as 'queen's colony', but locals rejected the idea and declared their loyalty to India. Arunachal attained statehood in 1987. Currently, there are 15 districts with a total population of 10.09 lakhs (2001). Forests cover 63% of total geographical area (ha. 83743) of the state. Though there is 'inner line regulation' number of people from plains have business establishments and economy is mostly controlled by non-tribal traders and officials. Initially, there were very few locals in government employment, but situation is fast changing. Arunachalis are mostly animists who believe in spirits. Other religions (Hindu, Muslim, and Christianity) are slowly penetrating into this hitherto unexplored, and protected area. Locals have variety of festivals and dances which relieves them from their drudgery. Almost all of them are non-vegetarians.

The society is patrilineal, patriarchal, and patrilocal. Women have freedom in selection of spouse, and household activities. Marriage is not regarded strictly as a socio-religious duty. Though polygyny is practiced by many tribes, monogamy is common form of marriage. Traces of polyandry are also found in certain places. The rule of endogamy is operative in selection of spouse. Pre-martial relations are not viewed seriously, but chastity is expected from a married woman. A man has considerable freedom in both the cases. Though men disagree, with little role in major decisions, in practice women are head of the households. They work from dawn to dusk with little recognition to their contribution. However, their status is better than the women of plains. Women of Arunachal are fine weavers and lovers of nature. Not many studies, however, are conducted to understand socio-economic status of these women. Present study is an attempt in that direction.

Objectives

The overall objective of the study is to capture the socio-economic conditions of tribal women in Arunachal Pradesh. Specific objectives of the study are:

1. to review various governmental programmes for development of tribal women in the state,
2. to study martial, and economic status of selected women,
3. to analyse time allocation, and participation in decision making process of tribal women,

4. to understand the awareness of respondents about cooperatives, health, ICDS, and government loaning,
5. to observe working of self-help groups in the state and to suggest a financial package for strengthening SHGs, and
6. to document case studies on typical tribal women.

Methodology

The study is conducted in Arunachal Pradesh. It is one of the seven sisters of north-eastern states. The region (NEFA) was formed as a full-fledged state on February 20, 1987. It is skirted by Bhutan in west, Tibet and China in north and north-east, Myanmar to east, and Assam in south. It is the largest state, area-wise, in north-eastern region. Monpas, Akas, Nishis, Apatanis, Adis, Miris, Wangchoos, Mishims, Nocktes, etc. of mongolian descent live here. In all, there are 3257 villages of which 3176 villages have less than 1000 population. Literacy rate is 41.6%. It is the most sparsely populated area of the country with 10 persons/sq.km. However, only 4% of the geographical area is under cultivation.

Both primary and secondary data were collected to address the stated objectives. Based on concentration of various tribes, 5 districts were selected (Lohit[1], Dibang Valley, Upper Siang, Lower Subansiri, and West Kameng). Further, eight Anganwadi centres drawn from two Integrated Child Development Services (ICDS) areas from each district were identified for a detailed study. The sample includes 200 women respondents spread over 40 Anganwadi centres, 10 ICDS project areas, and 5 districts. Presence of Anganwadi centre, number of households in the village, spread of distance from district headquarter, and concentration of a major tribe are the criteria used for inclusion of villages in the study. Pre-tested questionnaires were used to collect data on age, tribe, educational status, marriage profile, family income, time allocation, awareness about health, cooperatives, ICDS, and developmental programmes, role in household, agriculture, horticulture, animal husbandry, collection of forest produce, decision making process, etc. Primary data are supported by secondary data collected from state departments like social welfare, women and child development, family planning, education, agriculture, horticulture, animal husbandry, health, rural development, etc. Extensive discussions are also held with senior officers in-charge of various developmental programmes to elicit their opinions/suggestions to improve status of women in the society. Data are collected during October 2001-May 2002, and in all 80 days were spent in field. The report is presented in 10 Chapters, and summaries are given below.

An Overview of Arunachal Pradesh

People are changing and they are no longer what they were 50 years ago. The change was introduced by the administration and people are heading towards larger affiliation with nation to share its development and prosperity. This is basic for wider cohesion which goes to make a nation. The physiological integration is the greatest achievement to the credit of administrative policy followed in this region. In the new environment, new class alignment in offing; ministers and legislatures, officers and employees in government service; newly educated people; contractors; agents; traders; etc. have began to live a different life of their own forming a class of elite of society. Their mode of life in houses made of bricks, mortars, R.C.C. buildings, window curtains, bathrooms, and kitchens with most modern amenities, TV sets, VCR, cordless phones, air conditioners, maruti cars, gypsies, dress, diet, etc. are different from the rank and file who are still living age-old life in far flung areas.

Considerable amount of development has taken place during the planned era and lot more needs to carried out. It is to be considered as a joint effort of people, government, politicians, officials, state, and central governments. A holistic approach; by taking locals into confidence, and with their active participation; would go a long way in making this region a paradise.

Developmental Programmes for Women

A review of ongoing developmental programs for women revealed that both central and state governments have been providing assistance under various heads. Prominent among them are integrated child development services, IRDP/SGSY, DWCRA, MSS, BSY, etc. There are 57 ICDS projects operational in the state with a 2327 Anganwadi centres. As many as 1.33 lakh women, and children are covered under this scheme. The CDPOs, supervisors, and gramsevikas complained about non-availability of certain facilities which are hindering successful implementation of the scheme. Both IRDP and DWCRA programmes are now merged and are known as SGSY which is being implementing in the state since 1999-00. There are number of other schemes too for the benefit of women in the state.

Profiles of Selected Districts

Topography, status of agriculture, horticulture, animal husbandry, fishery, and potential sectors for development in the selected districts are discussed in this Chapter. Progress of IRDP/SGSY, and DWCRA is also covered. All the districts are located in high altitudes with little scope for terraced or wet rice cultivation. Jhumming is the life line followed by dependence on forests. Produce from jhumming is adequate for 3-4 months of a year. There is hardly any scope for industrial development. Communication and transport facilities are in nascent stage. On an average, 1/3rd of the beneficiaries from both IRDP and SGSY are women. The impact of DWCRA is less than marginal. West Kameng district is better placed compared to rest of the selected districts.

Martial and Economic Status of Women

An analysis of Chapter 5 revealed that selected respondents are young and majority of them are in the age group of less than 30 years. According to level of education, respondents of Lower Subansiri have highest number of illiterates followed by Upper Siang, Lohit, Dibang Valley, and West Kameng. These tribes have no written language and there are wide variations in their dialects. Districts with higher levels of education reported relatively higher ages at marriage. A variety of forms of marriages (arranged, love, love and arranged, elopement, and second marriage) are noticed in the study area. Nishi community preferred child marriages. Among preferred qualities of a prospective husband, majority of them reported that husband should have only one wife.

On an average, women have 3.5 living children and 2.6 expired, and 20% of them reported following family planning measures. It is a patriarchal society. Jhum cultivation is predominant in the study area and majority of respondents have plots ranging between 1-4. Almost all the respondents have some form of animals (mithun, yaks, cows, sheep, goat, pigs, and poultry). They fall in the income category of Rs. 15001-25000/annum. The percentage of respondents falling in this income bracket are more in Upper Siang, and Lower Subansiri. A large proportion of respondents are either purchasing packed powder salt or packed rock salt and 78% of them are purchasing more than 3 kgs. of salt/month. The percentage of respondents 'not familiar with iodized salt' are more in Lohit district. As many as 77.5% of respondents reported taps and borewells as the source of drinking water.

Workload and Participation in Decision-Making

Workload and participation in decision-making process by women revealed that majority of respondents are putting in, on an average, 8-12 hours of work/day. Women attended activities like cooking, fetching water, washing clothes, upkeep of house, collecting fire wood, collection of vegetables and fruits from forest, caring children, agriculture, feeding animals, preparation of rice beer, and social visits. Average workload (hours/day) of respondents hovered around 12 hours/day. There are minor variations in workloads across districts. As regards exchange labour, majority of respondents reported that there is a need for it. On an average, 4.5 days of advance notice is required for getting such labour. Factors like number of jhum plots, number of animals, years of schooling, and index of awareness are found to be positive and significant. Decision making in important activities are decided by husbands, while decisions associated with responsibility and duties of use value are left to women. There is a positive change among younger generations and are actively participating in making variety of decisions.

Awareness About Local Organisations

An observation of Chapter 7 revealed that women started slowly visiting number of institutions like bank, post office, panchayat, town, and cinema hall. Though most of women are not members of cooperatives, they have been utilizing its services. Respondents from below poverty line got a monthly ration of 25 kgs. of rice at subsidized prices. Women are not happy with quality, and price of items available at cooperatives. They felt that items of daily necessity with good quality should be supplied through cooperatives regularly at reasonable price. In majority of the cases, health care centres are not located in villages studied. Due to non availability, and socio- religious reasons, women depended both on doctor and priests. Respondents with literacy, educated husbands, and close to town have preferred doctors over priests. On the other hand, illiterate women from far flung areas preferred priest. Respondents are familiar with anganwadi centre and its activities. According to them, supply of nutritious food to children is the core activity of anganwadi centre. Almost all of them are beneficiaries of these centres. As many 12 suggestions were made to improve efficiency of anganwadi centre. About 44% of women had not availed any government loan during their life time. As regards repayment of loan, 20.5% of them repaid fully, 23.5% partly, and half of the respondents are averse to avail a new loan. Depending upon availability of local resources, skills, and market for final product, respondents opted for activities like horticulture, fish ponds, vegetable cultivation, and weaving. In all an amount of Rs. 10.07 lakhs is required to implement to these schemes.

Self-help Groups in Study Area

A close observation of Chapter 8 revealed that there are 9 SHGs working in the state. Women respondents are in favour of organizing SHGs. They are willing to have regular savings, meetings, and internal loaning. Women opted for schemes like fish ponds, vegetable cultivation, horticulture, garment shop, petty trade, weaving, and breeding mithuns to be taken up through SHGs. An amount of Rs. 45 lakhs would be required to implement these schemes on an experimental basis which would go a long way in improving socio-economic status of these women.

Case Studies

An observation of individual case studies revealed that all

tribes studied belong to patriarchal, patrilineal, and patrilocal societies. Barring Nishis, women from other tribes got married in the age varying between 14-18 years. In majority of the cases, they have freedom in selection of spouse. Though arranged marriages were practiced in ölden days love marriages and love and arranged marriages are accepted and followed now. Bride price is compulsory in almost all the tribes. But the form and amount is changing fast due to increased education. Infant mortality is very high and women prefer to have sons over daughters. However, neither daughters are ill treated nor there is any female infanticide. Women have full freedom in household and agricultural activities while they have little role in decision making pertaining to outside the household. More number of women are now visiting health care centres, and the role played by priest is relatively declining. Slowly and steadily women have started realising importance of education, family planning, health, and sanitation. They are participating in village cooperatives and anganwadi centres and demanding more facilities for their well being. Educated women also started bringing pressure against polygyny, and bride price. Due to all weather roads, and improved communication facilities women started moving out of their homesteads and as a result their outlook is broadening. Jhum lands, and mithuns as assets of prestige are loosing ground to well furnished houses in towns, bank balances, government jobs, consumer durables, etc. In majority of the cases income from jhum plots is sufficient only for 3-4 months. Women are also entering into politics, business, contracts, self-employment, service, community development, etc.

Recommendations

Women are part of the society and their problems should be treated as society's problems. Women's emancipation would lead to family emancipation, and ultimately emancipation of the country. Thus, it is in the men's interest that efforts should be made to improve women's social, economic, and political empowerment. Women, men, society, NGOs, state, and center are stake-holders in this exercise. Hence, stake-holder wise responsibilities are suggested below:

For Women to Act

Women's empowerment is in their hands. They should not misplace this opportunity. Once they get going, world will have to change. Inorder to make it a reality women have to discharge certain responsibilities. In seeking to empower women, let us not forget that it is mothers who are essentially bringing up children. Education is a crucial input in this direction. Women should change their attitude towards girl child and accordingly provide necessary education, health care, and affection on par with boys. Girl children should not be ill treated and mothers should ensure sending them to school. They should follow small family norms. Further, child marriages, polygyny, and bride prices should be discouraged. Women should organise themselves into self-help groups and take active part in village institutions like anganwadi centre, health care centre, cooperative, school, etc. Educated women voluntarily should come forward to conduct adult education classes, and awareness programmes on health care, sanitation, family planning, superstitions, etc. for women. Women have to stop feeling themselves as victims and that can only happen through education. Women should also convince their men folk about the advantages of educating girl child, monogamy, etc. Unless women become a political force, they cannot make an impact in this age of globalization. Transfer of power might lead to disruption of social system but we cannot expect men to change over night.

For Men to Act

Men should realise the contribution of women to the household. They should also appreciate special qualities of women. Men should encourage their spouses and children to take active part in decision making not only in house but also outside homestead. Women should be given equal treatment and that should start from the home. Men should try to modify according to the changing environment, and practices like polyandry, polygyny, child marriages, bride price, consumption of excess rice beer, etc. should be avoided.

For NGOs to Act

There are few genuine NGOs operating for emancipation of women in the state. Particulars of one such NGO and its activities was given in Chapter 9. Further, Vivekananda Kendra, Oju Welfare Association, and a number of other NGOs are in the field. They should collectively prepare an action plan for overall development of women. Exclusively schools and boarding hostels for girls, women's old age homes, organising self help groups, conducting health camps and adult education to women, taking up issues like child marriages, polygyny, polyandry, and bringing awareness among women about their position in society and expected roles should form agenda of these NGOs. Education and economic upliftment should form the first step in their overall objective of women's empowerment. Support from the state and central governments, and international agencies can be sought for this noble cause.

For State to Act

The state government has number of schemes for women. Of late, it has enacted state women's commission. However, progress in this regard is less than satisfactory. State should apportion atleast 30% of its total developmental expenses towards emancipation of women. Efforts should also be made to ensure that allotted amount reaches the target group. Further, police, district administration, and judiciary should help women's cause, and a speedy redressal mechanism should be worked out. Women's commission should be given adequate powers and resources to carry out its cherished goals. Appointments to the commission should be made non-political and chairperson be given the rank of a cabinet minister. State also may follow the precedence of Government of Haryana which announced an incentive of Rs. 500/month for opting family planning with two girl children. However, this amount may be deposited on the name of children in a national savings scheme which can be encashed after attaining majority. The state should give preference to girls in education, employment, and legislature. Thus, the state should not only create conducive environment for emancipation of women but also provide necessary financial support in achieving overall objective.

For Centre to Act

Centre should take the role of a friend, philosopher, and

guide. As it is aware Arunachal is a sensitive area located in the fragile Himalayas with numerous handicaps. Added to it, Arunachalis are yet to form part of national main stream. Further, women of Arunachal need a special attention of the government of India. ICDS is being implemented in the state with central assistance. There is a need to strengthen anganwadi centres with play materials, adequate timely, and quality medicines, SNP items, and necessary infrastructure. The rules followed in the rest of the country with regard to ICDS may not be applicable here. Arunachal is considered as a highly expensive area and such honorarium to worker and helper needs immediate hike. Further, it would be difficult for the locals to contribute towards construction of anganwadi centre. Government of India should consider providing 50% grants towards their construction in the state. There is neither office accommodation nor quarters for the staff of ICDS. In an undulated region like this, it is a difficult task for the staff to get quarters. Government should make necessary provision for providing quarters and office accommodation to ICDS staff. Efforts also should be made to extend scheme to hitherto uncovered villages, and population.

Vast majority of the women are interested in organising self-help groups. Women opted for schemes like fish ponds, vegetable cultivation, horticulture, garment shop, petty trade, weaving, and breeding mithuns to be taken up through SHGs. An amount of Rs. 45 lakhs would be required to implement these schemes on an experimental basis by the Government of India. This would go a long way in improving socio-economic status of these women. Government should also make available adequate grants for education of girl children, health care of girls, pregnant, nursing, and old women. Such a liberal attitude from Government of India would go a long way in not only improving emancipation of women but also building their loyalty towards India.

Summing-up

There is lot of difference between women described by Verrier Elwin, and the present women. They are marching towards progress, and are no longer passive spectators. There are women ministers, administrators, doctors, engineers, lawyers, nurses, typists, clerks, contractors, social workers, and they are in all fields. Selection of life partners is no longer restricted to rule of endogamy, many inter-tribal marriages have been taking place, and some of them got married to people from plains (rest of India). Young and educated women are crusading against polygyny. A good number of girl students are also studying outside the state. Due to rising unemployment and lack of alternative sources of income, there is unrest among educated youth. Many women have set up small businesses, and brought into focus irregularities practiced at fair price shops. They have also started literacy programmes for women, and children. We will be surprised to know that there are eight beauty parlours and a training centre to train beauticians at Itanagar/Naharlagun. They started wearing saree, bindi, and mehindi. Their verbal conversations are in Hindi, English, and of course in their dialect. Age old practices and traditions are coming on their way hindering progress. Thus, it is necessary to create congenial social, political, and economic environment to enable women to participate in decision making process. Whatever these women take up, they do it whole heartedly and this attitude pays dividends.

There has been a drastic reduction in periodicity of Jhum cycle. As a result, Jhum plots became private property. Now it is the productivity of the Jhum lands and not number of Jhum plots which is significant. Some of them are now using improved variety of seeds, and fertilizers, and even going for off-seasonal vegetables, and horticultural crops. Keeping in view of the topography and crops grown, agricultural tools may be developed. Women have to learn by doing, by using technology, and not merely by being told. The method and approach of teaching and convincing them of utilizing information must be enhanced. It is necessary to train women facilitators on improved tools and equipment. There is a need to develop and encourage time saving technologies that can help women find time to participate in social, economic, and political activities. There is a need to strengthen support services and provide necessary inputs at subsidised rates to make them self-sufficient.

Reservation for women in education, employment, and legislature is necessary to bring about equality. Present 33 % reservation for women in state and central government employment is an affirmative action. There is a need to build women's capacities through education, organising self-help groups, arranging economic activities, and providing agricultural extension activities. The aim should be to build women's capacities, give information, and construct a positive perspective of society. Eradication of illiteracy through education, and health care of pregnant, and lactating mothers alongwith newly born babies will have to be clubbed together to successfully impart family planning programmes. Efforts should be made to reduce/widening economic and social disparities between various tribes.

Money has replaced barter system. Waves of liberalisation are on the state. Industrially made cheap and alien goods are already made head way into Arunachal. There is a need to preserve their culture and heritage, at the same time adopting systems and procedures, with necessary modifications, of modern and vibrant India. Women would be the worst affected in this transitory stage. They have to remember that anything in excess is not good. Efforts should be made to evolve harmonious mechanisms so that balance between people and nature, men and women, old and young, and rich and poor could be maintained and ultimately leads to overall development of the state. We have to bridge communication divide that separated the region from rest of India.

NOTE

1. Initially, Tirap district was formed part of the study. However, due to insurgency and the resultant disturbances, it was replaced by Lohit district.

APPENDICES

Appendix 1.1
DISTRICT-WISE LIST OF SELECTED VILLAGES

District	*Village*
Lohit	1. Gundri
	2. Old Pukri
	3. Naraliang
	4. Suplang
	5. Meshei
	6. Sarti
	7. Yassong
	8. Quibang
Dibang Valley	1. Gupulin
	2. Mihundo
	3. Angolin
	4. Riyalin
	5. New Elope
	6. Brilin
	7. Hunli
	8. Kongo
Upper Siang	1. Gette
	2. Simong
	3. Ramsing
	4. Moying
	5. Damroh
	6. Millang
	7. New Millang
	8. Mariyang

Lower Subansiri	1. Tamen 2. Yattap 3. Kamporijo 4. Poku 5. Joram 6. Jara 7. Upper Talo 8. Lower Talo
West Kameng	1. Ankling 2. Dengzi 3. Morshing 4. Shergaon 5. Barchipam 6. Sagor/Skhrong 7. Yewang 8. Ramacamp

Source: Compiled by the author.

Appendix 1.2

OFFICIALS CONTACTED

Mrs. D.M. Mallo
Director
Department of social welfare, Women and child development,
Government of Arunachal Pradesh
Nagarlagun 791 110

Mrs. G.D. Panicker
Joint Director (ICDS)
Department of social welfare, Women and child development,
Government of Arunachal Pradesh
Nagarlagun 791 110

Shri S.C. Tok
Statistical Assistant (ICDS)
Directorate of Social Welfare, Women and Child Development
Naharlagun 791 110

Shri A.K. Mishra
Program Officer (ICDS)
Directorate of Social Welfare, Women and Child Development
Naharlagun 791 110

Dr. B.V.S Murthy
State Homeopathic and ISM Officer
Directorate of Health
Naharlagun 791 110

Shri H. Bhattacharjee
Joint Director
Directorate of Rural Development
Naharlagun 791 110

Shri D. Das
Senior Economic Investigator
Diretorate of Rural Development
Naharlagun 791 110

Shri S. Laskar,
A R C S,
Office of the Registrar of Cooperative Societies,
Government of Arunachal Pradesh
Naharlagun 791 111

Dr. D.K. Bora
Director (Research)
Directorate of Research
Government of Arunachal Pradesh
Itanagar 791 111

Shri Hage Khoda, IAS
Secretary
Department of Cooperation, Horticulture and Fisheries
Central Secretariat
Itanagar 791 111

Shri Vijay Swamy
Gyanodaya
C-Sector
Sunview Centre
Itanagar 791 111

Mrs. Nello Umbrey
CDPO (Hunli-Kronli)
ICDS project
Hunli 792 110
Dibang Valley District

Dr. Mika Umpo
Medical Officer
Hunli 792 110
Dibang Valley district

Mrs. A. Perme
CDPO (Anini)
Anini 792 101
Dibang Valley District

Shri P.S. Gogoi
A P O (Monitoring)
D R D A
Anini 792 101
Dibang Valley District

Dr. Brelee Mimi
Veterinary Officer
Hunli 782 110
Dibang Valley district

Mrs. Ume Pulu
Supervisor (ICDP)
Hunli 792 110
Dibang Valley district

Mrs. Mijihe Mewu
Gram Sevika
Hunli 792 110
Dibang Valley district

Mrs. Jena Dele
Community Teacher
New Elope
Hunli 792 110
Dibang Valley district

Mrs. Ruth Lego
Supervisor (ICDS)
Hunli 792 110
Dibang Valley district

Miss Savitri Chettry
Senior Gram Sevika
Hunli 792 110
Dibang Valley district

Shri Sushil Yadav
Senior Branch Manager,
Apex Bank, Roing
Dibang Valley District,

Shri Y.D. Thongchi, IAS
Deputy Commissioner,
Tezu 792 001
Lohit District

Shri Tamune Miso
Project Director (DRDA)
Tezu 792 001
Lohit District

Mrs. Nyapi Ringu,
Deputy Director (ICDS)
Divisional Cell,
Tezu 792 001
Lohit District

Mrs. Geyum Amo
C D P O (ICDS)
Wakro 792 104
Lohit District

Smt. Damang Tayeng
Junior Gram Sevika (ICDS)
Wakro 792 104
Lohit District

Miss Yobom Doke
Junior Gram Sevika (ICDS)
Wakro 792 104
Lohit District

Smt. Reeta Mansai
Supervisor (ICDS)
Wakro 792 104
Lohit District

Miss Y. Ronya
Gram Sevika (DWCRA)
Wakro 792 104
Lohit District

Shri Pailo Mihu
Statistical Assistant (ICDS)
Divisional Cell,
Tezu 792 001
Lohit District

Shri Solel Longling
C D P O (ICDS)
Hayuliang 792 102
Lohit district

Mrs. Deal Seal Burman
C D P O (ICDS)
Walang ICDS Project,
P.O. Hayuliang 792 102
Lohit District

Shri Songyalum Bellai
Statistical Assistant
C/o C D P O Walang
Post: Hayuliang 792 102
Lohit District

Mr. Arun Kumar Das,
Circle Officer,
Kibithoo
Lohit District

Shri Subedar G.K. Limba
29, Assam Rifles
C/o 99 APO
Kibithoo
Lohit District

Shri R. Bhattarcharjee
Supervisor
ICDS (Hayuliang)
Hayuliang, Lohit District
Smt. T. Partin
Deputy Director (ICDS)
Divisional cell
Pasighat 791 102
East Siang

Miss Ponu Moyang
CDPO (ICDS)
Pasighat 791 102
East Siang

Smt. Mukuta Saroh Devri
CDPO
Yingkiong 791 101
Upper Siang

Smt. T. Tabing
Supervisor (ICDS)
C/o CDPO
Yingkiong 791 101
Upper Siang

Mrs. O. Tarang
Gramsevika
C/o CDPO
Yingkiong 791 101
Upper Siang

Smt. K. Duggom
Gramsevika
C/o CDPO
Yingkiong 791 101
Upper Siang

Smt. N Yassung
Statistical Assistant
C/o CDPO
Yingkiong 791 101
Upper Siang

Shri S.K. Nath
Accountant
C/o CDPO
Yingkiong 791 101
Upper Siang

Shri G. Jiji
School Teacher
Gette
Yingkiong
Upper Siang

Smt. T. Tayang
CDPO, Mariyang
Upper Siang

Smt. K. Tayeng
Supervisor (ICDS)
C/o CDPO
Mariyang
Upper Siang

Mrs. Karoti Borang
Gramsevika
C/o CDPO
Mariyang
Upper Siang

Smt. Savita Bhagavati
CDPO (ICDS)
Raga
Lower Subansiri

Mrs. Tei Hampu
Statistical Assistant
Divisional ICDS cell
Ziro
Lower Subansiri

Mrs. Dani Yami
CDPO (ICDS)
Ziro II
Yachuli
Lower Subansiri

Mrs. Yatung Debom
Supervisor
C/o CDPO
Ziro
Lower Subansiri

Mrs. Lego Suchitra
Supervisor
C/o CDPO
Ziro
Lower Subansiri

Mrs. Nangaram Yabik
Gramsevika
Supervisor
C/o CDPO
Ziro
Lower Subansiri

Shri Habung Donyi
Project Director (DRDA)
Bomdila 792 001
West Kameng District

Mrs. Lian Moyee
CDPO (ICDS)
Kalaktang
West Kameng District

Mrs. Shermin Kharma
Supervisor
C/o CDPO (ICDS)
Kalaktang
West Kameng District

Mrs. Pema Monpa
Supervisor
C/o CDPO (ICDS)
Kalaktang
West Kameng District

Miss Durgavati Roy
Supervisor
C/o CDPO (ICDS)
Kalaktang
West Kameng District

Miss Mahi Megha
Statistical Assistant
C/o CDPO (ICDS)
Kalaktang
West Kameng District

Miss Sonam Drema
Gramsevika
C/o CDPO (ICDS)
Kalaktang
West Kameng District
Shri Sange Wangchu
Gram bura, Kalaktang
West Kameng District

Shri S.D. Kharme
Teacher
Middle School
Dengzi, Kalaktang
West Kameng District

Miss Pema Wangjom
Teacher (Middle School)
Dengzi, Kalaktang
West Kameng District

Mrs Kago Maya
CDPO (ICDS)
Dirang 790 002
West Kameng District

Shri Drogumbo
Supervisor (ICDS)
Dirang 790 002
West Kameng District

Miss Gachimy Yamchadu
Extension Officer (WCS)
C/o CDPO (ICDS)
Dirang 790 002
West Kameng District

Miss Kesang Dreama
Jr. Gramsevika
C/o CDPO (ICDS)
Dirang 790 002
West Kameng District

Mrs. Dexay Dreama
Jr. Gramsevika
C/o CDPO (ICDS)
Dirang 790 002
West Kameng District

Shri O.P. Singh
Teacher (Middle School)
Yewang
West Kameng District

Shri Tsaing Wangchu
Teacher (Middle School)
Yewang
West Kameng District

Mrs. Jaya Jawal Singh
Deputy Director (ICDS)
Bomdila 792 001
West Kameng District

Mrs Hage Yasse
Statistical Assistant
C/o Deputy Director (ICDS)
Bomdila 792 001
West Kameng District

Shri P. Chakhat
Deputy Resident
Commissioner
Government of Arunachal
Pradesh
Parvatinagar
Tezpur 784 001
Assam

Shri K.S. Gogai, APCS
Deputy Resident
Commissioner
Government of Arunachal
Pradesh
Mohanbari 786 012
Dibrugarh
Assam

Shri C.N. Bailung
Assistant Director (ST)
Government of Arunachal
Pradesh,
Mohanbari
Dibrugarh 786 012,
Assam

Shri R.K. Baidya
DRC
RG Baruva Road
Guwahati 780 121

Appendix 2.1
CHRONOLOGY OF CHANGES IN NOMENCLATURE OF VARIOUS REGIONS OF ARUNACHAL PRADESH

Period/ Year	*Existing name*	*New name*
Till 1914	NA	(a) Central and eastern (north-east frontier tract) (b) Western section (north- east frontier tract) (c) Lakhimpur frontier tract
1919	Central and eastern sectors Western section	Sadiya Frontier Tract Balipara Frontier Tract
1943	Sadiya Frontier Tract (part of Sadiya Frontier Tract & Lakhimpur Frontier Tracts were Combined)	(a) Tirap Frontier Tract (b) Sadiya Frontier Tract
1946	Balipara Frontier Tract	(a) Sela sub-agency (b) Subansiri area
1948	Sadiya Frontier Tract	(a) Abor Hills (b) Mishmi Hills
1954	Balipara Frontier Tract Abor Hills district Mishmi Hills Sela Sub-agency Tirap Frontier Tract Naga Tribal area	Kameng Frontier Division Siang Frontier Division Lohit Division Subansiri Frontier Division Tirap Frontier Division Tuensang Frontier Division
1965	Kameng Frontier Division Siang Frontier Division Lohit Division Subansiri Frontier Division Tirap Frontier Division	Kameng district Siang district Lohit district Subansiri district Tirap district
1972	NEFA	Union Territory of Arunachal Pradesh

Contd...

Appendix 2.1 *Contd...*

Period/ Year	*Existing name*	*New name*
1980	Kameng District	(a) East Kameng district (b) West Kameng district
	Siang District	(a) East Siang district (b) West Siang district
	Lohit District	(a) Dibang Valley district (b) Lohit district
	Subansiri District	(a) Lower Subansiri district (b) Upper Subansiri district
1984	West Kameng district	(a) West Kameng district (b) Tawang district
1987	Union Territory of Arunachal Pradesh	Arunachal Pradesh (Statehood)
1987	Tirap district	(a) Tirap district (b) Changlang district
1992	Lower Subansiri district	(a) Lower Subansiri district (b) Papum Pare district
1995	East Siang district	(a) East Siang district (b) Upper Siang district
2001	Dibang Valley district	(a) Upper Dibang Valley district (b) Lower Dibang Valley district

Source: Compiled by the author

Appendix 2.2

LIST OF TRIBES OF ARUNACHAL PRADESH

Sr. No.	Name	Sr. No.	Name	Sr. No.	Name
1	Abor	2	Adi	3	Adi Gallong
4	Adi Minyong	5	Adi Padam	6	Adi Pasi
7	Aka	8	Apatani	9	Ashing
10	Bagi	11	Bangni	12	Bangro
13	Bogum	14	Bokar	15	Bolok Tangse
16	Bomdo	17	Bori	18	But Monpa
19	Dagla	20	Dorak Tangsa	21	Deori
22	Digaru/Taraon Mishmi	23	Dirang Monpa	24	Gallong
25	Haisa Tangsa	26	Havi Tangsa	27	Hill Miri
28	Hotang Tangsa	29	Idu/Chulikata Mishmi	30	Janbo
31	Kaman/Miju Mishmi	32	Karka	33	Katin Tangsa
34	Kamsing Tangsa	35	Khalim Tangsa	36	Khamba
37	Khamiyang	38	Khampti	39	Khowa
40	Khrodeng Bangni	41	Komkar	42	Kongbo
43	Korang Tangsa	44	Longkai Tangsa	45	Libo
46	Lichi Tangsa	47	Liju Nocte	48	Lisha Monpa
49	Longchang Tangsa	50	Longin Tangsa	51	Longphi Tangsa
52	Longri Tangsa	53	Longsang Tangsa	54	Lowang Tangsa
55	Meyog	56	Miji	57	Mikir
58	Millang	59	Millang Abor	60	Minyong
61	Mishing/Miri	62	Mishmi	63	Moglum Tangsa
64	Momba	65	Monpa	66	Morang Tangsa
67	Mossang Tangsa	68	Muktum	69	Namsang Tangsa
70	Ngionong Tangsa	71	Nishang	72	Nissi
73	Nocte	74	Monong	75	Padam

Contd...

Appendix 2.2 *Contd...*

Sr. No.	*Name*	*Sr. No.*	*Name*	*Sr. No.*	*Name*
76	Pailibo	77	Panchen Monpa	78	Pangi
79	Rasi	80	Phong Monpa	81	Phongkong
82	Ponthai Nocte	83	Ramo	84	Rangai Tangsa
85	Rongran Tangsa	86	Sanka Tangsa	87	Sherdukpen
88	Simong	89	Simsa Tangsa	90	Singpho
91	Siram	92	Sulung	93	Sulung Bangni
94	Tagin	95	Tagin Bangni	96	Taisen Tangsa
97	Tangsam	98	Tangsa	99	Taram
100	Tawang Monpa	101	Thai Khampti	102	Tikhak Tangsa
103	Tutcha Nocte	104	Wancho	105	Yanoo Bangni
106	Yatong	107	Yabin	108	Yongkuk Tangsa
109	Yougli Tangsa	110	Zakhring	111	Any Naga Tribe

Source: Sengupta (1992).

REFERENCES

Araham, (2000), *The Woman's Way*, Discover India, 13(7): 6-7.

Banerjee, B., (1991), *Status of Women Among Bokars*, Resarun, 17 (1 and 2): 70-79.

Banthia, J.K., (2001), *Census of India 2001*, Series 1 (India), Provisional population totals, Paper 1 of 2001, Office of the Registrar General and Census Commissioner, (Government of India), New Delhi.

Bawa, P.S., (2001), *Shakti in Form and Spirit*, Discover India, 14(5):52-54.

Bhange, N.P., (1993), *Tribal Commissions and Committees in India*, Himalaya Publishing House, New Delhi.

Bhargava, R., (2001), *Protecting Children's Rights*, Employment News, 36(32):1-2.

Bhattacharya, R.P., (2000), *Economic Development of Arunachal Pradesh*, Himalayan Publishers, Itanagar.

Bora, D.K., and D.K. Duarah, (1999), *Health Status of the Arunachalee Women with Reference to the Nishings*, Resarun, 25 (1 and 2):39-45.

Bora, D.K., (2002), *Assam Pradishik Mahila Samity and the Great Earthquake of 1950 in NEFA* (Mimeo), Department of Research, Government of Arunachal Pradesh, Naharlagun.

Bose, M.L., (1997), *History of Arunachal Pradesh*, Concept Publishing Company, New Delhi.

Charlton, S.E.M., (1984), *Women in Third World Development*, Westview Press, London.

Chowdhury, J.N., (1996), *Arunachal Panorama*, Directorate of Research, Itanagar.

Dalvi, J.P., (undated), *Himalayan Blunder*, Hind Pocket Books (P) Limited, Bombay.

Department of Information and Public Relations (1988), *Discover Arunachal*, Government of Arunachal Pradesh, Naharlagun.

Department of Tourism, (1992), *Arunachal Pradesh (India)*, Government of Arunachal Pradesh, Thomson Press, Faridabad.

Department of Tourism, (2001), *Buddha Mahotsava*, Tawang, Arunachal Pradesh, Government of Arunachal Pradesh, Naharlagun.

Department of Tourism, (2001), *Brahmaputra Darshan*, Pasighat, Arunachal Pradesh, Government of Arunachal Pradesh, Naharlagun.

Deuri, R.K., (1986), *Marriage System of Idu Mishmis*, Resarun, 12 (1 and 2): 4-8.

Directorate of Census, (2001), *Census of India*, Series 13 Arunachal Pradesh, Provisional Population Tables, paper 1 of 2001, Government of Arunachal Pradesh, Shillong.

Directorate of Economics and Statistics, (1985 to 2002), *Economic Review of Arunachal Pradesh 2000*, Government of Arunachal Pradesh, Itanagar.

Directorate of Information, Public Relations, and Ministry, (2001), *Your Expectations our Endeavours*, Government of Arunachal Pradesh, Naharlagun.

Directorate of Rural Development, (1991), *A Report on Integrated Child Development Schemes*, Government of Arunachal Pradesh, Itanagar.

DRDA, (1998), *Panorama of West Kameng district*, Office of the Project Director, Government of Arunachal Pradesh, Bomdila.

District Statistical Office, (1998), *Upper Siang District: At a glance*, Directorate of Economics and Statistics, Yingkiong.

District Statistical Office, (1993), *Block Level Statistics of Dibang Valley District*, Directorate of Economics and Statistics, Anini.

District Statistical Office, (1994), *Socio-economic Review of West Kameng District 1994*, Directorate of Economics and Statistics, Bomdila.

District Statistical Office, (1994), *Socio-economic Review of Dibang Valley District*, Directorate of Economics and Statistics, Anini.

District Statistical Office, (2000), *Lohit District: At a Glance*, Directorate of Economics and Statistics, Tezu.

District Statistical Office, (1995), *District Statistical Handbook of Dibang Valley District*, Directorate of Economics and Statistics, Anini.

District Statistical Office, (1996), *Block Level Statistics of Lohit District 1996*, Directorate of Economics and Statistics, Tezu.

District Statistical Office, (1996), *Statistical Handbook of Lower Subansiri District*, 1996 (Arunachal Pradesh), Directorate of Economics and Statistics, Ziro.

District Statistical Office, (1997), *Statistical Handbook of Upper Siang District (1997)*, Directorate of Economics and Statistics, Yingkiong.

District Statistical Office, (1997), *Statistical Handbook of Lower Subansiri District (1997)*, Directorate of Economics and Statistics, Ziro.

District Statistical Office, (1997), *Lower Subansiri District: At a Glance*, Directorate of Economics and Satistics, Ziro.

District Statistical Office, (1997), *District Socio-economic Review: Upper Siang District (Arunachal Pradesh)*, Yingkiong.

District Statistical Office, (1997), *West Kameng District: At a Glance*, Directorate of Economics and Statistics, Bomdila.

District Statistical Office, (1997), *Dibang Valley District: At a Glance 1997*, Directorate of Economics and Statistics, Anini.

District Statistical Office, (1997, and 1999), *Statistical Handbook of Lohit District 1997*, Directorate of Economics and Statistics, Tezu.

District Statistical Office, (1998), *Upper Siang District: At a Glance*, Department of Economics and Statistics, Yingkiong.

District Statistical Office, (1998), *Profile of West Kameng District*, Directorate of Economics and Statistics, Bomdila.

District Statistical Office, (1998), *West Kameng District; At a Glance 1998*, Directorate of Economics and Statistics, Bomdila.

District Statistical Office, (2001), *District Socio-economic Review*, Lohit District (1999-00), Directorate of Economics and Statistics, Tezu.

District Information and Public Relations Office, (1998), *Parashuram Kund*, Government of Arunachal Pradesh, Tezu.

Duarah, D.K., (1998), *Women Movements in Arunachal Pradesh*, Resarun, 22 (1 and 2):39-42.

Dutta, P., (1975), *Women in Arunachal and their Status in the Socio-cultural Life*, Resarun (1): 68-76.

Dutta, S., (1997) (ed.), *Studies in the History, Economy, and Culture of Arunachal Pradesh*, Himalayan Publishers, Itanagar.

Elwin, V., (1955), *India's North-east Frontier in the Nineteenth Century*, Oxford University Press, Calcutta.

Elwin, V., (1959), *A Philosophy for NEFA*, NEFA, Shillong.

Elwin, V., (1959), *Myths of North-east Frontier India*, NEFA, Shillong.

Elwin, V., (1965), *Democracy in NEFA*, NEFA, Shillong.

Government of India, (1981), *Sixth Five Year Plan*, 1980-85, Planning Commissions, New Delhi, 167.

Hangen, W., (1963), *After Nehru, Who?* Rupert Hart-Davis, London.

Kaul, B.M., (1967), *The Untold Story*, Allied Publishers, Bombay.

Kaul, P.N., (1976), *Frontier Callings*, Vikas Publishing House Private Limited, Delhi.

Khera, S.S., (1968), *India's Difence Problem*, Orient Longmans, Bombay.

Kumar, P., (2002), *State Commission for Women bill 2002 Approved*, The Arunachal Times, March 22.

Leacock E., (1986), *Women Power and Authority*, in Dube, L. E. Leacock, and S. Ardener (eds.), Visibility and power, Oxford University Press, Delhi.

Mackenzie, A., (1989), *The North-east Frontier of India*, Mittal Publications, Delhi.

Mankekar, D.R., (1968), *The Guilty Men of 1962*, The Tulsi Shah Enterprises, Bombay.

Mantaw, N.H., and P. Priyadarshini, (2000), *Nutritional Status of Children in Arunachal Pradesh: An Overview*, Resarun, 26 (1 and 2):109-118.

Ministry of Information and Broadcasting, (1963a), *The Chinese Threat*, Publications Division, Government of India, Delhi.

Ministry of Information and Broadcasting, (1963b), *The sino-Indian Conflict: Question and Answers*, Publication Division, Government of India, Delhi.

Ministry of Information and Broadcasting, (1965), *NEFA*, Publications Division, Delhi.

Mishra, K., (1991), *Women in Tribal Community: A Study of Arunachal Pradesh*, Vikas Publishing House Private Limited, New Delhi.

Mitkong, N., (1996), *Women's Rights in Tagin and Hill-Miri Society of Arunachal Pradesh*, Resarun, 22 (1 and 2):31-33.

NABARD, (1997), *Base Potential Linked Credit Plan 1997-98 to 2001-2002 for West Kameng District*, NABARD, Itanagar.

NABARD, (1998), *Potential Linked Credit Plan of Lower Subansiri District, Arunachal Pradesh*, NABARD, Itanagar.

NABARD, (1998), *Potential Linked Credit Plan of West Kameng District* 1998-99, NABARD, Itanagar.

NABARD, (1998), *Potential Linked Credit Plan of Dibang Valley District, 1998-99*, NABARD, Itanagar.

NABARD, (1998), *Potential Linked Credit Plan of Lohit District, 1998-99*, NABARD, Itanagar.

NABARD, (2001), *Annual Report, 2000-01*, NABARD, Bombay, 147-156.

Nath, A., (2001), *The Forces of Mystery*, Discover India, 14(5):37-39.

North-eastern Council (various issues), *Basic Statistics of North-Eastern Region*, North-eastern Council Secretariat, Shillong.

Osik, N.N., (1996), *A Brief History of Arunachal Pradesh*, Himalayan Publishers, Itanagar.

Osik, N.N., (1999), *Modern History of Arunachal Pradesh (1825-1997)*, Himalayan Publishers, Itanagar.

Pandey, B.B., (1997) (ed), *Patterns of Change and Potential for Development in Arunachal Pradesh*, Himalayan Publishers, Itanagar.

Pandey, B.B., (ed.) (1997), *Status of Women in Tribal Society: Arunachal Pradesh*, Directorate of Research, Government of Arunachal Pradesh, Itanagar.

Pandey, B.B., (1997), *Arunachal Pradesh: A Village to Statehood*, Himalayan Publishers, Itanagar.

Parul, D., (1976), *Women in Arunachal Pradesh and Their Status in the Socio-cultural life*, Resarun, 8: 68-76.

Planning Commission, (1985), *Sixth Five Year Plan (1985-90)*, Volume 2, Sectoral programmes of development, Government of India, New Delhi, 323.

Rao, V.M., (2000a), Integrated Cooperative Development project for Arunachal Pradesh, VMNICM, Pune.

Rao, V.M., (2000b), Role ot LAMPs in tribal economy: A study in Arunachal Pradesh, *Kurukshetra*, 49 (3): 5-11.

Rao, V.M., (2001a), *Challenges Before Cooperative Movement*, in Goel, B.B. (ed), Reinventing Cooperatives: A 21st century vision, Deep and Deep Publications Private Limited, New Delhi, 309-318.

Rao, V.M., (2001b), *Integrated Cooperative Development Project: A Boost to Cooperative Movement in Arunachal Pradesh*, Souvenir of state level cooperative seminar on Prospects of Cooperative Sector in new millennium, APSCU, Naharlagun.

Riba, T., (2000), *The Tribals and their Changing Environment with Special Reference to Arunachal Pradesh*, Himalayan Publishers, Itanagar.

Sengupta, T., (1996), *Census of India 1991*, Series 3 (Arunachal Pradesh), Part 12, A and B, Census handbook of Dibang Valley, East Siang, Lohit, and West Kameng districts, Directorate of Census operations, Government of Arunachal Pradesh, Naharlagun.

Sen, G., (2001), *Gurgles of laughter*, Discover India, 14(5):35-36.

Shukla, S.P., (2000), *Tribal Women and their Empowerment: A Case Study of Arunachal Pradesh*, Resarun, 26 (1 and 2): 6-13.

Singh, V.P., (1991), *Impact of Shifting Cultivation on Eco-system in Arunachal Pradesh*, Resarun, 17 (1 and 2):38-42.

State income unit, (1998), *State Domestic Product of Arunachal Pradesh: 1980-81 to 1996-97 (Revised series)*, Directorate of Economics and Statistics, Government of Arunachal Pradesh, Itanagar.

State income unit, (1999), *Press Note on Quick Estimates of State Domestic Product: Arunachal Pradesh (1991-98)*, Directorate of Economics and Statistics, Government of Arunachal Pradesh, Itanagar.

Srutikar, P.K., (1990), *Traditional Status of Women Among the Nishing (Bangnis) of East Kameng:* Trends of change, Resarun, 16 (1 and 2): 15-23.

Tayeng, P., (2001), *Basic Information and a Guide to General Studies on Arunachal Pradesh*, Purbadesh Mudran, Guwahati.

INDEX